MENSA

Mind Challenge

Thunder Bay Press
An imprint of the Advantage Publishers Group
5880 Oberlin Drive, San Diego, CA 92121-4794
www.advantagebooksonline.com

Text copyright © 1995, 2002 Mensa Publications
Design copyright © 1995, 2002 by Carlton Books Limited

All notations of errors or omissions should be addressed to Thunder Bay Press, editorial department, at the above address. All other correspondence (author inquiries, permissions) concerning the content of this book should be addressed to Carlton Books Limited, 20 Mortimer Street, London W1T 3JW, United Kingdom.

ISBN 1-57145-883-2
Library of Congress Cataloging-in-Publication Data available upon request.

Printed in Great Britain.
1 2 3 4 5 06 05 04 03 02

MENSA® Mind Challenge

Robert Allen

THUNDER BAY
P·R·E·S·S

San Diego, California

CONTENTS

Believe it or not, there are people who do not regard writing or solving puzzles as suitable occupations for grown-ups. 'Pointless,' they say. 'Waste of time,' they sneer. 'Why can't you solve real world problems instead,' they harrumph. Well, tough! Puzzles have been around since the dawn of civilisation. The Babylonians had them. And what about the Riddle of the Sphinx? The truth is that people have been fascinated by puzzles ever since they learned to do joined-up thinking. Puzzles may have no practical value but, as bad habits go, they are entertaining and relatively harmless. Have you ever seen anyone overdose on puzzles? Has anyone contracted a life-threatening disease through excessive conundrum consumption? Of course they haven't.

In a little way puzzles reflect our fascination with the mystery of life. They demonstrate that very human curiosity that demands we get to the bottom of everything. They are a part of the intellectual curiosity that drives humans on.

Mensa has been in the puzzle business for over half a century. That may not be long in the history of puzzle development, but it is long enough for us to have built up a formidable collection of amusing, intriguing, fascinating, frustrating, infuriating puzzles.

This collection was great fun but also hard work. We had to come up with twenty ideas a day, which is easy in the beginning but gets harder as you go on. By the end we were even getting puzzle ideas from staring at the wallpaper. Almost anything becomes a puzzle if you work at it.

This collection should keep you occupied for many, many hours. Have fun, and enjoy.

ROBERT ALLEN
Editorial Director, Mensa Publications
June, 1995

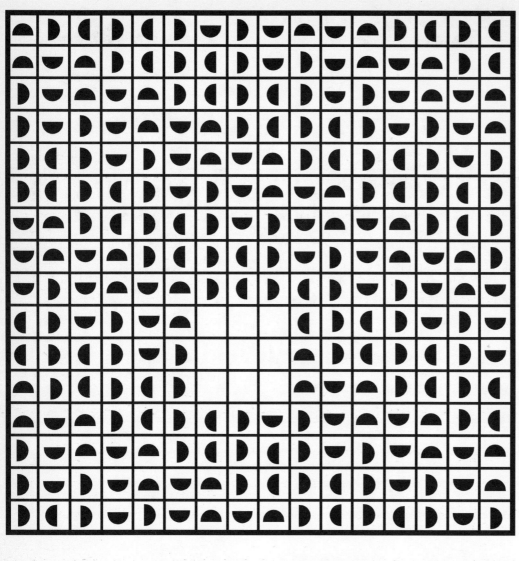

PUZZLE 1

Which of these patterns fits into the blank section?

See answer **25**

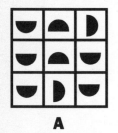

A

B

C

D

2   3   5   8   13   21   34   ?

PUZZLE 2

Can you find the number which comes next in this sequence?

See answer **81**

PUZZLE 3

Can you correct this equation by moving one match?

See answer **28**

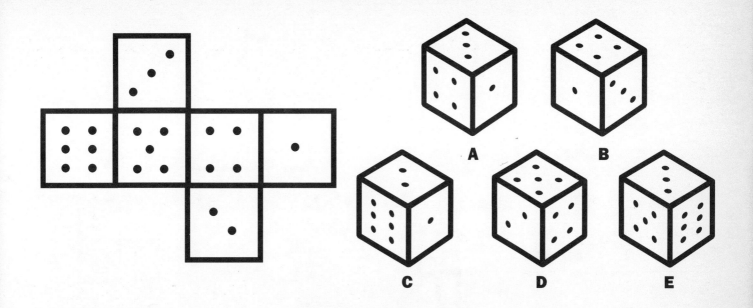

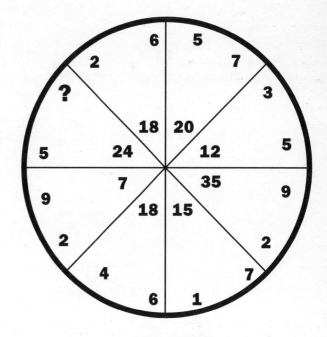

PUZZLE 4

Which of the following cubes cannot be
made from this layout?

See answer 15

I have five hands
but you would pass
me in the street
without comment.

Why?

PUZZLE 5

See answer 46

PUZZLE 6

Can you replace the question mark
with a number to meet
the conditions of the wheel?

See answer 58

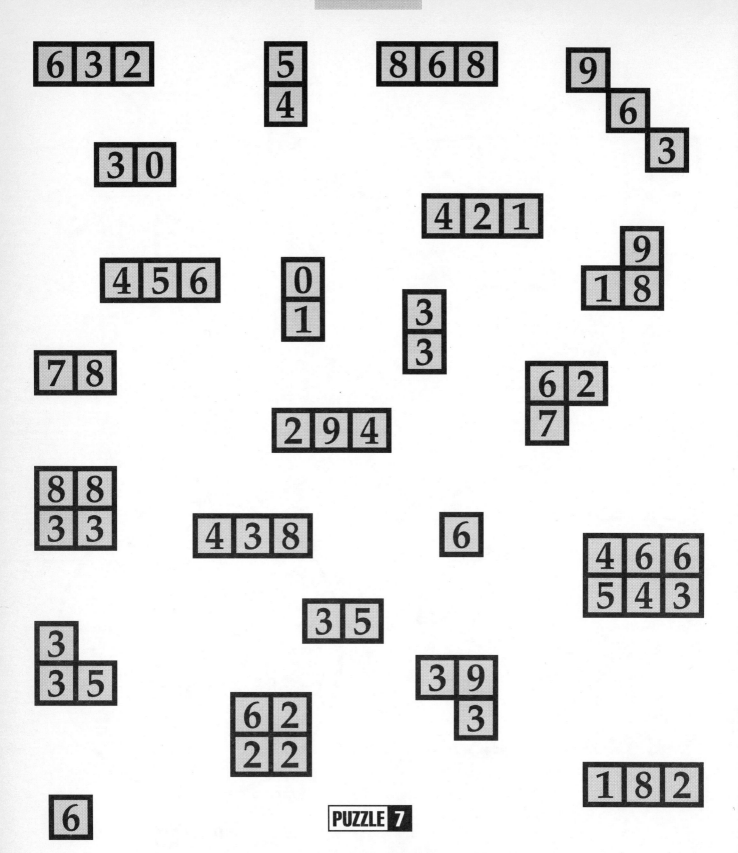

PUZZLE 7

These tiles, when placed in right order, will form
a square in which each horizontal line is
identical with one vertical line.
Can you successfully form the square?

See answer 33

ULFCHANIH
VYNBYMXU
WIFOGVCU JCEY
MCFPYL MJLCHA
GIOHN LUCHCYL
WBYPS WBUMY
AYILAYNIQH
UHUWIMNCU

PUZZLE 8

Here are the coded names of some places in or around Washington, D.C. Try to unravel them.

See answer 62

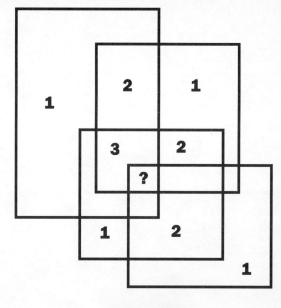

PUZZLE 9

This diagram was constructed according to a certain logic. Can you work out which number should replace the question mark?

See answer 104

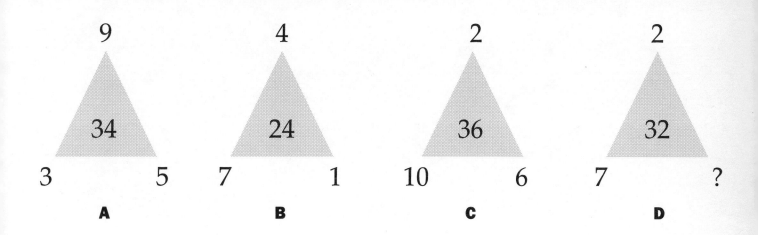

	A	B	C	D
top	9	4	2	2
middle	34	24	36	32
bottom	3 5	7 1	10 6	7 ?

PUZZLE 10

Can you find the number to go at the bottom of triangle D?

See answer 87

O Q L H R
I J F E Q
F G F C ?

PUZZLE 11

Can you find the letter which completes
the diagram?

See answer **22**

PUZZLE 12

Can you find out the relationship of the letters and
numbers in this square and find out which number
should replace the question mark?

See answer **35**

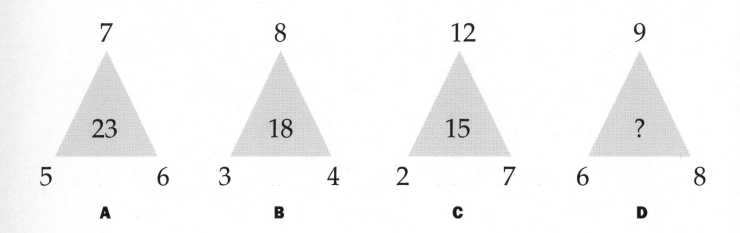

PUZZLE 13

Can you work out how the numbers in the triangles
are related and find the missing number?

See answer **39**

To celebrate her sixth birthday, Samantha planted a tree in her parents' garden.

She had often watched her dad plant things and she did it just right.

She even remembered to water it in.

Her mother was furious. She said that the tree belonged to her and Samantha had no business planting it.

However, her father thought it was funny but explained to her that the tree would never grow.

Why?

See answer 41

VKHEOHC (Russian)

THRBCE (German)

EWDIL (Irish)

TBTEEKC (Irish)

TGNEE (French)

EEOHTG (German)

NBESI (Norwegian)

CAIREN (French)

PUZZLE 15

The above are all anagrams of the names of famous playrights. The nationality is given in brackets to help you.

See answer 114

PUZZLE 16

Can you find the odd ball out?

See answer 122

PUZZLE 17

Can you work out the time on the blank clock face?

See answer 83

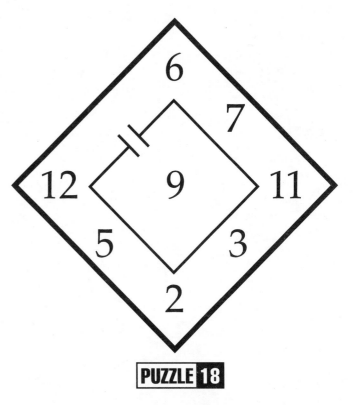

PUZZLE 18

In this diagram, starting from the top of the diamond and working in a clockwise direction, the four basic mathematical signs (+, −, x, ÷) have been omitted. Your task is to restore them so that the calculation, with answer in the middle, is correct.

See answer 6

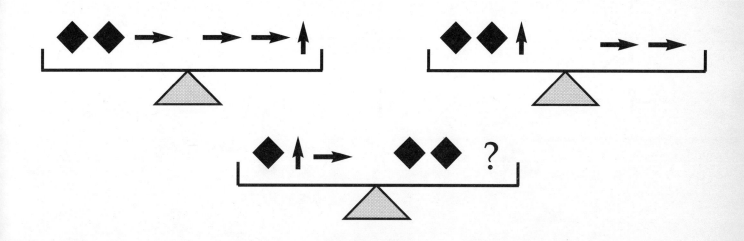

PUZZLE 19

Can you find the symbol that will balance the
last set of scales?

See answer 101

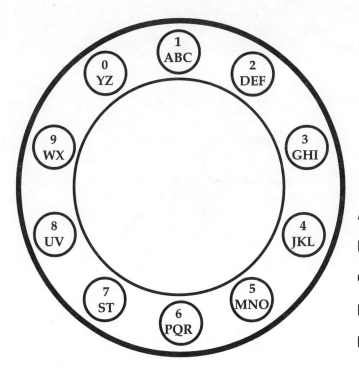

PUZZLE 20

The diagram represents an old-fashioned telephone
dial with letters as well as numbers. Below is a list of
numbers representing ten American States. Can you
use the diagram to decode them?

See answer 1

A.	1143256531	F.	562355
B.	72917	G.	83633531
C.	52161741	H.	2456321
D.	141741	I.	15456125
E.	32135	J.	1630551

A   is to   **B**   as   **C**   is to

D   **E**

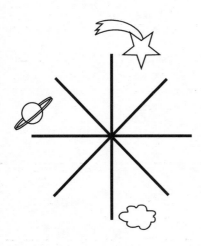

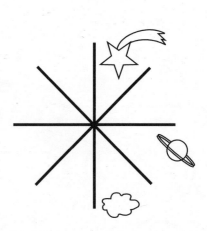

F   **G**

PUZZLE 21

See answer **127**

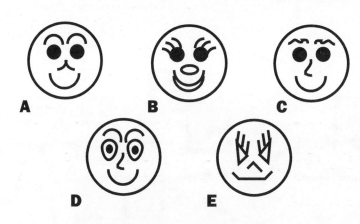

A   **B**   **C**

D   **E**

PUZZLE 22

Can you find the odd face out?

See answer 12

PUZZLE 23

YVRKYIFN
WFIK NFIKY
SVE XLIZFE
CRJ GRCDRJ
F'YRIV
XRKNZTB
YREVUR
JYREEFE

The above is a simple substitution code which conceals the names of eight international airports. See if you can crack the code.

See answer 128

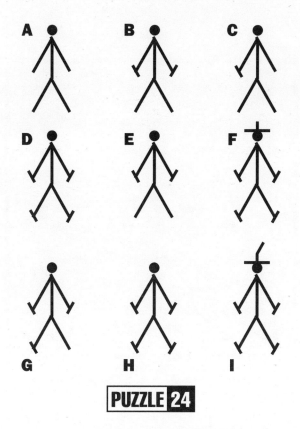

A   **B**   **C**

D   **E**   **F**

G   **H**   **I**

PUZZLE 24

Which matchstick man, G, H or I, would carry on the sequence?

See answer 49

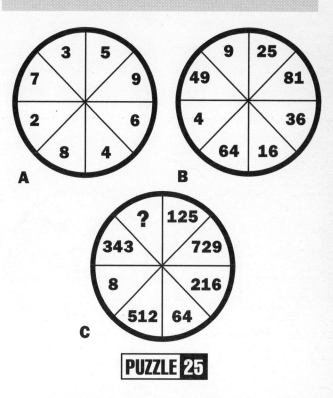

Circle A: 3, 5, 7, 9, 2, 6, 8, 4

Circle B: 9, 25, 49, 81, 4, 36, 64, 16

Circle C: ?, 125, 343, 729, 8, 216, 512, 64

PUZZLE 25

A curious logic governs the numbers in these circles. Can you discover what it is and then work out what the missing number should be?

See answer 9

PUZZLE 26

These tiles, when placed in right order, will form
a square in which each horizontal line is
identical with one vertical line.
Can you successfully form the square?

*See answer **51***

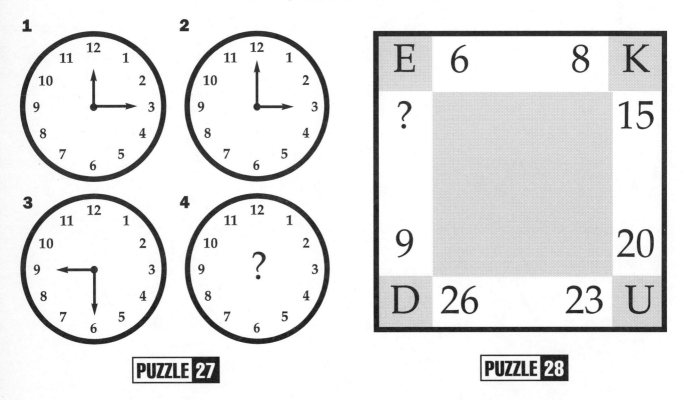

PUZZLE 27

The above clocks move in a certain pattern.
Can you work out the time on the last clock?

*See answer **100***

PUZZLE 28

The letters and numbers in this square follow
a pattern. Can you work out which number
represents the question mark?

*See answer **19***

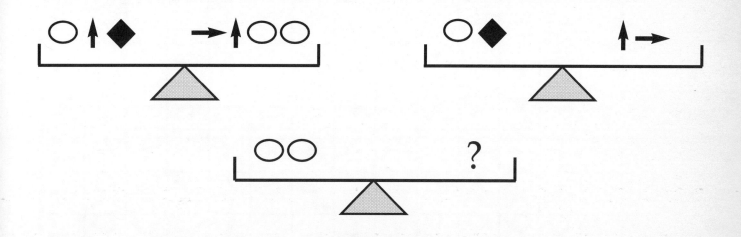

PUZZLE 29

Can you find out which symbol would
balance the third scale?

See answer 96

2

5

9

14

20

?

PUZZLE 30

Can you complete this series?

See answer 106

ACCOHGI
WLKEEMUIA
UTSOONH
GNHIAMMRBI
RTOEIDT
AAATTNL
XPEHOIN
PMHEIMS

PUZZLE 31

The above are all anagrams of the names of American
cities. Can you work out which they are?

See answer 105

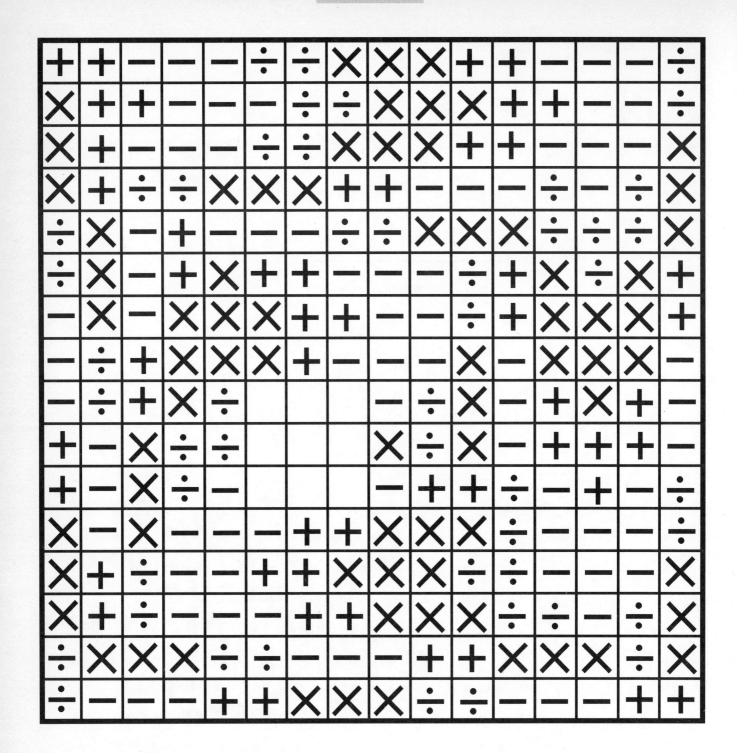

PUZZLE 32

A section of this grid has been removed and its symbols deleted. Can you replace the symbols so that the logic of the grid is restored?

See answer 27

20

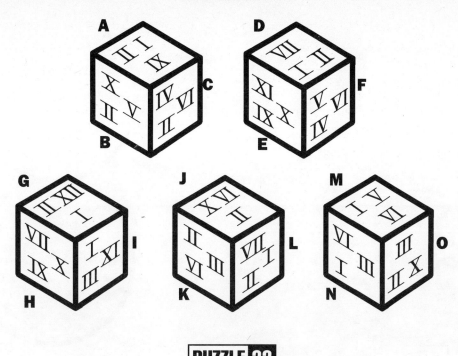

PUZZLE 33

Can you work out which two sides on these cubes
have identical numbers?

See answer 130

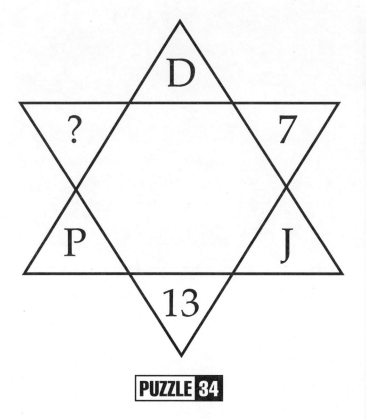

PUZZLE 34

Can you find the number to complete the diagram?

See answer 21

7 1 26 16 1 3 8 15
13 21 12 12 9 7 1 20 1 23 14 25
2 15 18 19 3 8 20
13 9 14 5 19 20 18 15 14 5
3 8 15 23 4 5 18
1 22 7 15 12 5 13 15 14 15
3 15 3 11 - 1 - 12 5 5 11 9 5
2 15 21 9 12 12 1 2 1 9 19 19 5

PUZZLE 35

The above is a substitution code which
uses numbers in place of letters. The words that
have been encoded are all types of soup
from around the world.

See answer 119

E O G O N R
A R B S E N A K
A V D N E A
C I S N O W N I S
R I O D A L F
I G N R I I A V
X S T E A
O O O A D R L C

PUZZLE 36

The above are anagrams of the names of American states. Can you work them out?

See answer 113

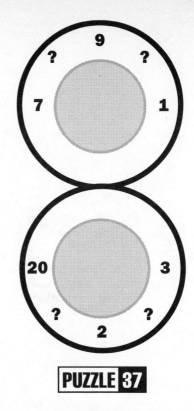

PUZZLE 37

Can you work out whether + or − should replace the question marks in this diagram so that both sections arrive at the same value?

See answer 136

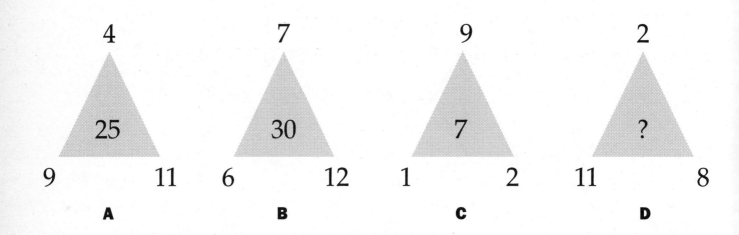

4	7	9	2
25	30	7	?
9 11	6 12	1 2	11 8
A	**B**	**C**	**D**

PUZZLE 38

The above triangles follow a pattern. Can you work it out and find the missing number?

See answer 97

Jim sat in the bedroom watching the never-ending rain morosely.

Jt had fallen on his home town for three weeks without cease and there were now floods everywhere.

In most places the water was several feet deep and rising rapidly.

Everyone had been forced to live upstairs.

Just then his wife walked in but, try as he might, Jim couldn't get her to take the situation seriously.

Why not?

*See answer **42***

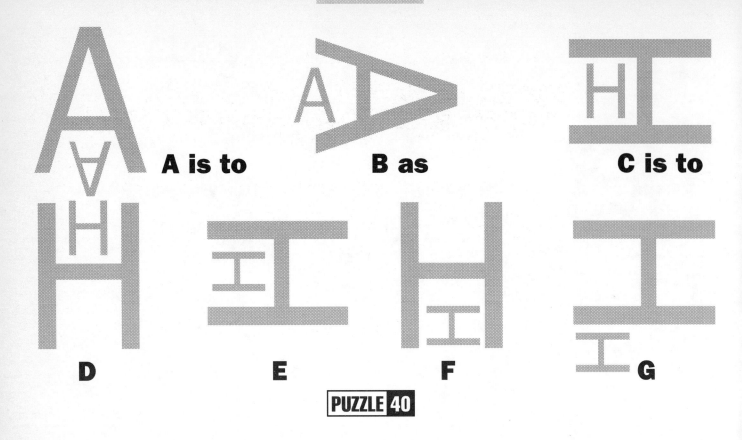

A is to B as C is to

D E F G

See answer **110**

PUZZLE 40

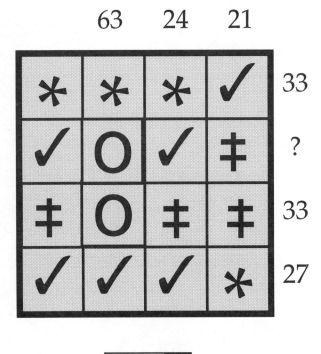

63 24 21

✱	✱	✱	✓	33
✓	O	✓	‡	?
‡	O	‡	‡	33
✓	✓	✓	✱	27

PUZZLE 41

Each symbol in this square represents a value. Can you work out how much the question mark is worth?

See answer **94**

NUCXW SXQW
OANMMRN VNALDAH
URBJ BCJWBORNUM
BRWNJM X'LXWWXA
VNJCUXJO
VJMXWWJ
VRLQJNU SJLTBXW
AXM BCNFJAC

PUZZLE 42

The above is a simple substitution code which conceals the names of eight pop singers. See if you can work out who they are.

See answer **109**

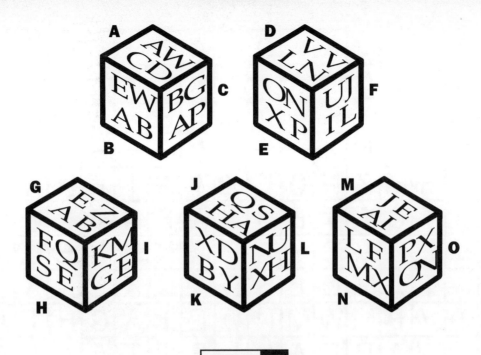

Two sides of these cubes contain the same letters. Can
you spot them?

See answer 82

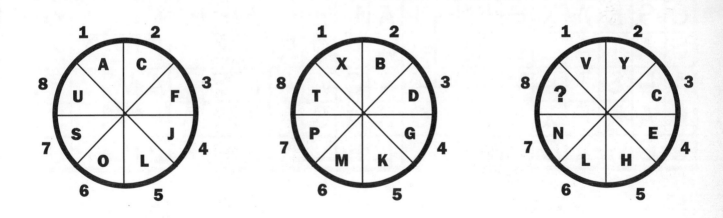

Can you find the letter which fits in
the missing segment?

See answer 16

C	W	C	O	A	L	M	K	W	O	E	A	C	K	L	G	O	Z	A	N
L	H	E	M	I	N	G	W	A	Y	N	E	I	Y	L	M	O	X	A	E
L	E	E	C	M	O	X	K	W	A	X	F	E	X	A	N	B	K	O	S
C	F	A	K	K	E	N	Z	A	E	X	L	A	E	B	L	P	E	F	B
A	I	E	L	H	M	Z	N	O	E	X	I	A	I	F	H	R	K	L	I
M	O	Q	V	T	O	A	T	E	U	I	W	E	H	T	E	O	G	M	O
A	T	K	V	L	A	V	C	H	A	E	M	N	O	L	E	U	A	B	C
F	S	I	A	T	A	M	Q	L	S	D	I	C	K	E	N	S	S	T	A
A	L	S	T	V	E	M	W	M	N	O	E	I	A	C	H	T	A	C	T
F	O	O	X	W	A	B	E	A	L	L	E	I	T	A	W	W	A	C	G
G	T	O	X	A	E	A	K	F	A	K	I	L	A	A	S	T	A	W	N
O	N	F	B	C	H	J	K	W	L	L	T	J	I	I	E	X	G	H	I
E	N	O	L	F	M	G	O	Z	X	A	Y	N	A	E	B	E	C	W	L
R	V	O	L	F	I	G	A	E	Z	I	U	I	E	J	C	C	K	T	P
E	W	U	V	E	C	U	O	P	T	E	G	B	P	N	H	T	S	E	I
C	S	E	W	X	H	L	H	J	A	L	E	C	E	K	L	T	U	Z	K
U	A	T	A	E	E	C	K	U	W	P	Q	R	A	R	A	E	P	A	Z
A	U	S	T	E	N	X	A	T	A	Q	W	A	L	E	T	A	W	V	E
H	A	P	E	X	E	A	B	C	B	A	C	A	E	W	W	E	X	L	E
C	C	W	A	O	R	W	E	L	L	K	M	N	O	P	P	E	L	T	U

Austen	**Hemingway**	**Michener**
Chaucer	**Huxley**	**Orwell**
Chekhov	**Ibsen**	**Proust**
Dickens	**Kafka**	**Tolstoi**
Flaubert	**Kipling**	**Twain**
Goethe	**Lawrence**	**Zola**

PUZZLE 45

In this grid are hidden the names of 18 famous authors. Can you detect them? You can go forward or in reverse, in horizontal, vertical and diagonal lines.

See answer 38

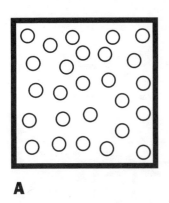
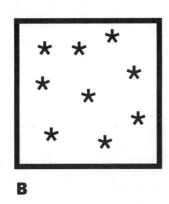

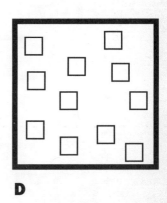

A   **B**   **C**   **D**

PUZZLE 46

There is a logic to the patterns in these squares but one
does not fit. Can you find the odd one out?

See answer 3

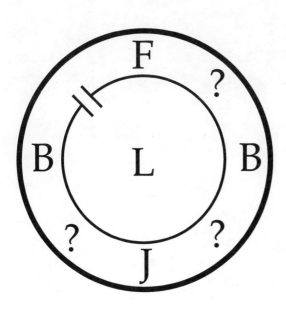

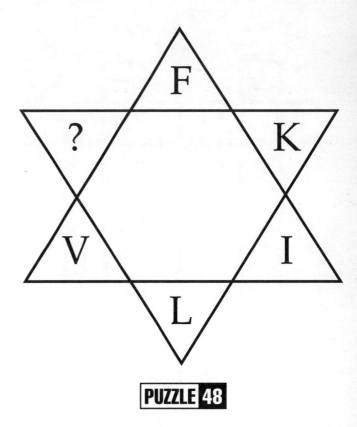

PUZZLE 47

Can you work out which mathematical signs should
replace the question marks in this diagram? You have
a choice between – or +.

See answer 10

PUZZLE 48

Which letter replaces the question mark in this star?

See answer 30

PUZZLE 49

These tiles, when placed in right order, will form
a square in which each horizontal line is
identical with one vertical line.
Can you successfully form the square?

*See answer **88***

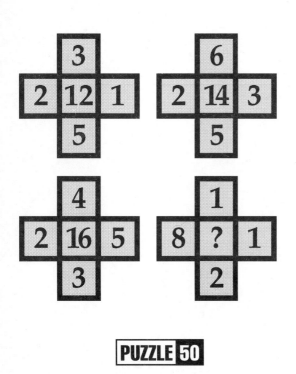

PUZZLE 50

Find a number to replace the question mark

*See answer **20***

I L V A V I D   **(Italian)**

G G E I R   **(Norwegian)**

E H E T B N V O E   **(German)**

T Z E B I   **(French)**

L H R E M A   **(Austrian)**

G R E N A W   **(German)**

Z R O T M A   **(Austrian)**

R A L G E   **(English)**

PUZZLE 51

Here are some anagrams of the names
of famous composers. The nationality
is given in brackets to help you.

*See answer **123***

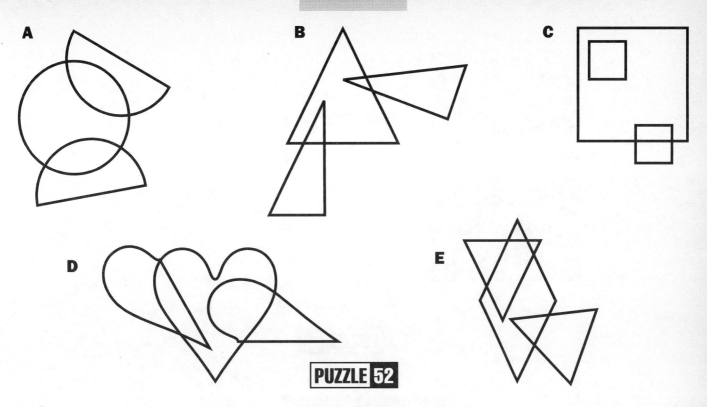

A

B

C

D

E

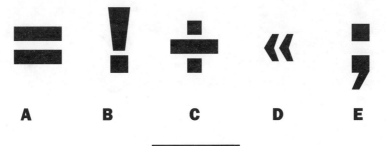

PUZZLE 52

Can you work out which of these diagram is
the odd one out?

See answer **138**

1 3 2 6 4 12 8 24 ?

PUZZLE 53

What comes next in this sequence?

See answer **63**

A   **B**   **C**   **D**   **E**

PUZZLE 54

Can you work out which of these symbols
is the odd one out?

See answer **140**

41 34 12 14 52 52 42
53 24 44 13 53 14 43 11 51
22 14 64 22 34 43
31 24 42 43 14 53 11 42
12 42 43 52 51 14 13 31 24
53 14 41 21 14 24 31
63 14 43 22 42 22 21
44 14 51 34 52 52 24

PUZZLE 55

This is a simple grid code. The encoded words are all names of famous painters.

See answer 115

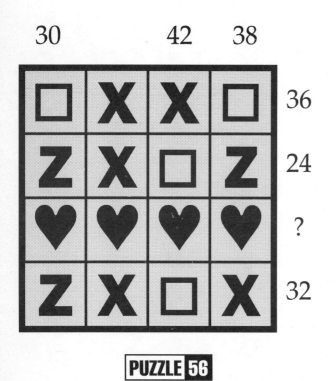

PUZZLE 56

Each symbol in the above square represents a number. Can you find out how much the question mark is worth?

See answer 98

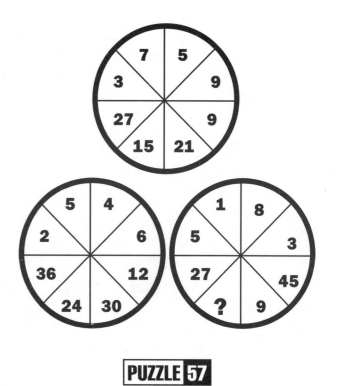

PUZZLE 57

Can you find the missing number that fits into the sector of the last wheel?

See answer 55

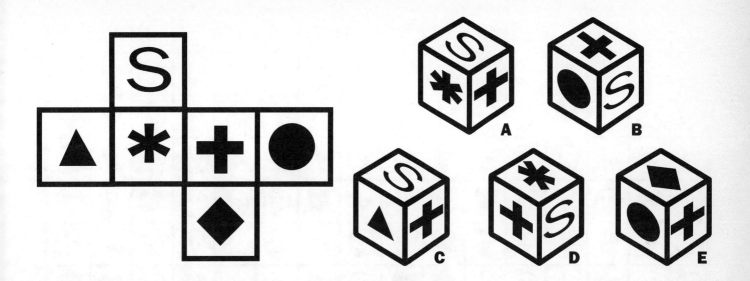

PUZZLE 58

Which of these cubes cannot be made
from this layout?

See answer 36

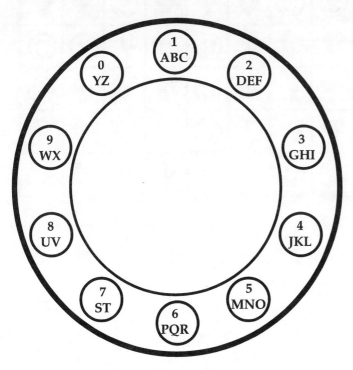

PUZZLE 59

The diagram represent an old-fashioned telephone
dial with letters as well as numbers. Below is a list of
numbers representing 10 American towns or cities.
Can you decode them?

See answer 48

A.	214417	F.	65674152
B.	7217742	G.	2276537
C.	1331135	H.	1741571
D.	534918422	I.	1351355173
E.	53552165437	J.	352315165437

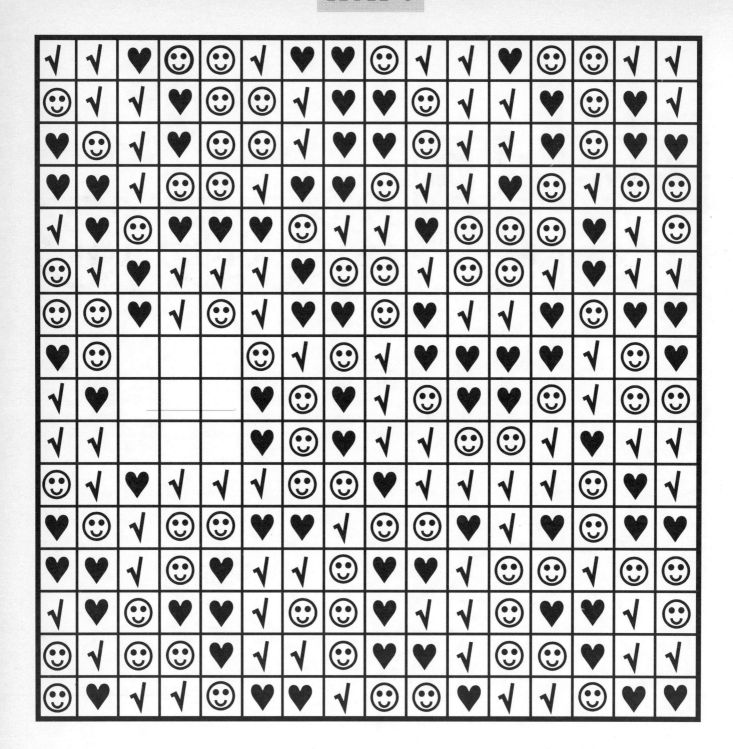

PUZZLE 60

The symbols in the above grid follow a pattern. Can you work it out and find the missing section?

See answer 60

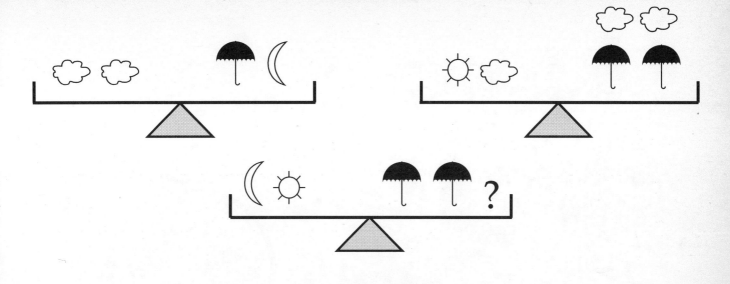

PUZZLE 61

The first two sets of scales are in balance.
Which symbol is needed to balance the third set?

See answer 5

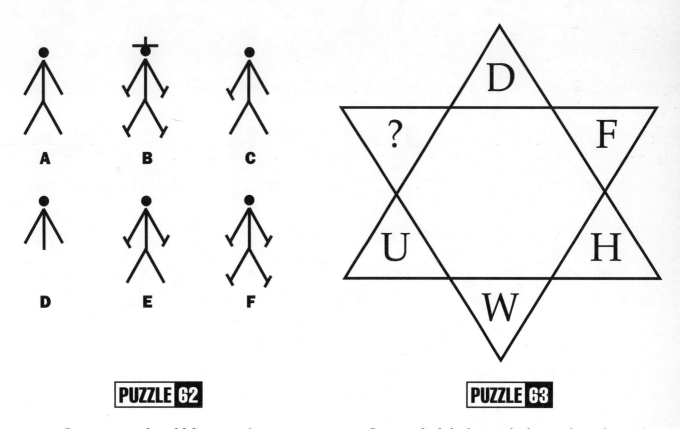

PUZZLE 62

Can you spot the odd figure out?

See answer 137

PUZZLE 63

Can you find the letter which completes the star?

See answer 47

ΜΙΥΥΜΕ ΙΥΑΜΥ
ΗΣΕΕΞΨΙΓΘ ΧΙΜΜΑΗΕ
ΝΑΞΘΑΥΥΑΞ
ΥΙΝΕΤ ΤΡΦΑΣΕ
ΗΣΑΝΕΣΓΥ ΠΑΣΛ
· ΤΟΘΟ
ΓΕΞΥΣΑΜ ΠΑΣΛ
ΓΘΙΞΑΥΟΨΞ

PUZZLE 64

Above are the coded names of some places in
New York. Can you work out their names?
Vowels A, E, I and O are correct.

See answer 75

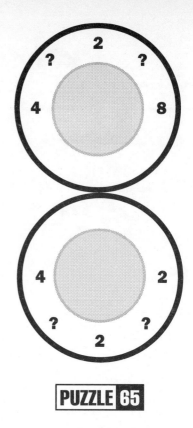

PUZZLE 65

Can you work out what mathematical signs should
replace the question marks so that both sections of the
diagram arrive at the same value. You have a choice
between ÷ or x.

See answer 89

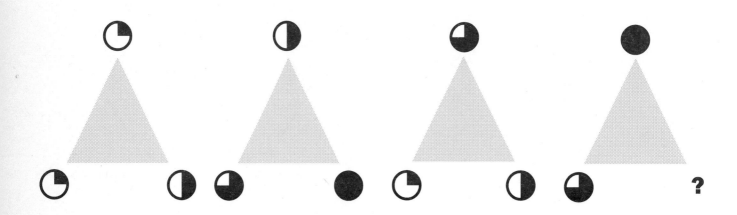

PUZZLE 66

Can you find the missing symbol in the last triangle?

See answer 76

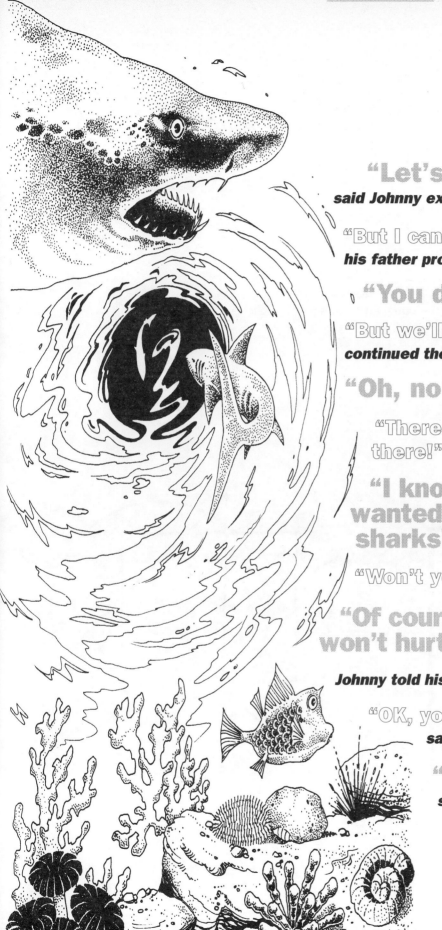

PUZZLE 67

"Let's go under the sea!"
said Johnny excitedly to his dad.

"But I can't swim,"
his father protested.

"You don't have to."

"But we'll get wet,"
continued the reluctant parent.

"Oh, no we won't."

"There are sharks down there!"

"I know – I've always wanted to see real sharks!"

"Won't you be scared?"

"Of course not, they won't hurt us."

Johnny told his dad where he meant to go.

"OK, you win,"
said the relieved parent.

"Let's go!"
said Johnny.

Johnny and his dad are not going diving, or taking a trip in a glass-bottomed boat. So how are they going under the sea without coming to any harm?

PUZZLE 68

MATCH POINTS

Can you correct this equation by moving six matches?

See answer 26

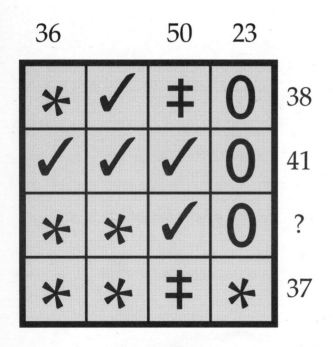

36   50   23

38

41

?

37

PUZZLE 69

Each symbol in this square represents a value.
Can you find out which number should replace the
question mark?

See answer 23

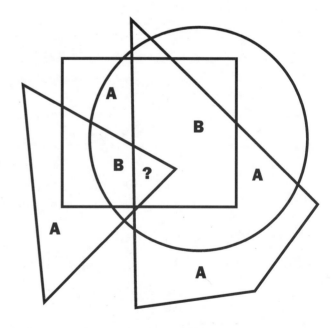

PUZZLE 70

A certain logic has been used in making this diagram.
Can you work out what the secret is and replace the
question mark with a letter?

See answer 131

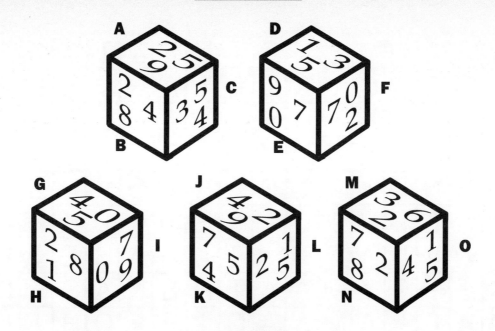

PUZZLE 71

Two sides on these cubes contain the same numbers.
Can you spot them?

See answer 107

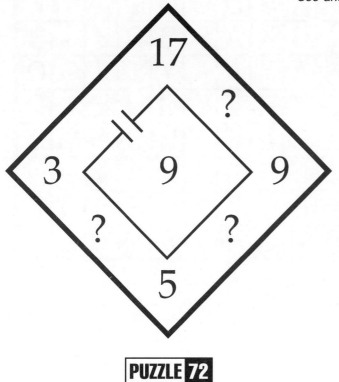

PUZZLE 72

The mathematical signs in this diamond have been
left out. Reading clockwise from the top can you work
out what the question marks stand for?

See answer 108

PUZZLE 73

OPLNNOEA	**(France)**
RCLUCHIHL	**(GB)**
MATNRU	**(USA)**
EDLAGELU	**(France)**
NNEEYDK	**(USA)**
OHHICHNIM	**(Vietnam)**
INHDAG	**(India)**
LEDAANM	**(South Africa)**

Here are anagrams of famous statesmen. Their
nationalities are given to help you.

See answer 37

P	B	A	W	N	W	O	C	H	K	T	V	E	N	T	A	C	Y	X	O
A	A	D	E	F	W	O	Y	J	U	L	I	A	R	O	B	E	R	T	S
C	D	U	S	T	I	N	H	O	F	F	M	A	N	B	R	M	O	N	L
K	A	O	L	W	O	L	N	N	Y	G	O	R	E	S	O	T	U	V	D
K	M	G	E	N	E	W	I	L	D	E	R	W	O	L	O	Z	B	R	R
C	A	S	K	L	E	M	U	O	T	L	B	W	J	L	K	K	E	G	O
P	C	M	W	V	U	W	E	A	I	J	L	G	A	H	E	T	E	B	F
E	L	K	E	F	O	Z	M	A	A	T	H	E	N	A	S	E	R	O	D
E	S	O	A	L	L	A	M	A	A	O	I	E	E	O	H	I	L	L	E
R	T	A	S	E	G	F	A	A	N	T	O	E	F	L	I	S	T	R	R
T	O	M	C	R	U	I	S	E	S	R	S	E	O	T	E	E	E	P	T
S	A	O	E	E	B	W	B	I	M	Q	I	A	N	E	L	G	N	O	R
L	A	A	O	H	E	H	R	S	T	D	A	B	D	C	D	O	A	T	E
Y	A	F	G	S	V	H	T	E	O	I	B	K	A	R	S	C	E	J	B
R	B	P	O	A	C	F	A	J	Z	N	A	Y	A	A	Y	I	X	Q	O
E	N	O	Z	E	A	L	M	A	O	C	Y	H	F	O	G	H	E	L	R
M	A	E	I	N	A	Z	E	N	I	A	C	L	E	A	H	C	I	M	B
C	P	L	M	A	N	N	V	W	X	I	E	R	S	F	L	A	Z	O	N
N	U	W	M	J	F	G	Q	S	R	A	E	L	L	A	E	S	S	O	E
J	O	N	Y	F	G	I	N	O	S	P	M	O	H	T	A	M	M	E	F

Jane Asher	**Richard Gere**
Julia Roberts	**Michael Caine**
Mel Gibson	**Brooke Shields**
Julie Christie	**Dustin Hoffman**
Meryl Streep	**Tom Cruise**
Paul Newman	**Emma Thompson**
Jane Fonda	**Robert Redford**
Gene Wilder	**Jodie Foster**

PUZZLE 74

Hidden in this grid are the names of 16 well-known actors. Can you spot them? You can move in horizontal, vertical and diagonal lines in a forward or backward direction.

See answer 61

**JWQA LM JWCTWOVM
UWVBXIZVIAAM
UILMTMQVM
XMZM TIKPIQAM
KPIUXA MTGAMMA
OIZM LM TGWV
IZK LM BZQWUXPM
UWVBU IZBZM**

PUZZLE 75

Here are the coded names of some places in Paris.
Can you discover their identity?

See answer 66

PUZZLE 76

Which of the faces A, B or C would carry
on the sequence above?

See answer 90

7		14	4		8	6		12	3		6
	35			20			30			?	
28		21	16		12	24		18	12		9

PUZZLE 77

Can you work out which number should go into
the last square?

See answer 52

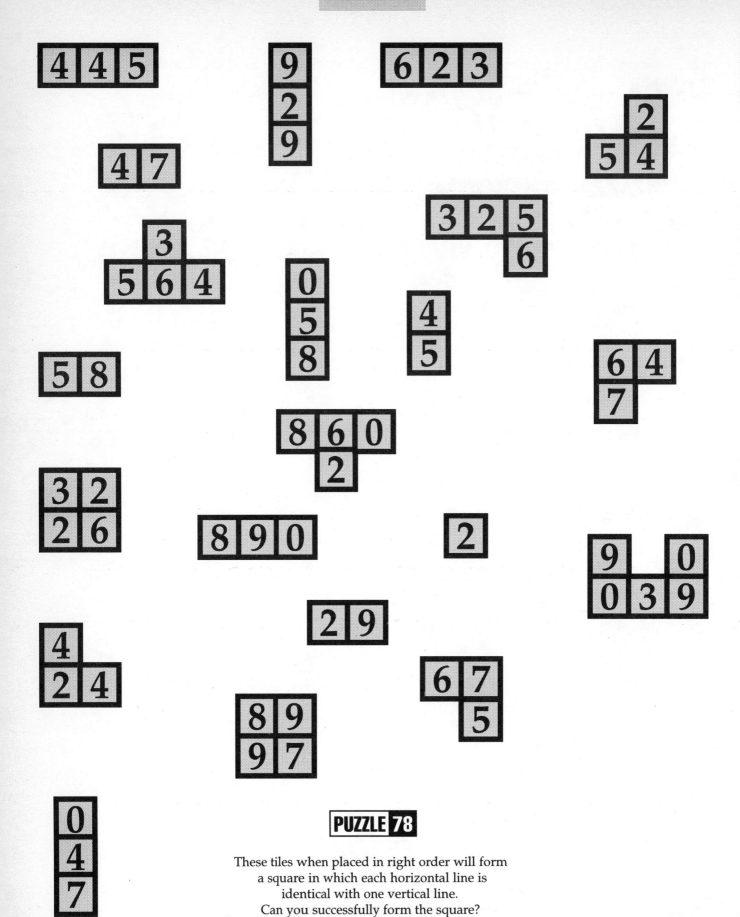

PUZZLE 78

These tiles when placed in right order will form
a square in which each horizontal line is
identical with one vertical line.
Can you successfully form the square?

See answer 77

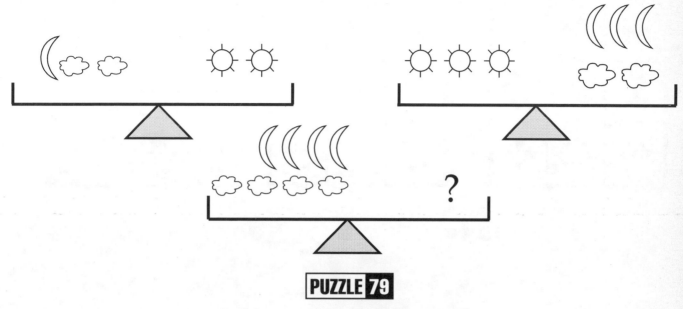

PUZZLE 79

Can you work out which symbols you need
to balance the scale?

See answer 31

PUZZLE 80

Can you work out what the blank clockface
should look like?

See answer 64

AJILU TREBORS
RUBT NOYLEDRS
CAKJ OHLCSIONN
VDAID EVNIN
IRLANYM RNOOME
MERYJE NSORI
URYEDA BPEHRNU
NNOAIW DYRER

PUZZLE 81

The above are anagrams of the names of film
stars. Both the first and second names are given.

See answer 132

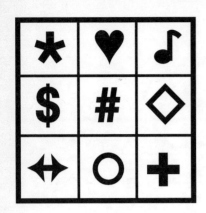

A   is to   B   as   C   is to

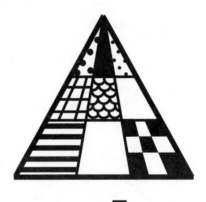

D   **E**

F   **G**

PUZZLE 82

See answer 121

42

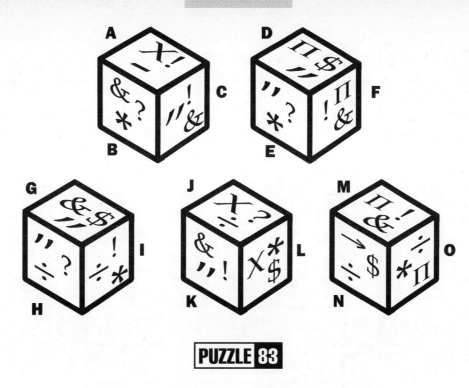

PUZZLE 83

Can you find the two sides on these cubes which
contain exactly the same symbols?

See answer 134

36   23   24   ?

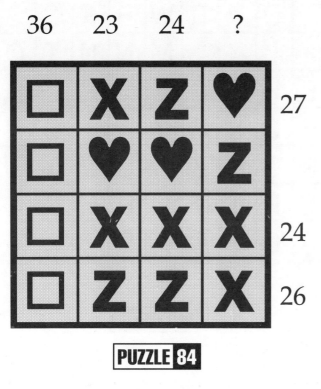

PUZZLE 84

Each symbol in the grid has a numerical value.
Work out what those values are and replace the
question mark with a number.

See answer 7

CCDALLYIIP	**(London)**
POCACAANAB	**(Rio)**
GGGNEUMEHI	**(New York)**
OITEEL	**(Paris)**
ETIHWLLHA	**(London)**
DAEMNIELE	**(Paris)**
NECRALT RAKP	**(New York)**
OOLSMEUCS	**(Rome)**

PUZZLE 85

The above are all anagrams of places or sights
to be found in cities around the world.
The location is given as a clue.

See answer 95

K	L	N	B	C	E	W	O	P	Q	B	A	I	K	M	O	L	C
G	A	E	C	C	W	V	R	A	E	I	X	C	M	O	L	A	D
B	E	F	H	A	E	L	E	H	A	R	U	O	H	N	K	M	X
O	A	B	A	C	H	A	N	A	E	X	T	A	T	O	T	E	W
R	L	O	N	E	F	A	G	E	T	W	Y	A	E	X	P	M	M
O	N	A	D	E	A	G	A	H	A	D	H	E	L	L	E	I	E
D	A	C	E	F	G	E	W	A	N	E	A	E	I	M	C	O	N
I	U	F	L	I	S	Z	T	B	E	N	T	V	O	W	L	C	D
N	A	E	K	M	O	Z	G	A	V	E	A	Z	C	K	L	P	E
Q	S	K	A	E	K	E	B	E	O	H	A	R	T	U	E	K	L
L	W	A	A	E	I	P	Q	R	H	R	A	E	T	X	C	K	S
A	C	E	I	R	V	O	S	P	T	Q	V	R	W	B	R	C	S
S	D	A	G	E	O	K	W	O	E	L	X	I	M	N	U	T	O
M	O	V	X	Z	K	V	M	N	E	K	E	C	V	A	P	J	H
H	L	W	X	Q	W	A	D	E	B	U	S	S	Y	A	T	O	N
A	O	W	P	X	B	E	I	E	P	Q	O	Z	A	C	L	T	W
R	A	C	A	S	C	H	U	B	E	R	T	T	O	R	H	D	A
B	B	C	F	K	L	M	N	T	A	C	T	O	A	R	Z	W	I

Bach   **Dvorak**   **Mendelssohn**

Beethoven   **Grieg**   **Mozart**

Borodin   **Handel**   **Purcell**

Brahms   **Haydn**   **Schubert**

Chopin   **Lehar**   **Vivaldi**

Debussy   **Liszt**   **Wagner**

PUZZLE 86

Hidden in this grid are 18 names of well-known composers. Can you find them? You can move horizontally, vertically or diagonally and in a forward or backward direction.

See answer 68

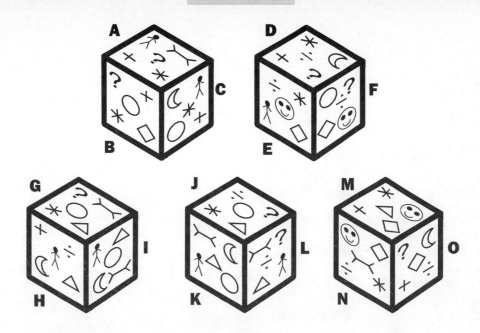

PUZZLE 87

There are two sides on those cubes that contain exactly
the same symbols. Can you spot them?

See answer 99

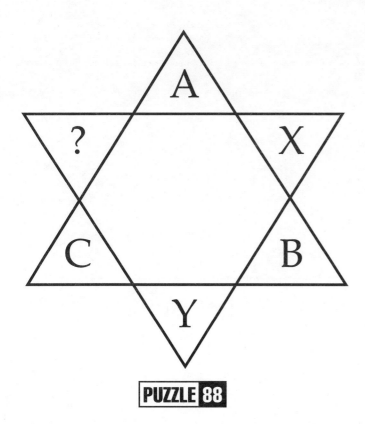

PUZZLE 88

Can you find the letter to complete the star?

See answer 86

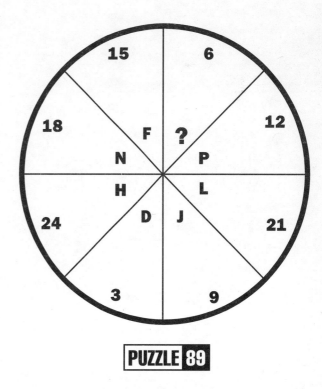

PUZZLE 89

The letters and numbers in this wheel are related in
some way. Can you find which letter should replace
the question mark?

See answer 18

VMASIO (American)
ZLBACA (French)
YHAEWMGIN (American)
CYOEJ (Irish)
MHUAMAG (English)
RELIML (American)
STRUPO (French)
NWITA (American)

PUZZLE 90

The above are anagrams of the names of famous novelists. The nationality is given in brackets to help you.

See answer 141

? 7 4 8 9 0
3 5 0 2 6 7
1 2 4 6 2 3

PUZZLE 91

Can you find the missing number which would complete the diagram?

See answer 34

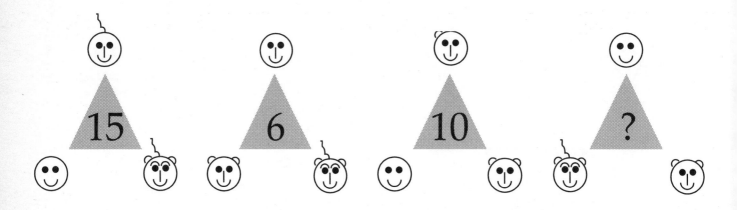

PUZZLE 92

Can you work out which number the question mark in the triangle stands for?

See answer 24

Dr Arnold Gluck, a psychiatrist in New York, came across the world's most enthusiastic bookworm during the course of his work.

He had been one since infancy. All he ever did was devour books.

Yet he never held down a proper job and he didn't go to the public library.

He hadn't inherited money, in fact he was penniless.

So how could he get through all those books?

See answer 44

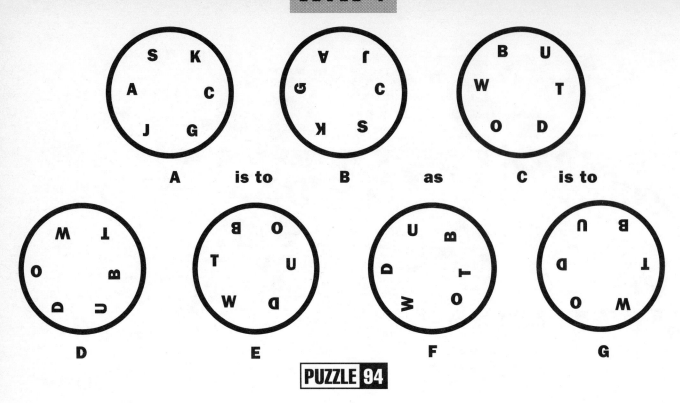

A   is to   B   as   C   is to

D   E   F   G

PUZZLE 94

See answer 116

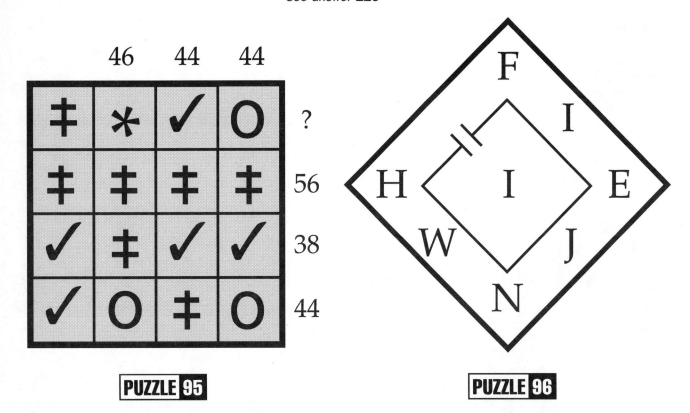

PUZZLE 95

PUZZLE 96

Each symbol in this square represents a number. Can you work out which number should replace the question mark?

In this diagram the mathematical signs (+ and − only) between each letter (which has a value equal to its position in the alphabet) have gone missing. Can you restore them in a way that you arrive at the letter in the middle of the diamond?

See answer 78

See answer 53

PUZZLE 97

Can you find the two sides on these cubes that contain
exactly the same symbols?

See answer 125

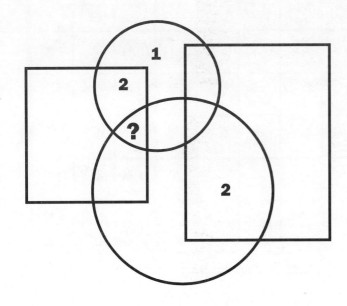

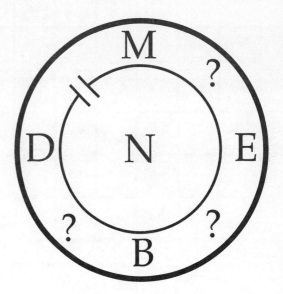

PUZZLE 98

This diagram was constructed according to a certain
logic. Can you work out which number should
replace the question mark?

See answer 124

PUZZLE 99

Can you work out whether + or − should replace the
question mark to arrive at the letter in the middle of
the circle?

See answer 143

LEVEL 1

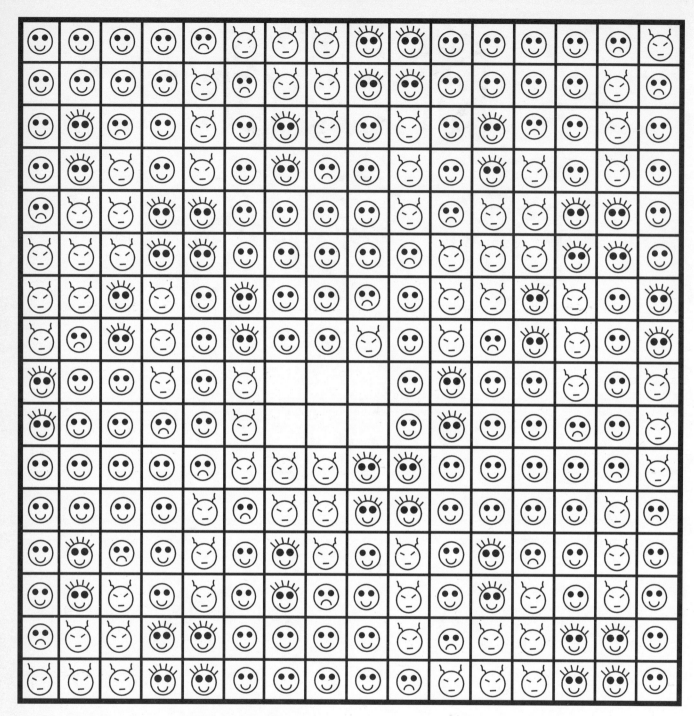

 **A**

 **B**

PUZZLE 100

The symbols in the above grid follow a pattern. Can you work it out and find the missing section?

*See answer **84***

 **C**

 **D**

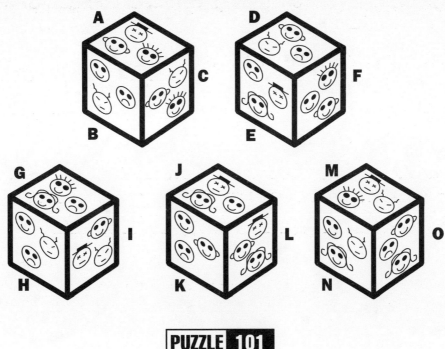

PUZZLE 101

Can you work out which two sides on these cubes
contain the same symbols?

See answer 13

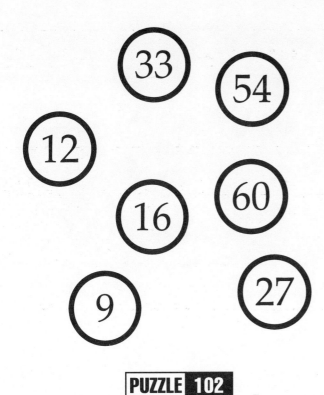

PUZZLE 102

Can you work out which is the odd ball out?

See answer 71

ΨΘΙΥΕΘΑΜΜ
ΥΣΑΖΑΜΗΑΣ ΤΡΦΑΣΕ
ΛΕΞΤΙΞΗΥΟΞ ΗΑΣΔΕΞΤ
ΝΑΣΒΜΕ ΑΣΓΘ
ΒΦΓΛΙΞΗΘΑΝ ΠΑΜΑΓΕ
ΠΙΓΓΑΔΙΜΜΥ ΓΙΣΓΦΤ
ΗΣΟΤΧΕΞΟΣ ΤΡΦΑΣΕ
ΥΘΑΝΕΤ ΕΝΒΑΞΛΝΕΞΥ
ΨΑΥΕΣΜΟΟ ΤΥΑΥΙΟΞ
ΛΙΞΗΤ ΓΣΟΤΤ

PUZZLE 103

The above are the coded names of places in London.
Can you decode them? Only the vowels
A, E, I, and O and consonant B are correct.

See answer 54

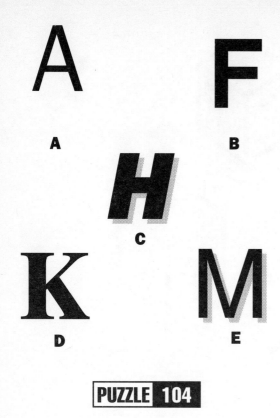

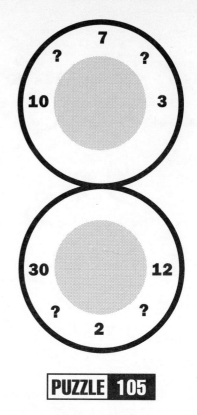

PUZZLE 104

Can you work out which of these letters is the odd one out?

*See answer **133***

PUZZLE 105

Can you replace the question marks with + or – so that both sections in this diagram add up to the same value.

*See answer **126***

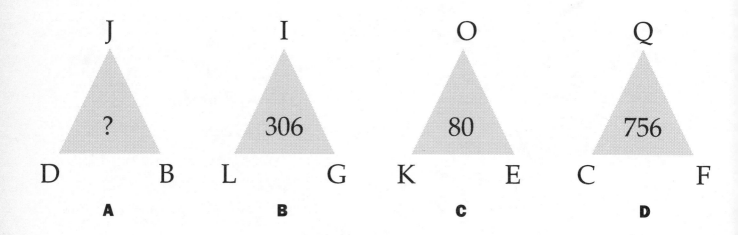

PUZZLE 106

Can you work out which number fits into the first triangle?

*See answer **56***

PUZZLE 107

A man came home to find himself locked out of his house and his back yard full of water.

An upstairs window was open, but he had no ladder to help him reach it.

However, if he could just reach the top of his front porch he'd be able to reach the window.

Then he had an idea.

What was it?

It did not involve ladders, steps or climbing up the walls of the house.

See answer 40

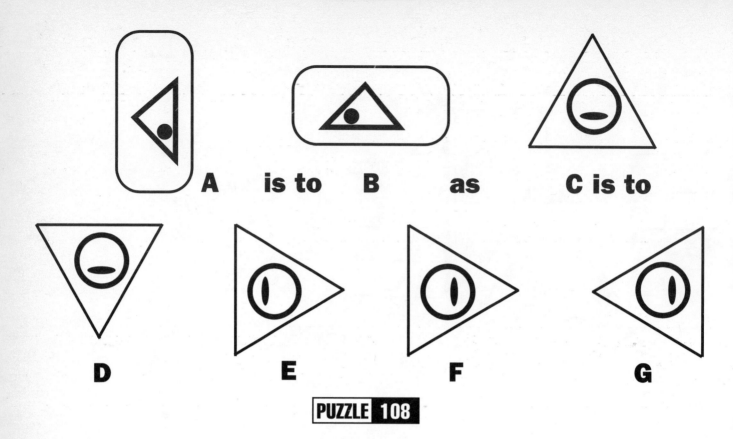

A is to **B** as **C is to**

D **E** **F** **G**

PUZZLE 108

See answer 8

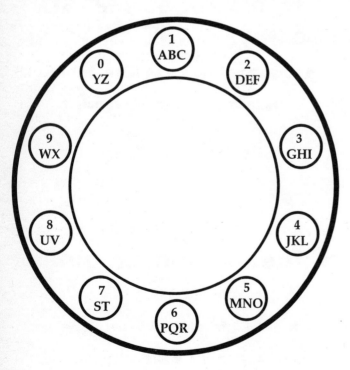

PUZZLE 109

The diagram represents an old-fashioned telephone dial with letters as well as numbers. Below is a list of numbers representing 10 large cities from around the world. Can you use the diagram to decode them?

See answer 92

A.	5151327726	F.	1153454
B.	3417359	G.	11418771
C.	75845872	H.	524158652
D.	75542574	I.	116124551
E.	815158826	J.	7116152575

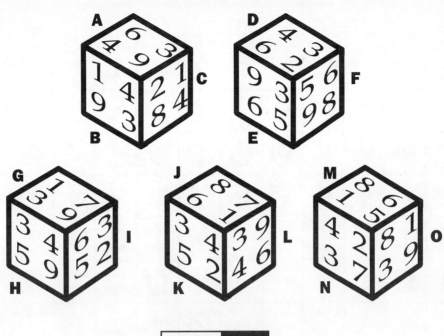

PUZZLE 110

Two sides of these cubes contain exactly the same numbers. Can you spot them?

See answer 57

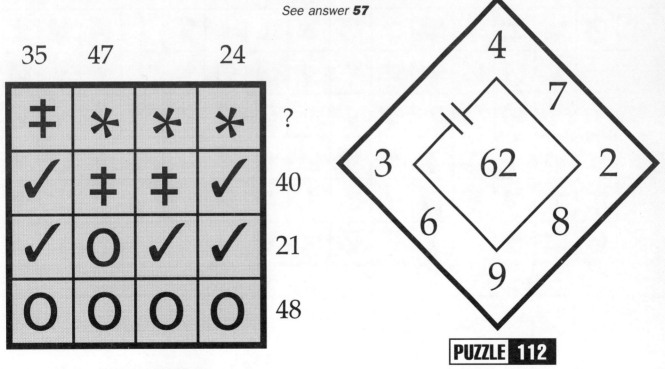

35   47   24

?

40

21

48

PUZZLE 111

Can you work out what number each symbol represents and find the value of the question mark?

See answer 59

PUZZLE 112

In this diamond the four mathematical signs +, −, x and ÷ have been left out. Can you work out which sign fits between each pair of numbers to arrive at the number in the middle of the diagram?

See answer 17

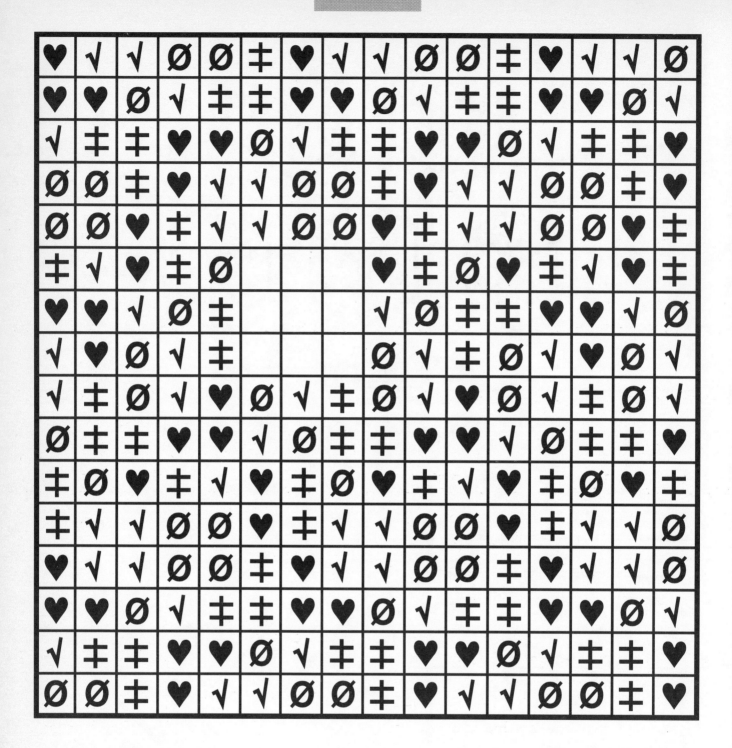

PUZZLE 113

The symbols in this grid follow a pattern. Can you work it out and complete the missing section?

*See answer **74***

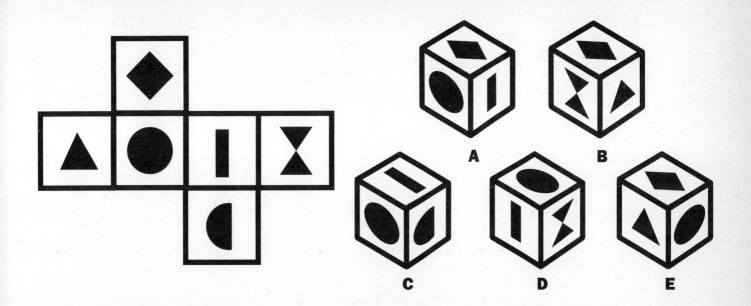

PUZZLE 114

Which of these cubes cannot be made from this layout?

See answer **65**

12		4	7		14	4		7	14		7
	60			28			56			?	
15		5	2		4	8		14	6		3

PUZZLE 115

Can you work out the number needed to
complete the square?

See answer **80**

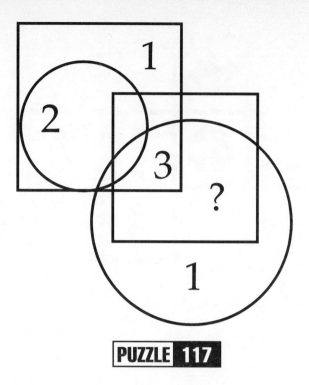

PUZZLE 116

Can you find the mathematical signs which should replace the question marks in this diagram?

See answer 129

PUZZLE 117

Can you crack the logic of this diagram and replace the question mark with a number?

See answer 112

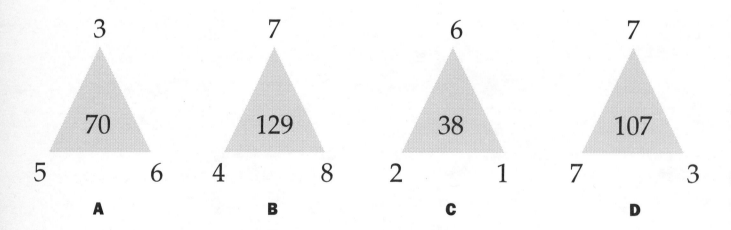

A   B   C   D

PUZZLE 118

The four triangles are linked by a simple mathematical formula. Can you discover what it is and then find the odd one out?

See answer 2

Old Silas Greenfield died and left each of his grandchildren the same bequest.

Sam spent all his having a good time, Dave wasted his and Suzy used hers wisely.

The old man had been determined to treat the grandchildren equally, and in a way he did, **but each got a different sum of money.**

Why?

See answer 43

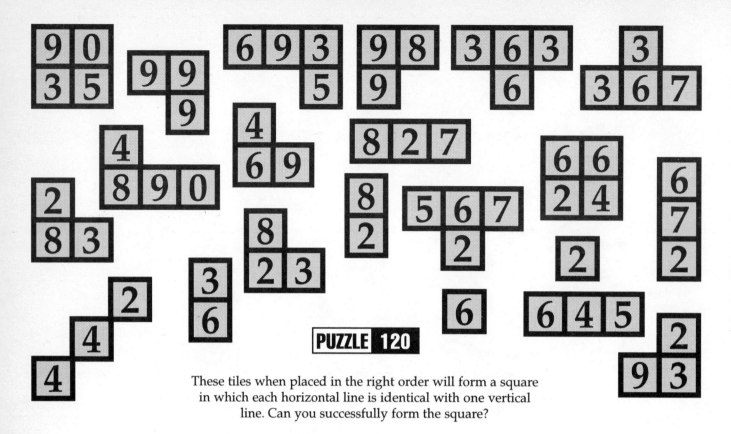

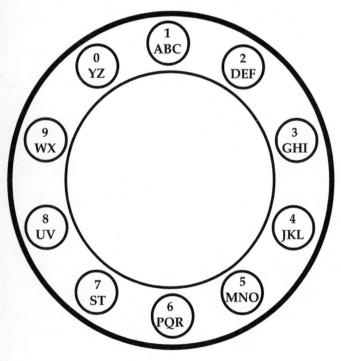

PUZZLE 120

These tiles when placed in the right order will form a square in which each horizontal line is identical with one vertical line. Can you successfully form the square?

See answer 85

PUZZLE 121

The diagram represents an old-fashioned telephone dial with letters as well as numbers. Below is a list of numbers representing 10 international capital cities. Can you use the diagram to decode them?

See answer 79

A.	**1562531325**	**F.**	**157726215**
B.	**661382**	**G.**	**775143545**
C.	**455255**	**H.**	**1545515**
D.	**126435**	**I.**	**512632**
E.	**75405**	**J.**	**154161**

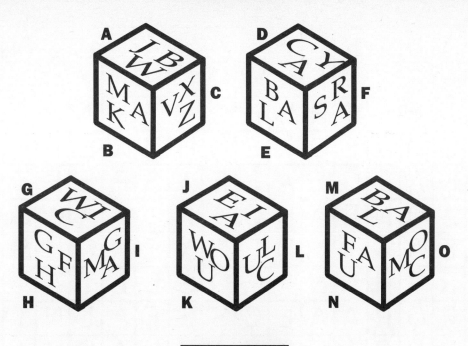

PUZZLE 122

Can you work out which sides on these cubes contain the same letters?

See answer 142

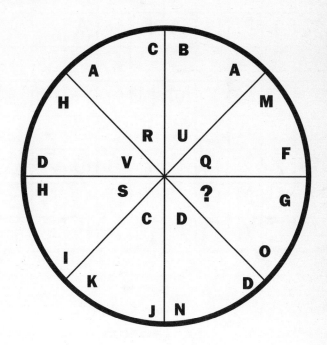

22 8 10 20 14 5 2 7
9 20 24 5 5 20
23 2 6 12 14 6
12 14 12 1 2
21 11 20 13 16 14 11 12 13
1 20 6 21 14 11 26 24 11
12 9 20 26 1 24 13 13 2
15 2 7 23 20 5 8 8

PUZZLE 123

This is a simple substitution code that uses numbers instead of letters. The coded words are all well-known foods from around the world.

See answer 135

PUZZLE 124

Can you find out which letter completes the wheel?

See answer 29

```
M O X A L T E F E I C H A L P X N O N S
F A L E F T I E X W K C R A M S I B P X
A L L L I H C R U H C E T P W O L I J L
M O N E D A L O X E G H N X E F A L A E
A X O N A E C E A L E I S P E E T F A E
G I A A O N E A B C A F I A A W S U P V
N G T E A A I Y D E N N E K O U S L E E
U S A R G H A N F A O S E L T A I X O H
T P F E Q R A A E C S E F A L N T A U C
E F A H S R A E H E A E N A C H I A E A
S A E C E A F E A E O N S O A T N A F B
T L O T A O T E A D F A L P E R I T O R
O L T A A S A A F E G N A E R L L O M O
A I N H O F S A F G P Q R N A E O M E G
M E A T B C E A D A D A U I F O S P X M
L M O X M N O P Q U R S T S A U S X A O
W V A E X F O H J L A A T T U B U C W N
O Z X A E F A O Z L A E H L U F M R A Z
A E N O I R U G N E B F A E E E A K L M N
O Z A D A C A H P T S R S Y T R A E L M
```

Arafat   **Gandhi**

Mussolini   **Ben Gurion**

Gorbachev   **Napoleon**

Bismarck   **Kennedy**

Pinochet   **Churchill**

Lincoln   **Stalin**

De Gaulle   **Mao Tse Tung**

Thatcher   **Franco**

Mitterand   **Yeltsin**

PUZZLE **125**

The above grid contains the names of 18 famous statesmen. Can you discover them?

See answer 93

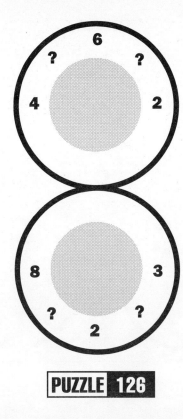

PUZZLE 127

PUZZLE 126

Can you work out which of these balls is the odd one out?

See answer **111**

Can you replace the question marks in this diagram with the symbols x and ÷ so that both sections arrive at the same value?

See answer **117**

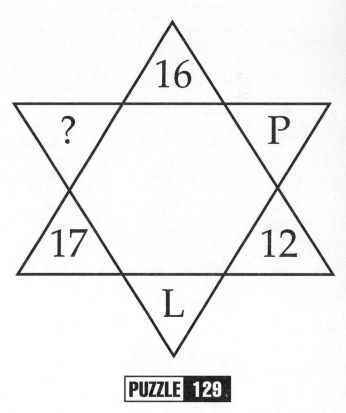

PUZZLE 128

Can you work out which is the odd number out?

See answer **118**

PUZZLE 129

Can you find the missing letter in this star?

See answer **70**

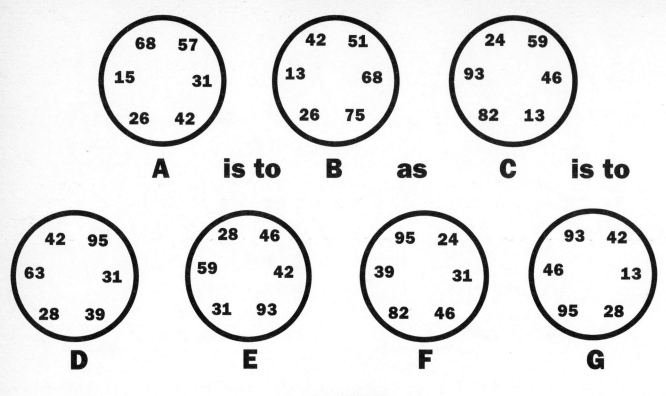

A   is to   B   as   C   is to

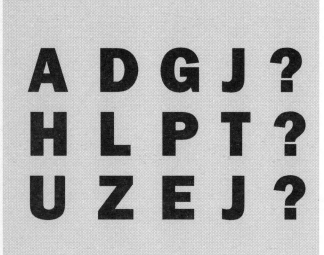

D   E   F   G

PUZZLE 130

See answer 103

A D G J ?
H L P T ?
U Z E J ?

PUZZLE 131

Each of the lines in this diagram follows a pattern.
Can you find the missing letters?

See answer 72

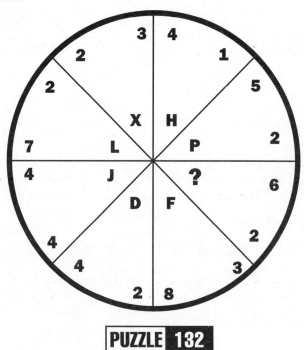

PUZZLE 132

Can you unravel the reasoning behind
this diagram and find the correct letter to replace
the question mark?

See answer 4

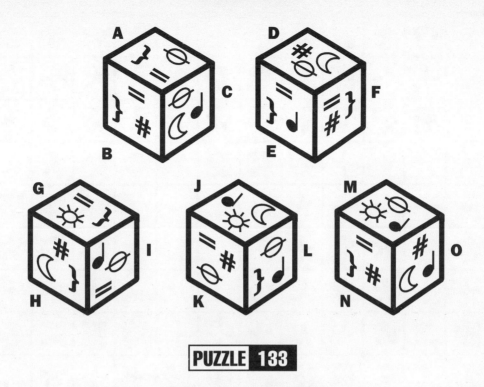

PUZZLE 133

Can you work out which three sides of these cubes
contain the same symbols?

See answer 102

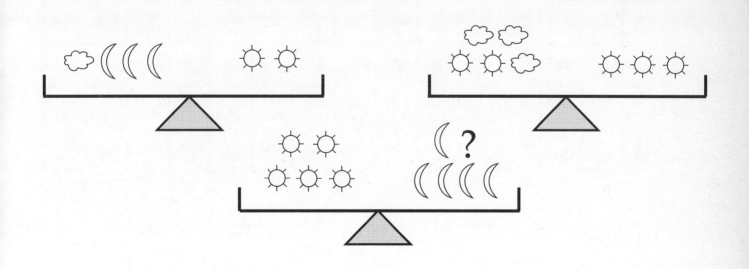

PUZZLE 134

Each of the symbols represents a value. Which symbols
would you need to add to balance the last scale?

See answer 14

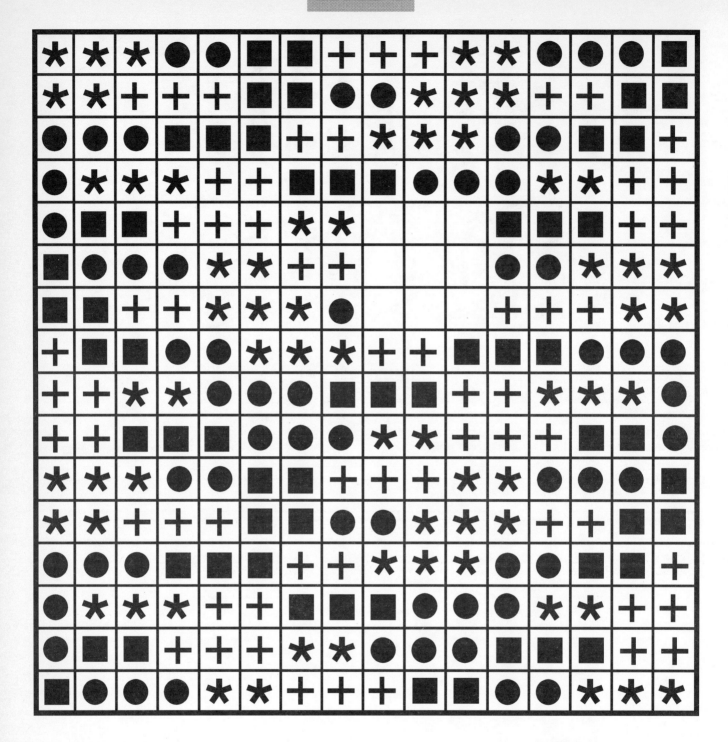

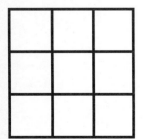

PUZZLE 135

The symbols in this grid behave in a predictable manner. When you have discovered their sequence it should be possible to fill in the blank segment.

See answer 11

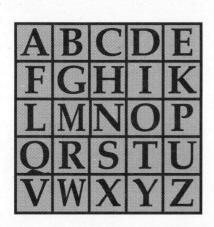

D2 C4 A2 A5 D2 D4

C5 B4 A5 D2 D2 A5

C2 B4 A3 B3 A5 C1 C1 A5

E2 C4 C1 B1 B2 A1 C3 B2

A4 C4 C1 C4 D2 A5 D3

D3 B4 C3 A5 A1 A4

D2 A1 A3 B3 A5 C1

C2 A1 B2 C3 D5 D3

PUZZLE 136

This time the code is a little more difficult. To help you we will give you a clue. The coded words are first names from around the world.

See answer **139**

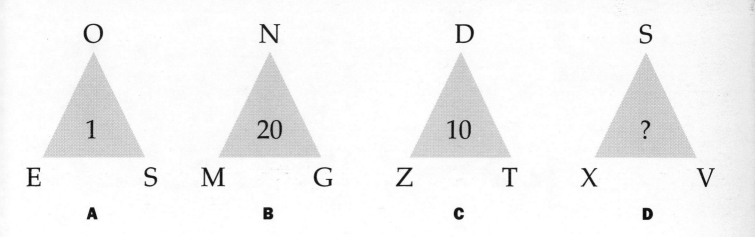

PUZZLE 137

Can you work out the rule these triangles follow and find the missing number?

See answer **69**

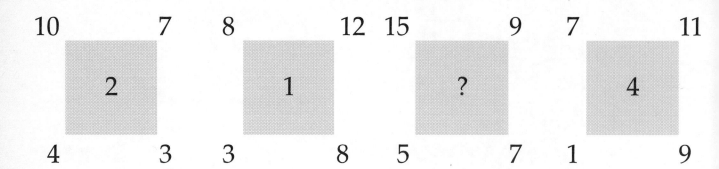

10   7   8   12 15   9   7   11

2   1   ?   4

4   3   3   8   5   7   1   9

PUZZLE 138

Can you work out which number should replace the
question mark in the square?

See answer **67**

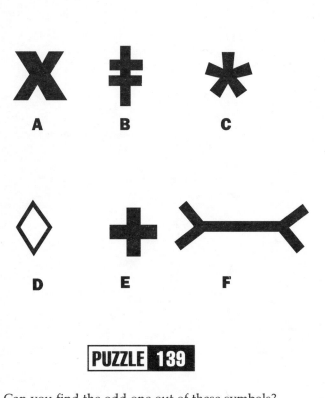

A   B   C

D   E   F

PUZZLE 139

Can you find the odd one out of these symbols?

See answer **120**

P U Z T N
A G M B G
P C B J ?

PUZZLE 140

Can you find the letter that should replace the
question mark?

See answer **50**

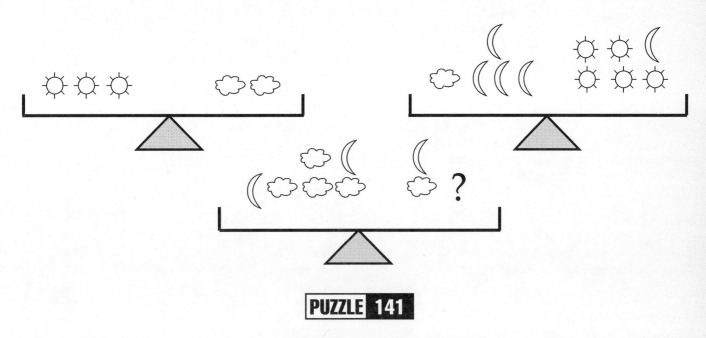

PUZZLE 141

Can you work out which symbols should replace the
question mark, so that the scales balance?

See answer 73

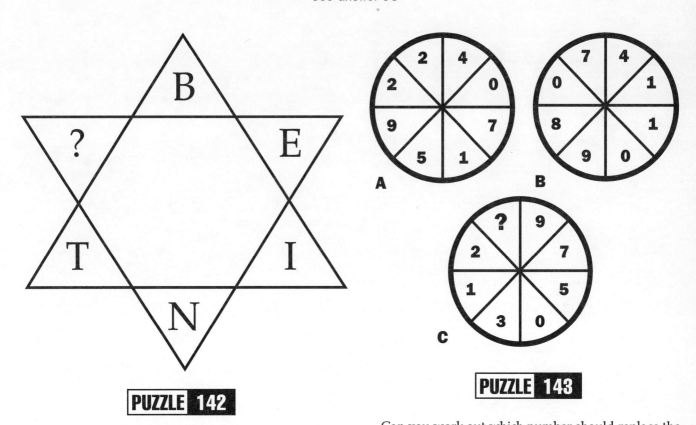

PUZZLE 142

Can you find the letter that would complete the star?

See answer 91

PUZZLE 143

Can you work out which number should replace the
question mark to follow the rules of the other wheels?

See answer 32

Answer 1

A.	California	F.	Oregon
B.	Texas	G.	Virginia
C.	Nebraska	H.	Florida
D.	Alaska	I.	Colorado
E.	Idaho	J.	Arizona

Answer 2

C. The number in the middle is the sum of the squares of the numbers at the points of the triangles. C does not fit this pattern.

Answer 3.

B. The number of sides of the internal figures should increase by one each time. B is the odd one out because its internal figures should have 2 sides.

Answer 4

N. Multiply the two numbers in each segment. Their product is used to represent a letter (based on its numerical position in the alphabet). This letter is put in the segment diametrically opposite the original numbers.

Answer 5

One sun. The values are: Cloud = 3; Umbrella = 2; Moon = 4; Sun = 7.

Answer 6

$6 + 7 + 11 \div 3 \times 2 + 5 - 12 = 9$.

Answer 7

23. Square = 9; Cross = 5; Z = 6; Heart = 7.

Answer 8

E. Turn the diagram by 90° clockwise.

Answer 9

27. A number in the first circle is squared and the product is put in the corresponding segment of the second circle. The original number is then cubed and that product is put in the corresponding segment of the third circle.

Answer 10

$F - B + J - B = L$.

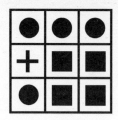

Answer 11

The pattern is a horizontal boustrophedon starting at the top left. The sequence is: 3 stars, 2 circles, 2, squares, 3 crosses, 2 stars, 3 circles, 3 squares, 2 crosses, etc.

Answer 12

E. It contains no curved lines.

Answer 13

B and **H**.

Answer 14

4 moons. Sun = 9; Moon = 5; Cloud = 3.

Answer 15

E.

Answer 16

Q. The letters are in the following alphabetical order: miss one, miss two, miss three, miss one etc.

Answer 17

$4 \times 7 \div 2 + 8 + 9 \times 6 \div 3 = 62$.

Answer 18

B. The value of each letter in the alphabet is two-thirds of the number in the opposite segment.

Answer 19

10. Replace each letter by the value of its position in the alphabet. Start at E and add 1, then 2, then 3, then 4, then 5, then 1, then 2 etc. When you reach 26 (Z), go back to 1 (A).

Answer 20

11. Add all the outside numbers then place the total in the centre of the cross diagonally opposite.

Answer 21

19. Starting from D, each number, or its alphabetic equivalent, advances three.

Answer 22

A. Letters represent values based on their position in the alphabet. In each column, subtract the letter in the middle row from the letter in the top row and place the answer in the bottom row.

Answer 23

33. Star = 8; Tick = 12; Cross = 13; Circle = 5.

Answer 24

2. The faces represent numbers, based on the elements in or around the face (excluding the head). Multiply the top number with the bottom right number and divide by the bottom left number. Place the answer in the middle.

Answer 25

A. Pattern is: 2 by arch on top, 4 by arch at right, 3 by arch on bottom, 2 by arch at left. Start at the top left corner and move down the grid in vertical lines, reverting to the top when of the next column when you reach the bottom.

Answer 26

Answer 27

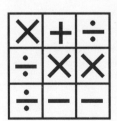

The order is 2 +, 3 –, 2 ÷, 3 x. The puzzle goes in an inward clockwise spiral starting from the top left corner.

Answer 28

Answer 29

L. Add the value of the two letters in each outer segment, based on their position in the alphabet, and place the answer letter in the opposite inner segment.

Answer 30

R. Multiply the value of the three earliest letters, based on their value in the alphabet, by 2. The answer goes in the opposite tip. I (9) x 2 = 18 (R).

Answer 31

Five suns. Moons = 2; Cloud = 3; Sun = 4.

Answer 32

3. The numbers in each wheel add up to 30.

Answer 33

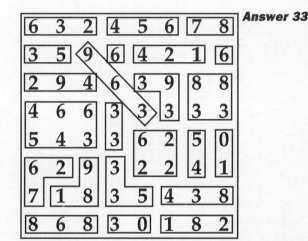

Answer 34

4. Imagine these are six-digit numbers. Add the bottom line to the middle line to get the top line.

Answer 35

8. Starting at H, and working clockwise, subtract the value of second letter, based on its value in the alphabet, from the value of the first letter, and put sum in following corner.

Answer 36

C.

Answer 37

Napoleon, Churchill, Truman, De Gaulle, Kennedy, Ho Chi Minh, Gandhi, Mandela.

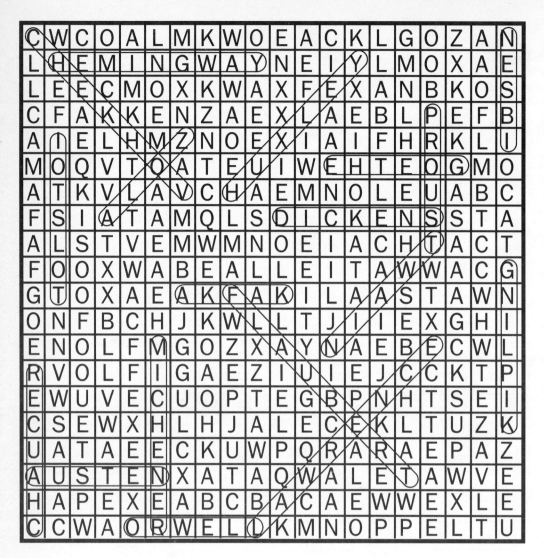

Answer 38

Austen
Hemingway
Michener
Chaucer
Huxley
Orwell
Chekov
Ibsen
Proust
Dickens
Kafka
Tolstoi
Flaubert
Kipling
Twain
Goethe
Lawrence
Zola

Answer 39

21. Add all the numbers of each triangle together and place the sum in the middle of next triangle. When you reach D put the sum in A.

Answer 40

The water in his garden was snow. He rolled several giant snowballs, built a pyramid and climbed onto the porch.

Answer 41

She was planting her mother's shoe tree.

Answer 42

Jim had moved from his home town years ago. He was watching the floods on the TV news. His wife had never liked the place anyway.

Answer 43

The old man had given them time. He left each of them the equivalent of their annual salary so that they could have a year to do what they liked.

Answer 44

This was a real bookworm, a bug that nibbles its way through books. Dr Gluck found him dining off his reference books.

Answer 45

Johnny wants to go through the glass tunnel at an aquarium.

Answer 46

Because three of them are on my wrist watch.

Answer 47

S. Look at opposite triangles. D is 4th letter of the alphabet, W is 4th from the end. F is 6th letter, while U is 6th from the end. H is the 8th letter, thus the missing letter is the one which is 8th from the end.

Answer 48

A. Dallas
B. Seattle
C. Chicago
D. Milwaukee
E. Minneapolis
F. Portland
G. Detroit
H. Atlanta
I. Cincinnati
J. Indianapolis

Answer 49

G. Add 2 elements to the body, take away 1, add 3, take away 2, add 4, take away 3.

Answer 50

B. In each column, divide the value of letter on the top row, based on its position in the alphabet, by the value of the second row letter to get the letter on the bottom row.

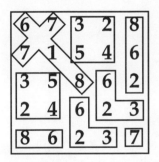

Answer 51

Answer 52

15. Start at the top left corner and add that number to each corner in a clockwise direction, eg. 7 + 7 = 14 + 7 = 21 + 7 = 28 + 7 = 35.

Answer 53

F + I + E − J + N − Y + H = I.

Answer 54

Whitehall, Trafalgar Square, Kensington Gardens, Marble Arch, Buckingham Palace, Piccadilly Circus, Grosvenor Square, Thames Embankment, Waterloo Station, Kings Cross.

Answer 55

72. Multiply all the numbers in the top sections to arrive at the number in the opposite bottom section. Multiply by 3 in the first circle, by 6 in the second one, and by 9 in the third circle.

Answer 56

825. Multiply the value of the letters, based on their value in the alphabet, from each triangle and place the product in the next but one triangle to the right.

Answer 57

A and **L**. The numbers are 3, 4, 6 and 9.

Answer 58

4. Multiply the two numbers in the outer circle of each spoke and place the product in the inner circle two spokes on in a clockwise direction.

Answer 59

35. Star = 6; Tick = 3; Cross = 17; Circle = 12.

Answer 60

Start at the top right corner and work in an inward spiral. The pattern is: two ticks, one heart, two faces, one tick, two hearts, one face, etc.

Answer 61 – See page 74

Answer 62

Arlington, Bethesda, Columbia Pike, Silver Spring, Mount Rainier, Chevy Chase, Georgetown, Anacostia. U = A, Z = F, A = G, T = Z, etc.

Answer 63

16. Add 2, subtract 1, add 4, subtract 2, add 8, subtract 4, add 16, subtract 8.

Answer 64

6.50. The minute hand moves back 5, 10 and 15 minutes, while the hour hand moves forward 1, 2 and 3 hours.

```
P B A W N W O C H K T V E N T A C Y X O
A A D E F W O Y J U L I A R O B E R T S
C D U S T I N H O F F M A N B R M O N L
K A O L W O L N N Y G O R E S O T U V D
K M G E N E W I L D E R W O L O Z B R R
C A S K L E M U O T L B W J L K K E G O
P C M W V U W E A I J L G A H E T E B F
E L K E F O Z M A A T H E N A S E R O D
E S O A L L A M A A O I E E O H I L L E
R T A S E G F A A N T O E F L I S T R R
T O M C R U I S E S R S E O T E E E P T
S A O E E B W B I M Q I A N E L G N O R
L A A O H E H R S T D A B D C D O A T E
Y A F G S V H T E O I B K A R S C E J B
R B P O A C F A J Z N A Y A A Y I X Q O
E N O Z E A L M A O C Y H F O G H E L R
M A E I N A Z E N I A C L E A H C I M B
C P L M A N N V W X I E R S F L A Z O N
N U W M J F G Q S R A E L L A E S S O E
J O N Y F G I N O S P M O H T A M M E F
```

Answer 61

Jane Asher
Richard Gere
Julia Roberts
Michael Caine
Mel Gibson
Brooke Shields
Julie Christie
Dustin Hoffman
Meryl Streep
Tom Cruise
Paul Newman
Emma Thompson
Jane Fonda
Robert Redford
Gene Wilder
Jodie Foster

Answer 65
D.

Answer 66
Bois de Boulogne, Montparnasse, Madeleine, Pere Lachaise, Champs Elysees, Gare de Lyon, Arc de Triomphe, Montmartre. The code here is: I = A, Z = R, A = S, H = Z, etc.

Answer 67
8. Subtract the bottom left corner from the top left corner. Now subtract the bottom right corner from the top right corner, then subtract this answer from the first difference and put the number in the middle.

Answer 68 – See opposite page

Answer 69
21. Find the value of each letter based on its position in the alphabet, then add the values of the top and left corner together. Subtract the bottom right corner from this number and place the new value in the middle of the triangle.

Answer 70
Q. Reading clockwise from the top, numbers correspond to the alphabetic position of the following letter.

Answer 71
16. All the other numbers can be divided by 3.

Answer 72
M X O. The first line values of letters, based on their position in the alphabet, increase by 3. The

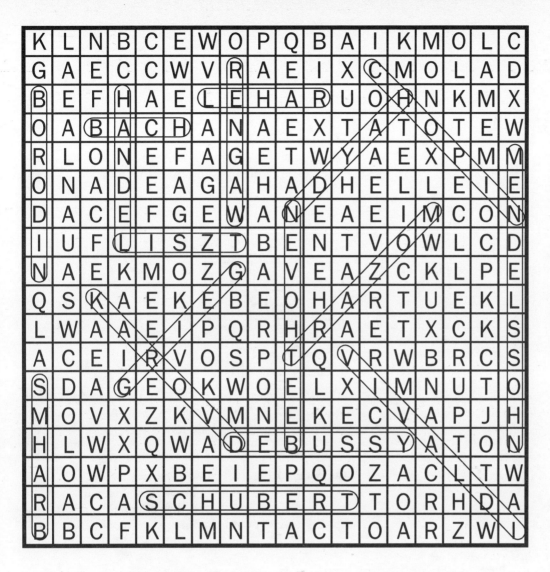

Answer 68

Bach
Dvorak
Mendelssohn
Beethoven
Grieg
Mozart
Borodin
Handel
Purcell
Brahms
Haydn
Schubert
Chopin
Lehar
Vivaldi
Debussy
Liszt
Wagner

second line values increase by 4 and the third line values increase by 5.

Answer 73

One cloud and one sun. Sun = 6; Moon = 7; Cloud = 9.

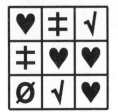

Answer 74
Start at top left corner and move in a vertical boustrophedon. The order is two hearts, one square root, two crossed circles, one cross, one heart, two square roots, one crossed circle, two crosses, etc.

Answer 75
Little Italy, Greenwich Village, Manhattan, Times Square, Gramercy Park, Soho, Central Park, Chinatown.

Answer 76
Go first along the top of the triangles, then along the bottoms. Each circle is filled one quarter more until the circle is complete, then reverts to one quarter filled.

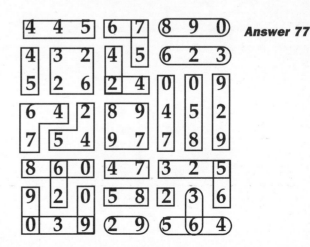

Answer 77

Answer 78
40. Star = 7; Tick = 8; Cross = 14; Circle = 11.

Answer 79
Copenhagen, Prague, London, Berlin, Tokyo, Amsterdam, Stockholm, Colombo, Madrid, Ankara.

Answer 80
42. Take the number in the middle of the square, divide it by the number in the top left corner and place the new number in the bottom right corner. Again take the middle number, but now divide it by the number in the top right corner and place this new number in the bottom left corner.

Answer 81
55. Add the two last numbers together.

Answer 82
E and **O**. The letters are N, O, P and X.

Answer 83
1.00. The minute hand moves forward 20 minutes, the hour hand moves back 1 hour.

Answer 84
B. Start from top left corner and move in a vertical boustrephedon. Order is: 4 smiley face, 1 sad face, 3 straight mouth, 2 face with hair, etc.

Answer 85

Answer 86
Z. Take the value of the letters, based on their position in the alphabet. A back 3 is X; X forward 4 is B; B back 3 is Y; Y forward 4 is C, etc.

Answer 87
7. Add the three numbers at the corner of each triangle, multiply by 2 and place that number in the middle.

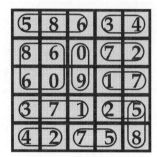

Answer 88

Answer 89
Top half: ÷ **x**; bottom half: **x x**.

Answer 90
A. Add one new element to the face, then add one hair and an element to the face, then a hair, then a hair and an element to the face, repeat sequence.

Answer 91
A. Based on the alphabet, starting at B miss 2 letters, then 3, then 4, etc.

Answer 92

A.	Manchester	F.	Bangkok
B.	Glasgow	G.	Calcutta
C.	Toulouse	H.	Melbourne
D.	Smolensk	I.	Barcelona
E.	Vancouver	J.	Sacramento

Answer 93 – See opposite page

Answer 94
39. Star = 9; Tick = 6; Cross =3; Circle = 24.

Answer 95
Piccadilly, Copacabana, Guggenheim, Etoile, Whitehall, Madeleine, Central Park, Colosseum.

```
M O X A L T E F E I C H A L P X N O N S
F A L E F T I E X W K C R A M S I B P X
A L L I H C R U H C E T P W O L I J L
M O N E D A L O X E G H N X E F A L A E
A X O N A E C E A L E I S P E E T F A E
G I A A O N E A B C A F I A A W S U P V
N G T E A A I Y D E N N E K O U S L E E
U S A R G H A N F A O S E L T A I X O H
T P E E Q R A A E C S E F A L N T A U C
E F A H S R A E H E A E N A C H I A E A
S A E C E A F E A E O N S O A T N A F B
T L O T A O C E A D F A L P E R I T O R
O L T A A S A A F E G N A E R L L O M O
A I N H O F S A F G P Q R N A E O M E G
M E A T B C E A D A D A U I F O S P X M
L M O X M N O P Q R S T S A U S X A O
W V A E X F O H J L A A T T U B U C W N
O Z X A E F A O Z L A E H L U F V R A Z
A E N O I R U G N E B F A E E A K L M N
O Z A D A C A H P T S R S Y T R A E L M
```

Answer 93

Arafat
Gandhi
Mussolini
Ben Gurion
Gorbachev
Napoleon
Bismarck
Kennedy
Pinochet
Churchill
Lincoln
Stalin
De Gaulle
MaoTse Tung
Thatcher
Franco
Mitterand
Yeltsin

Answer 96
One arrow pointing up.

Answer 97
14. Multiply the number on the left of the triangle by the number on top, take away the number on the right from this product and put this number in the middle.

Answer 98
68. Square = 7; X = 11; Z = 3; Heart = 17.

Answer 99
I and **K**. The figures are: matchstick man, triangle, half-moon, circle, stile.

Answer 100
6.45. The minute hand moves back 15, 30 and 45 minutes. The hour hand moves forward 3, 6 and 9 hours.

Answer 101
A diamond.

Answer 102
B, F and **N**.

Answer 103
F. The numbers made up of odd numbers are reversed.

Answer 104
4. The number relates to the number of shapes in which the number is enclosed.

Answer 105
Chicago, Milwaukee, Houston, Birmingham, Detroit, Atlanta, Phoenix, Memphis.

Answer 106
27. 2 + 3 = 5 + 4 = 9 + 5 = 14 + 6 = 20 + 7 = 27.

Answer 107
E and **I**.

Answer 108
– – X.

Answer 109
Elton John, Freddie Mercury, Lisa Stansfield, Sinead O'Connor, Meatloaf, Madonna, Michael Jackson, Rod Stewart. A = J, Z = I.

Answer 110
D. The large letter turns 90° clockwise, the small letter turns 180°.

Answer 111
26. The digits in each of the other balls add up to 10.

Answer 112
2. Relates to the number of shapes which enclose each figure.

Answer 113
Oregon, Nebraska, Nevada, Wisconsin, Florida, Virginia, Texas, Colorado.

Answer 114
Chekhov, Brecht, Wilde, Beckett, Genet, Goethe, Ibsen, Racine.

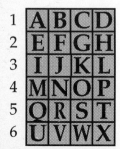

Answer 115
Picasso, Rembrandt, Gaugin, Leonardo, Constable, Raphael, Van Gogh, Matisse. A = 1:4; B = 1:3; C = 1:2; D = 1:1; E = 2:4, etc.

Answer 116
D. Letters with only curves stay the same, letters with curves and straight lines turn by 90° and letters with only straight lines by 180°.

Answer 117
Top half: **X ÷**; bottom half: **÷ X**.

Answer 118
31. In all the other numbers the first digit is smaller than the second one.

Answer 119
Gazpacho, Mulligatawny, Borscht, Minestrone, Chowder, Avgolemono, Cock-a-Leekie, Bouillabaisse. A = 1, Z = 26.

Answer 120
The diamond. It is a closed shape.

Answer 121
G. The internal patterns are reversed.

Answer 122
15. All the other numbers have not got a divisor.

Answer 123
Vivaldi, Beethoven, Grieg, Bizet, Mahler, Wagner, Mozart, Elgar.

Answer 124
3. The numbers refer to the number of shapes which surround each digit.

Answer 125
K and **O**.

Answer 126
Top half: **+ +**; bottom half: **+ –**.

Answer 127
F. The symbols are reflected over a vertical line.

Answer 128
Heathrow, Fort Worth, Ben Gurion, Las Palmas, O'Hare, Gatwick, Haneda, Shannon. A = R; B = S, etc.

Answer 129
5 x 4 ÷ 2 + 7 = 17.

Answer 130
D and **L**.

Answer 131
C. The letters represent values based on their position in the alphabet. They represent the number of straight-sided figures in which they are enclosed. The circle is a red herring.

Answer 132
Julia Roberts, Burt Reynolds, Jack Nicholson, David Niven, Marilyn Monroe, Jeremy Irons, Audrey Hepburn, Winona Ryder.

Answer 133
K. Only the K has serifs.

Answer 134
C and **K**.

Answer 135
Coq au vin, Paella, Dim sum, Sushi, Bratwurst, Hamburger, Spaghetti, Vindaloo. A = 20, B = 21.

Answer 136
Top half: **+ −**; bottom half: **– –**.

Answer 137
C. It has an odd number of elements, the others all have an even number.

Answer 138
C. In the others the small shapes added together result in the large shape.

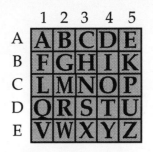

Answer 139
Robert, Pierre, Michelle, Wolfgang, Dolores, Sinead, Rachel, Magnus.

Answer 140
C. The symbol consists of 3 parts, the others only of 2.

Answer 141
Asimov, Balzac, Hemingway, Joyce, Maugham, Miller, Proust, Twain.

Answer 142
E and **M**.

Answer 143
M − E + B + D = N.

GARGANTUA MIND MAZE

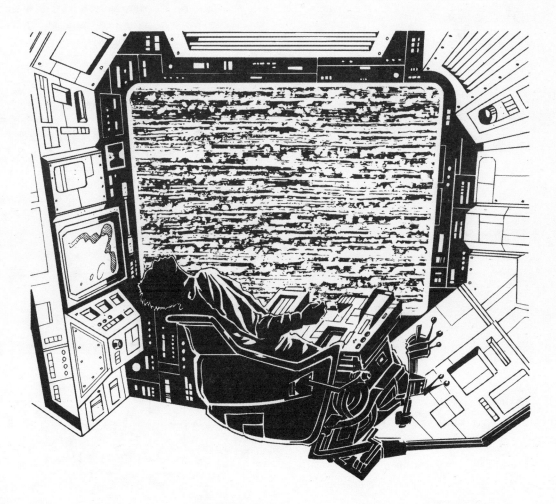

GARGANTUA, the super-computer that controls communications and transport in most of the developed world, has gone haywire. Dr Ben Eischrank, the computer's inventor and guardian, was carrying out routine maintenance when a freak electric shock hit him. Now the world is plunged into chaos. Only you, Eischrank's trusted assistant, can restore the computer to normality. But there is a problem. The doctor was so insanely jealous of anyone touching his invention that he guarded it with a fiendishly intricate system of enigmas to prevent unauthorized access.

Can you penetrate this mental maze and save the world? The solution to each puzzle will tell which you should tackle next. When you have worked your way around the maze you will receive a code number which allows access to the computer. But hurry, for as you work a video screen on the laboratory wall shows the devastation which is sweeping the earth. Planes plunge from the sky, whole cities are blacked out, panic and devastation are spreading like the plague. Don't delay, begin now! It is vital that you write down the number of every puzzle you complete in the order in which you complete it.

Five boys are going to visit relatives.
Tom goes to Georgia, Sid goes to Hawaii, William
goes to Dakota, and Orville goes to Louisiana.
Does George go to

A) Wyoming
B) California
C) Tennessee
D) Oregon
E) Alaska?

If you choose A, go to 22.
If you choose B, go to 11.
If you choose C, go to 7.
If you choose D, go to 16.
If you choose E, go to 10.

PUZZLE 1

See answer 1

This diagram represents a treasure map.
The treasure is under the square marked with
an asterisk. You are allowed to stop on each
square only once (though you may cross
a square as often as you like). When you
stop on a square you must follow the
instructions you find there. The letters
stand for points of the compass

N = North; S = South; E = East; W = West

and the numbers stand for the number of
squares you must travel (e.g. a square marked
3SW would instruct you to move three
squares South West). In order to find the
treasure which square would you start on?
When you have the co-ordinate
(one letter and one number) add 15
to the number and go to the
corresponding puzzle.

	A	B	C	D	E	F	G	H	
	2E	2SE	3S	4E	1S	1SE	4S	1W	**1**
	1SE	1N	3S	3W	3W	2S	1S	2S	**2**
	4E	4E	4S	3SW	2S	3S	1NW	1N	**3**
	3NE	2SE	3NE	1NW	2NW	4W	2W	3NW	**4**
	4N	1S	2NW	2W	3SW	2NE	2SW	1SW	**5**
	2S	1SW	2NW	4N	3E	2SE	2S	1S	**6**
	3E	*	3E	3N	3W	1S	3N	2NW	**7**
	3E	3E	2N	3NW	2N	1NE	4W	3N	**8**

PUZZLE 3

See answer 3

Below are seven 6-digit numbers all of which can be
divided by 136 with no remainder. They all begin with
117 but the other digits have been concealed. Can you
work out what they are? When you have done so, add
together the final digits of all seven numbers, subtract
2 and go to the puzzle indicated.

```
        ???
        ???
117     ???
        ???
        ???
        ???
        ???
```

See answer 2

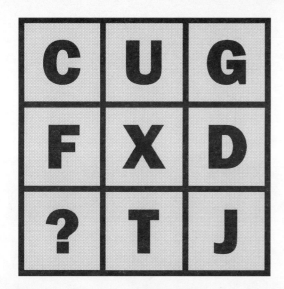

Look at the grid. Can you discover the logic used in its construction? When you have done so you will be able to replace the question mark with a letter. If you choose B, go to 35. If you choose H, go to 23. If you choose J, go to 17.

See answer **4**

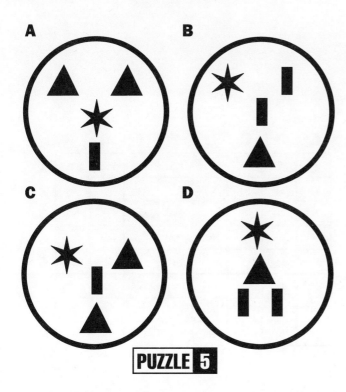

PUZZLE 5

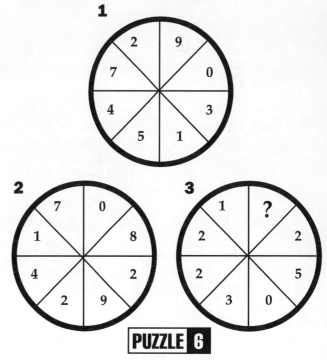

PUZZLE 6

Find the odd one out. If you choose A, go to 14. If you choose B, go to 17. If you choose C, go to 20. If you choose D, go to 15.

See answer **5**

Which number replaces the question mark? Add 24 and go to a new puzzle.

See answer **6**

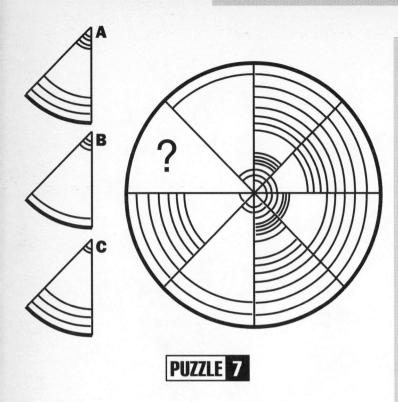

PUZZLE 7

Which sector correctly fills the blank? If you choose A, go to 10. If you choose B, go to 13. If you choose C, go to 34.

See answer 7

PUZZLE 8

Al's Diner has a unique menu. Al has his own special way of calculating his prices. Can you work out what it is and discover what he charges for Doner Kebab? Add the digits in that number, add 17 and go to the next puzzle.

See answer 8

The diagram on the right represents a treasure map. The treasure lies under the square with an asterisk. You are allowed to stop on each square only once (though you may cross a square as often as you like). When you stop on a square you must follow the instructions you find there. The letters stand for points of the compass

N = North; S = South; E = East; W = West

and the numbers for the number of squares you must travel (e.g. a square marked 3SW would instruct you to move three squares South West). Which is the starting square? When you have the co-ordinates 12 to the digit and go to the puzzle of that number.

A	B	C	D	E	F	G	H	
2S	1SE	2W	3S	4S	2W	1SE	3W	**1**
4E	2E	2SW	2SW	2S	1E	1S	4S	**2**
1NE	4S	3S	2W	2W	*	4S	2NW	**3**
1SE	4S	1NE	3NE	3SE	3W	1SE	3N	**4**
3N	1S	4N	2NE	3SE	3N	2NW	1SW	**5**
4E	2E	2SW	2NE	1NE	2NE	2S	2SW	**6**
2NE	1SE	2NW	4NE	1W	1N	3N	2W	**7**
1N	1NE	2NW	3N	1N	2W	3N	3W	**8**

PUZZLE 9

See answer 9

1

25	1
21	6
16	10
15	13

2

46	28
45	30
43	31
40	36

3

?	51
70	55
66	58
61	60

PUZZLE 10

Can you work out the logic of this diagram and replace the question mark with a number? When you have the correct number subtract 45 and go to the puzzle of that number.

See answer 10

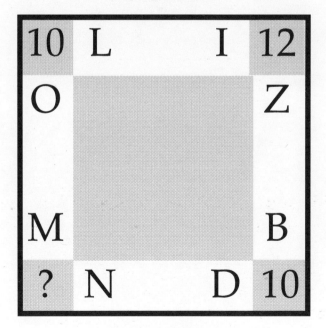

10	L		I	12
O				Z
M				B
?	N		D	10

PUZZLE 11

Look at the grid and work out what should go in place of the question mark? Subtract 5 and go to the puzzle whose number you now have.

See answer 11

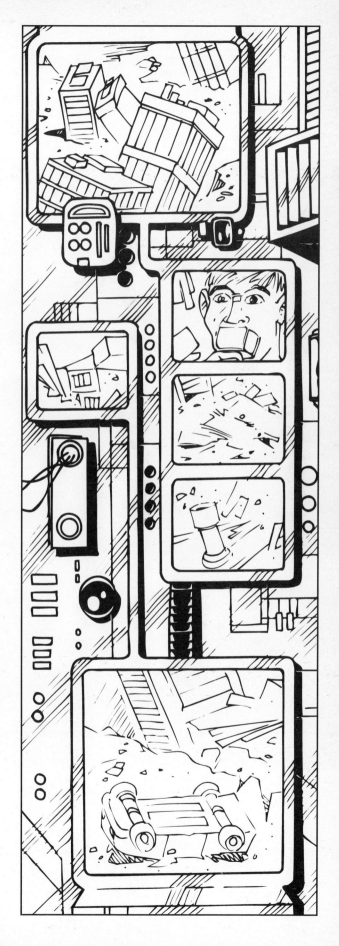

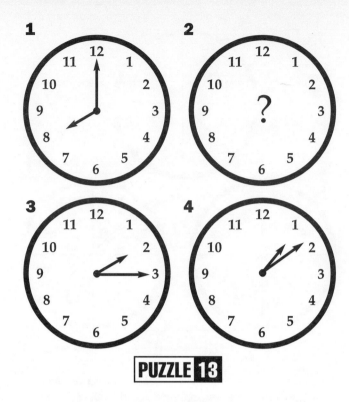

PUZZLE 12

The shapes in this grid appear in a set order. Work out what that order is and fill in the last square. If you choose Diamond, go to 16. If you choose Circle, go to 5. If you choose Heart, go to 13. If you choose Triangle, go to 17. If you choose Moon, go to 10.

See answer 12

PUZZLE 13

These clock faces follow a pattern. Can you work out what the second clock face should look like? Add the number indicated by the hour hand to the number indicated by the minute hand, add 12 to that sum and go to the puzzle indicated.

See answer 13

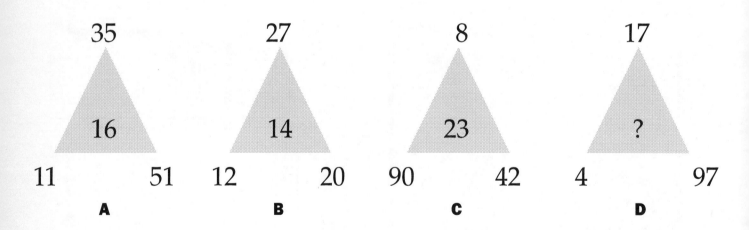

PUZZLE 14

Find a number to replace the question mark in Triangle D. Add 6 to your answer and go to that puzzle.

See answer 14

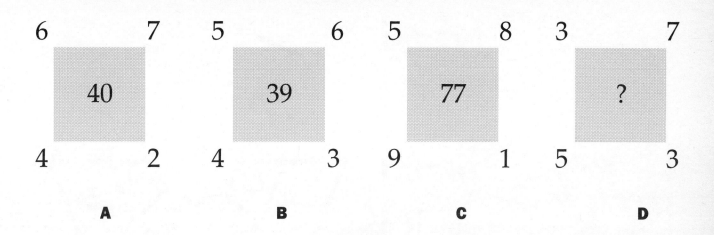

PUZZLE 15

Can you work out which number should replace the question mark in the last square? When you have the number subtract 36 and go to the next puzzle.

See answer 15

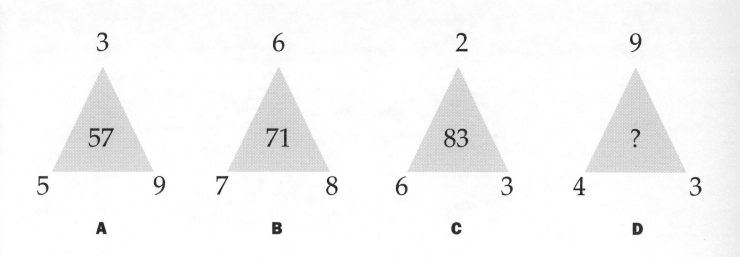

PUZZLE 16

Can you work out which number should replace the question mark? When you have the number subtract 21 and go to the puzzle of the resulting number.

See answer 16

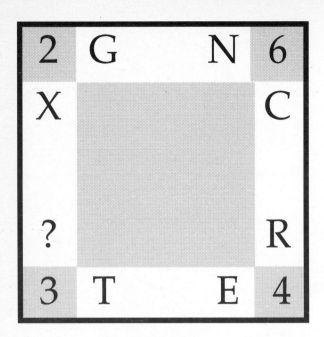

PUZZLE 17

This square follows a certain pattern. Can you work it out and replace the question mark with a letter? If you choose M, go to 16. If you choose D, go to 30. If you choose H, go to 27. If you choose F, go to 2.

See answer 17

PUZZLE 18

Can you crack the reasoning behind this spider's web and find the missing letter? If you choose Z, go to 31. If you choose V, go to 23. If you choose M, go to 13.

See answer 18

Sherry	$1.70
Sambucco	$2.10
Grand Marnier	$3.20
Chianti	$1.80
Cognac	$1.60

PUZZLE 19

In Maria's Bar the prices for drinks are calculated in an unusual way. Can you work it out and find out the price Maria charges for Whiskey? When you have the price discard the dollars and subtract 66 from the remaining cents.
You will then have the number of the next puzzle.

See answer 19

Five boys travel abroad by ship. Andy boards the *Elizabeth II*, John travels on the *Norway*, Peter sails on the *Tasmania*, Nick chooses the *Rover*. Which ship does Larry board?

A) Enterprise
B) Sea Sprite
C) Panama
D) Neptune
E) Iolanthe

If you choose A, go to 19.
If you choose B, go to 6.
If you choose C, go to 32.
If you choose D, go to 28.
If you choose E, go to 5.

PUZZLE 20

See answer 20

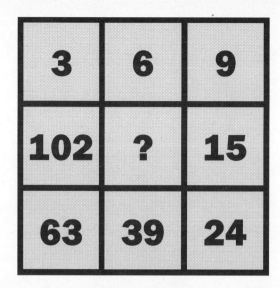

PUZZLE 21

Can you work out the logic of this square and find the missing number? When you have your answer subtract 163 and go to the puzzle of that number.

See answer 21

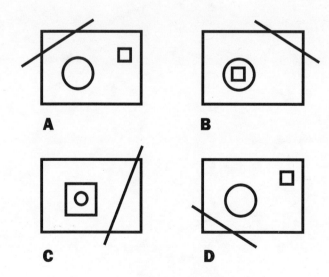

A   **B**

C   **D**

PUZZLE 22

Which of the above diagrams does not follow the same rule as the others? If you choose A, go to 17. If you choose B, go to 6. If you choose C, go to 29. If you choose D, go to 30.

See answer 22

PUZZLE 23

Each of the following girls has to work on a project about a famous statesman. Yvonne chooses Bismarck, Henrietta chooses Stalin, Trudie decides to work on Gandhi, Irene picks Roosevelt and Virginia chooses Eisenhower. Who of the following does Natasha choose:

a) Churchill
b) Mao
c) Charlemagne
d) Reagan
e) Sadat

If you think the answer is A, go to 6.
If B, go to 19. If C, go to 31.
If D, go to 34. If E, go to 15.

See answer 23

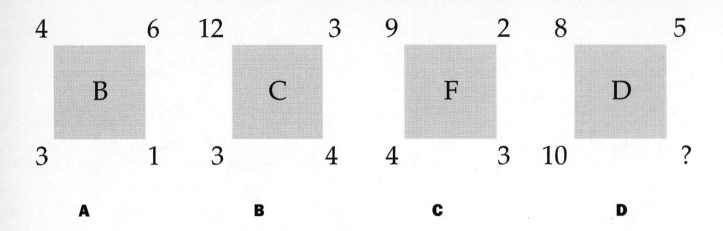

| 4 | | 6 | 12 | | 3 | 9 | | 2 | 8 | | 5 |

B   C   F   D

| 3 | | 1 | 3 | | 4 | 4 | | 3 | 10 | | ? |

A　　　　**B**　　　　**C**　　　　**D**

PUZZLE 24

Can you find the number which should replace the
question mark? When you have it add 2 and go to
the next puzzle.

See answer 24

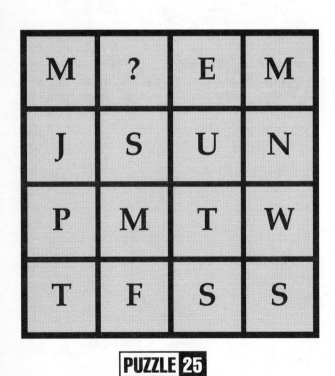

M	?	E	M
J	S	U	N
P	M	T	W
T	F	S	S

PUZZLE 25

Look at the diagram and replace the question mark
with a letter. When you have the answer convert the
letter into a number by using its position in the
alphabetical order (A=1, B=2… Z=26), subtract five
and then go to the puzzle of that number.

See answer 25

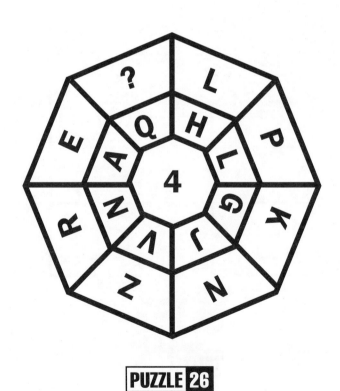

PUZZLE 26

Can you find out which letter should replace the
question mark in this spider's web?
If your answer is K, go to 29. If you choose U,
go to 18. If your answer is G, go to 7.

See answer 26

This is the end of the Mind Maze. To find the code that will allow you to access Gargantua you must add up the numbers of all the puzzles on your route between puzzles 16 and 23 inclusive. The sum of these numbers will give you the code.

PUZZLE 27

See answer 27

```
        ???
        ???
115     ???
        ???
        ???
        ???
```

PUZZLE 28

Above are six 6-digit numbers each beginning with 115. All the numbers are divisible by 173 with no remainder. Which digits do you need to complete the numbers? Add the last digits of all six numbers together, add 8 and go to the puzzle whose number you now have.

See answer 28

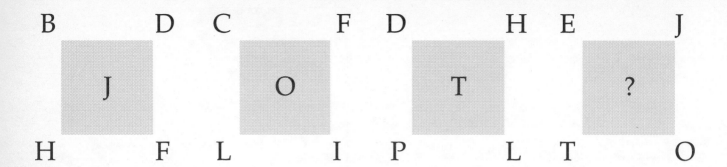

B   D   C   F   D   H   E   J

J   O   T   ?

H   F   L   I   P   L   T   O

PUZZLE 29

Can you work out the logic behind the letters on these squares and find the one that should replace the question mark? If you choose F, go to 23. If you choose K, go to 16. If you choose Y, go to 3.

See answer 29

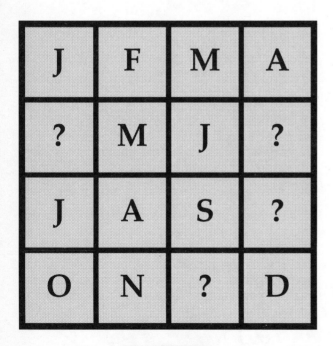

PUZZLE 30

The question marks in this grid have a numerical significance. In fact they are all related to the same number. When you know what that number is, subtract 7 and go to the next puzzle.

See answer 30

PUZZLE 31

This diagram represents a treasure map. The treasure lies under the square marked with an asterisk. You are allowed to stop on each square only once (though you may cross a square as often as you like). When you stop on a square you must follow the instructions you find there. The letters stand for points of the compass

N = North, S = South, E = East, W = West

and the numbers stand for the number of squares you must travel (e.g. a square marked 3SW would instruct you to move three squares South West). In order to find the treasure which square would you start on? When you have the co-ordinate, add 10 to the digit and go to the next puzzle.

See answer 31

	A	B	C	D	E	F	G	H	
	2SE	4E	1S	1S	2W	1SW	1SE	4W	**1**
	2S	1SW	1SE	2SW	2SE	4S	3S	2SW	**2**
	1N	2N	3S	4SE	2SW	2E	1NW	1NW	**3**
	2E	✱	3S	3NE	3S	4S	4S	3NW	**4**
	4N	4E	1W	2NW	2N	1SE	3W	4N	**5**
	2SE	4N	2SE	2W	4W	2NE	2NW	2S	**6**
	3E	1S	1W	3N	2E	4N	4N	2W	**7**
	1N	3NE	2W	3NW	3NE	2NE	2NW	4W	**8**

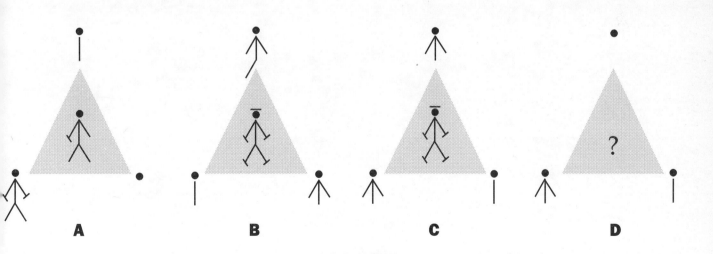

A **B** **C** **D**

PUZZLE 32

Can you work out what the matchstick man in the middle of the last triangle should look like? Take the number of elements in the matchstick man, add 4 and go to the next puzzle.

See answer 32

Each of the following girls have to name their favourite pop group.

**Jessica's is Genesis,
Elspeth's is Bon Jovi,
Zoe's is Wet Wet Wet,
Patricia's is Meatloaf and
Gwendoline's favourite
band is Dire Straits.
Which of these girls chooses Queen?
A) Annabelle B) Roberta C) Barbara
D) Dolly E) Trixie.**

If you choose A, go to 8.
If you choose B, go to 32.
If you choose C, go to 26.
If you choose D, go to 3.
If you choose E, go to 21.

PUZZLE 33

See answer 33

??? ??? 124 ??? ??? ??? ???

PUZZLE 34

Above are six 6-digit numbers each beginning with the numbers 124. Each of the numbers is divisible by 149 with no remainder. Which digits do you need to complete the numbers? Add all the last digits together, subtract 16 and go to the next puzzle.

See answer 34

PUZZLE 35

Can you work out the sequence of this snake and find the missing shape. If you choose Diamond, go to 12. If you choose Heart, go to 16. If you choose Cross, go to 9. If you choose Circle, go to 17. If you choose Arrow, go to 3.

See answer 35

Answer 1

C, go to 7. G (the first letter of George) is the 7th letter from the beginning of the alphabet, T (for Tennessee) is 7th from the end.

Answer 2

117096, 117232, 117368, 117504, 117640, 117776 117912. Divide 117000 by 136. Round the number up to the next full number, then multiply it by 136, then keep adding 136 to this number.
6 + 2 + 8 + 4 + 0 + 6 + 2 = 28. 28 – 2 = 26.

Answer 3

D5. Work backward from the ✱ (Finish) square.
5+15=20.

Answer 4

B, go to 35. The letters represent numbers based on their position in the alphabet. Those in the left column and multiplied by those in the right to give the letters in the middle.

Answer 5

D, go to 15. The diagrams make "faces", D is upside down.

Answer 6

1. The corresponding sections of the three wheels add up to 10. 1 + 24 = 25.

Answer 7

A, go to 10. The outer lines of one sector added to the inner lines of the sector opposite always add up to 9.

Answer 8

$5.80. Vowels = 7, Consonants = 5. 5 + 8 + 17 = 30.

Answer 9

B1. Work back from the ✱ (Finish) square. 1 + 12 = 13.

Answer 10

73. Starting at 1 add 5, then 4, then 3, then 2, then 1, and repeat order. When you arrive at the highest number move on to the lowest number in the next wheel. 73 – 45 = 28.

Answer 11

9. Take the value of each letter, add their digits together and put number in space to the right.
9 – 5 = 4.

Answer 12

Circle, go to 5. The basic sequence is Heart, Circle, Diamond, Triangle, Moon. Take the first symbol and put a line through it. The rest of the sequence then repeats in reverse order. Repeat this with each symbol in turn.

Answer 13

4.30. The numbers are divided by 2 on each clock.
4 + 6 + 12 = 22.

Answer 14

28. Add individual digits of each number on edge of triangle and place their sum in the middle. 28 + 6 = 34

Answer 15

44. Multiply the diagonals of each square, then add both values together and put this number in the middle. 44 – 36 = 8.

Answer 16

30. Multiply the numbers at the bottom of each triangle, reverse the digits in the answer and add number on top of triangle. This number goes in the middle. 30 – 21 = 9.

Answer 17

H, go to 27. Start at top left hand corner, multiply number by value of following letter (based on its position in the alphabet), find new letter equivalent to that value and place in next space.

Answer 18

Z, go to 31. Subtract inner letter from outer, based on their position in the alphabet. The result of each calculation is 3.

Answer 19

$1.90. Vowel = 2, consonant = 3. Add all values together and multiply by 10. 90 – 66 = 24.

Answer 20
C, go to 32. The initial letter of each ship is four places down the alphabetical order from the initial letter of the boy's name.

Answer 21
165. 3 + 6 = 9, 6 + 9 = 15, 9 + 15 = 24, 15 + 24 = 39, 24 + 39 = 63, 39 + 63 = 102, 102 + 63 =165. 165 – 163 = 2.

Answer 22
C, go to 29. The line should cut off a triangle at one corner.

Answer 23
B, go to 19. In each pair, the girl's initial and the statesman's is the same number of letters from either the beginning or the end of the alphabet. Natasha, 13 letters from the end, studies Mao, 13 from the beginning.

Answer 24
4. Multiply the numbers on each left side and each right side of the square and divide the new value on the left by the new value on the right. 4 + 2 = 6.

Answer 25
V, go to 17. The letters are the initials of the planets in the solar system, followed by the days of the week. The order is a horizontal boustrophedon, starting from top left. Venus is missing, so V (22nd letter) – 5 = 17.

Answer 26
U, go to 18. Based on their position in the alphabet the inner letter is four places behind the outer letter.

Answer 27
The code number to access Gargantua is 335.

Answer 28
115045, 115218, 115391, 115564, 115737, 115910. Divide 115000 by 173 and round the answer up to the nearest whole number. Now multiply this number by 173 and add 173 to it until you reach 115910.
5 + 8 + 1 + 4 + 7 + 0 = 25. 25 + 8 = 33.

Answer 29
Y, go to 3. Based on the letters position in the alphabet and starting at the top left hand corner, in the first square add 2 to each value, in the second square add 3, in the third square add 4 and in the fourth square add 5.

Answer 30
The letters refer to the months of the year. A question mark appears after each 30-day month and therefore the number you need is 30.

Answer 31
D6. Work back from the ✳ (Finish) square. 6 + 10 = 16.

Answer 32
He should have 10 elements. Add the elements of matchstick men on each side of triangle and place new figure in middle of following triangle. Put figure based on corners of last triangle in middle of first triangle. 10 + 4 = 14.

Answer 33
E, go to 21. The initial letter of the girls name is three places ahead in the alphabet to the initial letter in the groups name.

Answer 34
124117, 124266 124415, 124564, 124713, 124862. Divide 124000 by 149 and round the answer up to the nearest whole number. Now multiply this number by 149 and add 149 to it until you reach 124862.
7 + 6 + 5 + 4 + 3 + 2 = 27. 27 – 16 = 11.

Answer 35
Diamond, go to 12. The sequence is Heart, Cross, Circle, Arrow, Diamond. Repeat sequence omitting the first symbol, then add first symbol with extra line around. Repeat with each symbol.

ORDER IS

1	7	10	28	33	21			
2	26	18	31	16	9	13	22	
29	3	20	32	14	34	11	4	35
12	5	15	8	30	23	19	24	6
25	17	27						

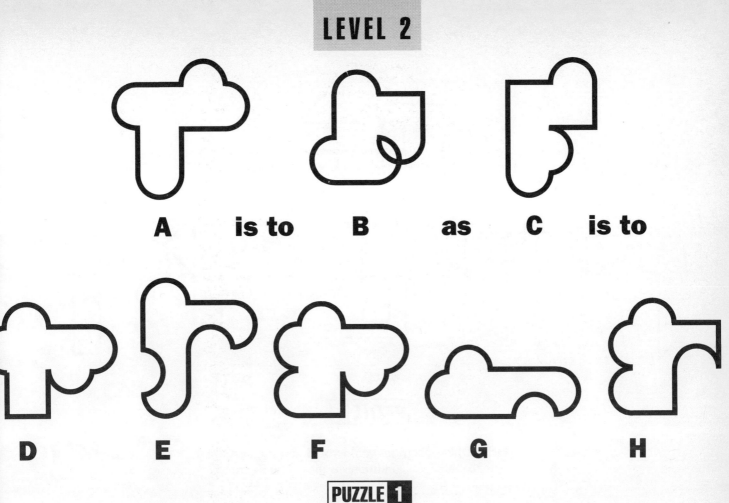

A   is to   B   as   C   is to

PUZZLE 1

See answer 117

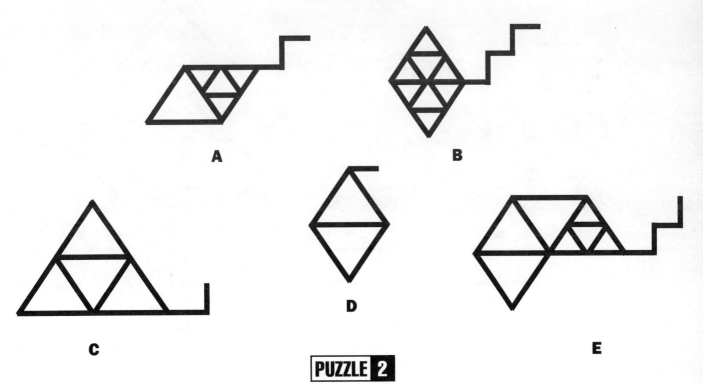

PUZZLE 2

Can you find the odd shape out?

See answer 170

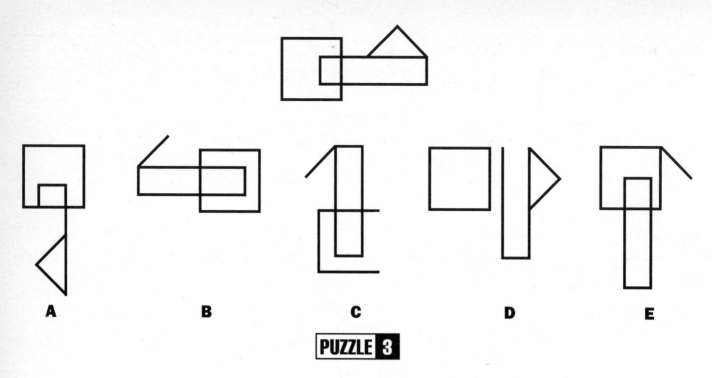

A   **B**   **C**   **D**   **E**

PUZZLE 3

To which of these diagrams could you add a single straight
line to match the conditions of the above figure?

*See answer **145***

J Q G O T D

Y N S Z P

W K M V H F

PUZZLE 4

Most anagrams give you a heap of mixed up
letters and ask you to sort them out. This one is
different. The letters above are the ones you do
NOT need to complete the puzzle!

*See answer **176***

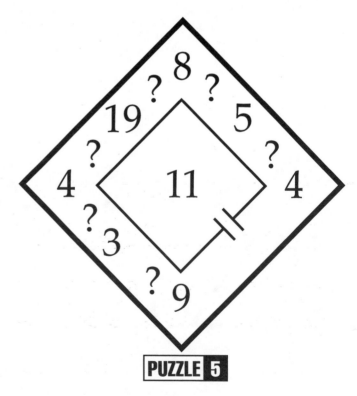

PUZZLE 5

The four main mathematical signs have been left out
of this equation. Can you replace them?

*See answer **184***

A. Los Angeles

B. Dallas

C. Houston

D. Kansas

E. Chicago

PUZZLE 6

Can you unravel the logic behind these domino pieces and fill in the missing letter?

See answer **122**

PUZZLE 7

All the suitcases are shown with their destinations. Which is the odd one out?

See answer **60**

PUZZLE 8

Can you find the shape that should replace the question mark ?

See answer **9**

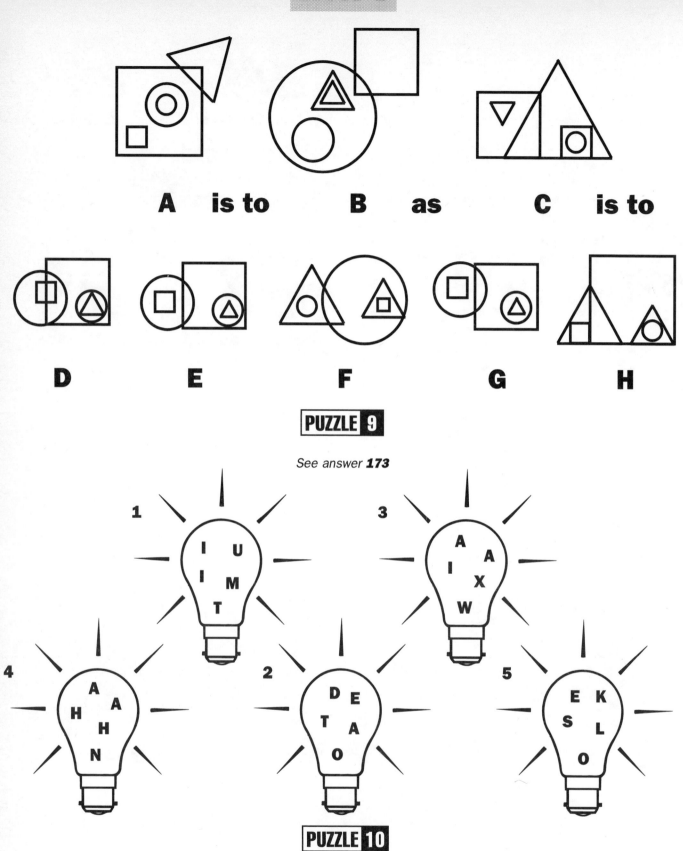

A   is to   B   as   C   is to

D   E   F   G   H

PUZZLE 9

See answer 173

PUZZLE 10

Pick up one letter from each bulb in numerical order. You should find the names of five US states and two dummy letters. What are they?

See answer 46

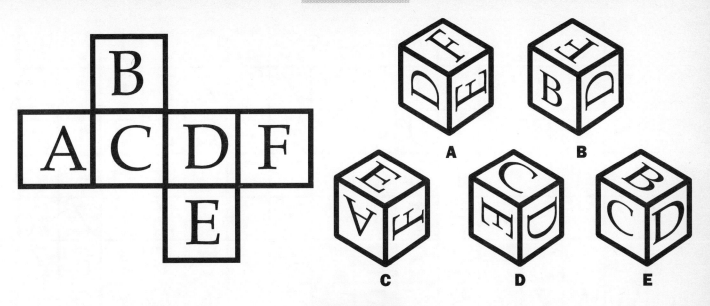

PUZZLE 11

Can you spot the cube that cannot be made
from the layout above?

See answer 167

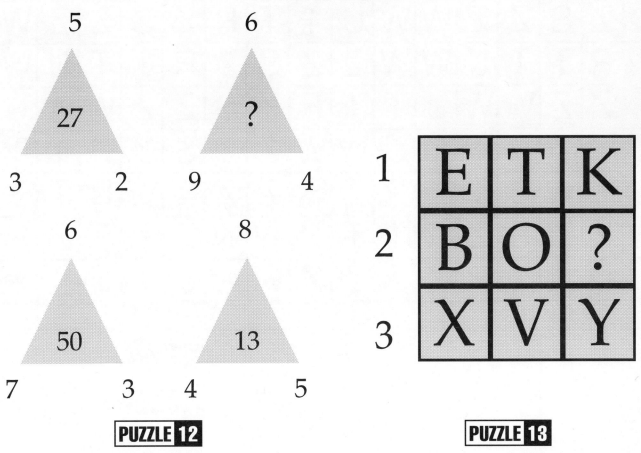

PUZZLE 12

Find a letter to replace the question mark.

See answer 137

PUZZLE 13

Can you unravel the logic behind this square and
find the missing letter?

See answer 91

LEVEL 2

Z	R	T	T	U	W	W	Z	Z	S	Z	R	T	T	U	W
S	Z	Z	W	W	U	T	T	R	Z	S	Z	Z	W	W	U
Z	S	Z	R	T	T	U	W	W	Z	Z	S	Z	R	T	T
Z	W	W	U	T	T	R	Z	S	Z	Z	W	W	U	T	T
W	Z	Z	S	Z	R	T	T			Z	Z	S	Z	R
W	U	T	T	R	Z	S	Z			U	T	T	R	Z
U	W	W	Z	Z	S	Z	R			W	W	Z	Z	S
T	T	R	Z	S	Z	Z	W	W	U	T	T	R	Z	S	Z
T	T	U	W	W	Z	Z	S	Z	R	T	T	U	W	W	Z
R	Z	S	Z	Z	W	W	U	T	T	R	Z	S	Z	Z	W
Z	R	T	T	U	W	W	Z	Z	S	Z	R	T	T	U	W
S	Z	Z	W	W	U	T	T	R	Z	S	Z	Z	W	W	U
Z	S	Z	R	T	T	U	W	W	Z	Z	S	Z	R	T	T
Z	W	W	U	T	T	R	Z	S	Z	Z	W	W	U	T	T
W	Z	Z	S	Z	R	T	T	U	W	W	Z	Z	S	Z	R
W	U	T	T	R	Z	S	Z	Z	W	W	U	T	T	R	Z

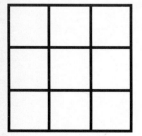

PUZZLE 14

Can you spot the pattern of this grid and complete the missing section?

See answer 115

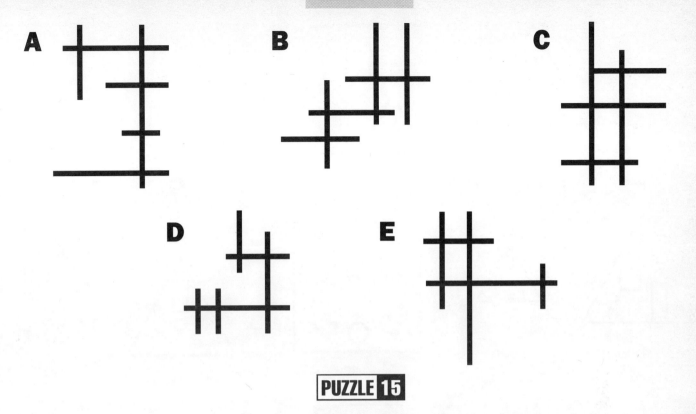

PUZZLE 15

Can you work out which diagram is the odd one out?

See answer 179

A. 4 hrs 20 min ?

B. 3 hrs 15 min 80

C. 6 hrs 14 min 60

D. 7 hrs 13 min 42

E. 4 hrs 12 min 78

PUZZLE 16

Each tractor has been working for the time shown. The figure under the tractor shows how many tons of potatoes have been gathered. Clearly some strange logic is at work! How many tons has tractor A gathered?

See answer 90

A is to **B** as **C** is to

D   **E**   **F**   **G**   **H**

PUZZLE 17

See answer 106

F C J Z I E

W K L P Y

Q H B V G X

PUZZLE 18

This is another anagram in which we have given you only the letters that are NOT used. When you have the correct letters you should be able to make the name of an astrologer. Take care! Two letters are used twice.

See answer 177

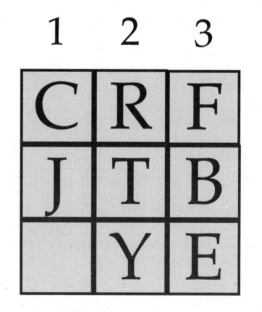

1   2   3

C	R	F
J	T	B
	Y	E

PUZZLE 19

Can you work out the logic behind this square and complete the missing section?

See answer 93

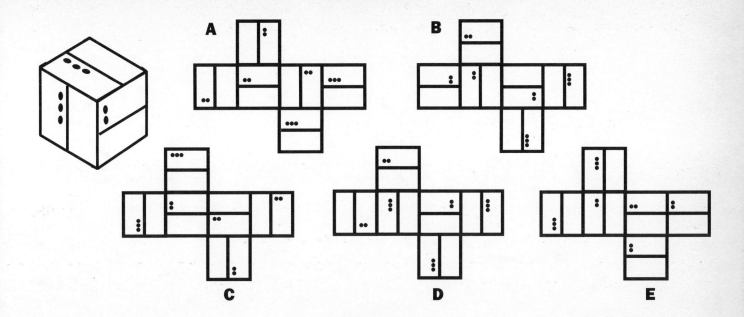

A B

C D E

PUZZLE 20

Which of these layouts could be used to make the
above cube?

See answer 149

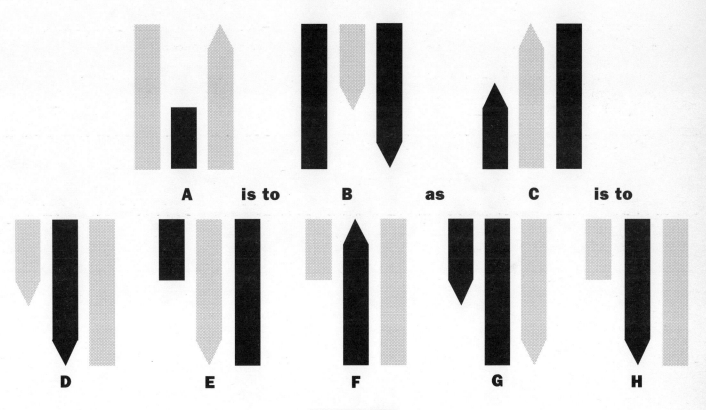

A   is to   B   as   C   is to

D   E   F   G   H

PUZZLE 21

See answer 178

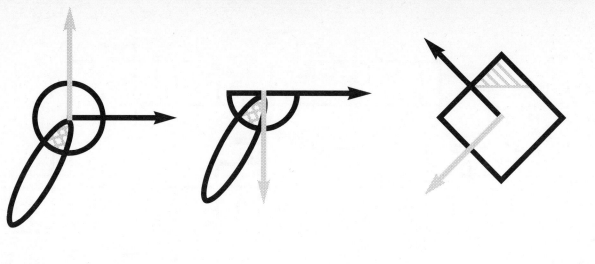

A   **is to**   **B**   **as**   **C**   **is to**

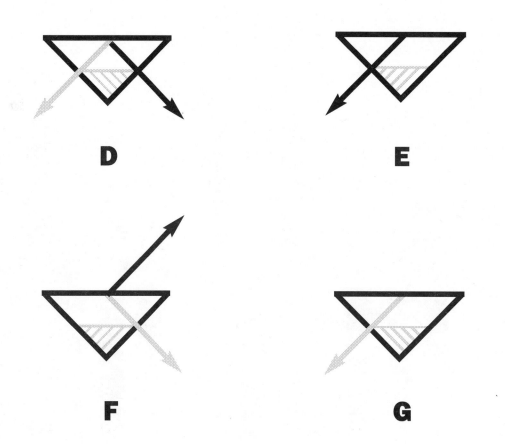

D   **E**

F   **G**

PUZZLE 22

See answer 86

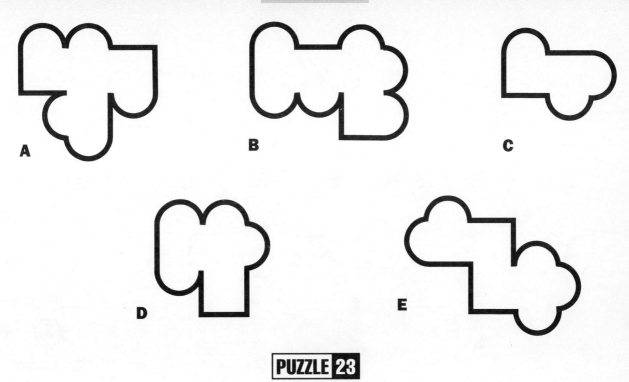

A

B

C

D

E

PUZZLE 23

Can you find the odd shape out?

See answer 185

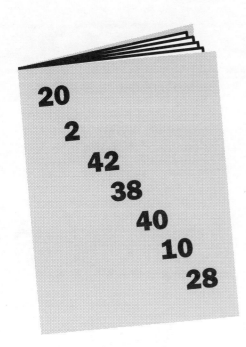

20
2
42
38
40
10
28

PUZZLE 24

Can you unravel the code on this book to find its famous author?

See answer 131

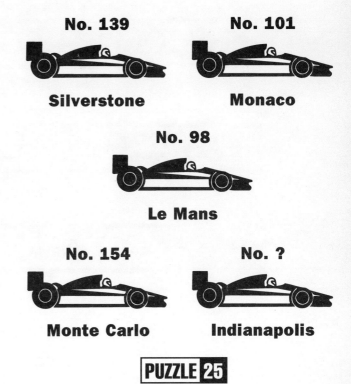

No. 139
Silverstone

No. 101
Monaco

No. 98
Le Mans

No. 154
Monte Carlo

No. ?
Indianapolis

PUZZLE 25

These cars are all racing at famous circuits. Can you work out the number of the car at Indianapolis?

See answer 85

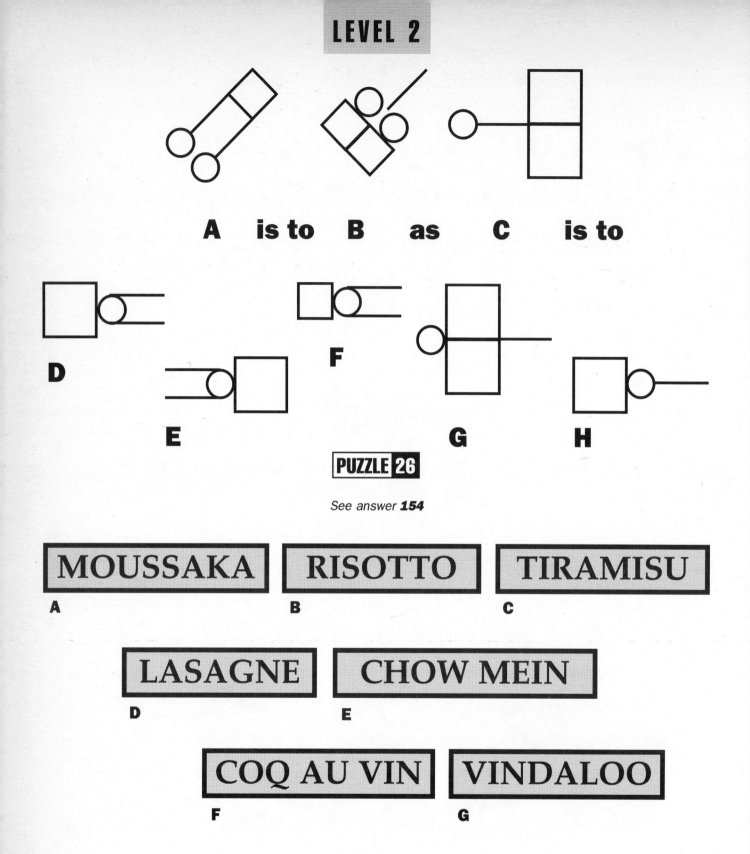

A is to **B** as **C** is to

PUZZLE 26

See answer 154

MOUSSAKA	RISOTTO	TIRAMISU
A	B	C

LASAGNE	CHOW MEIN
D	E

COQ AU VIN	VINDALOO
F	G

PUZZLE 27

Can you work out which of the above dishes is
the odd one out?

See answer 35

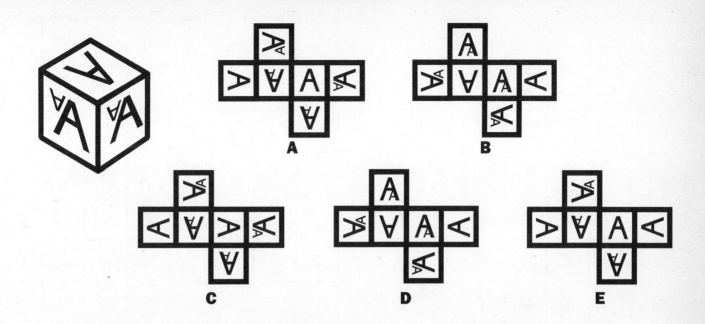

PUZZLE 28

Which of the following layouts could be used to make the above cube?

See answer 181

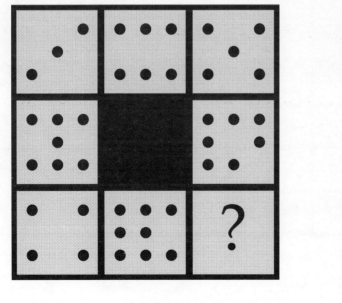

PUZZLE 29

Can you work out the logic behind this square and fill in the missing section?

See answer 92

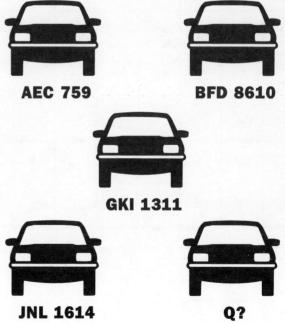

AEC 759

BFD 8610

GKI 1311

JNL 1614

Q?

PUZZLE 30

The registration plates of all these cars conform to a certain logic. Can you work out the final plate?

See answer 84

LEVEL 2

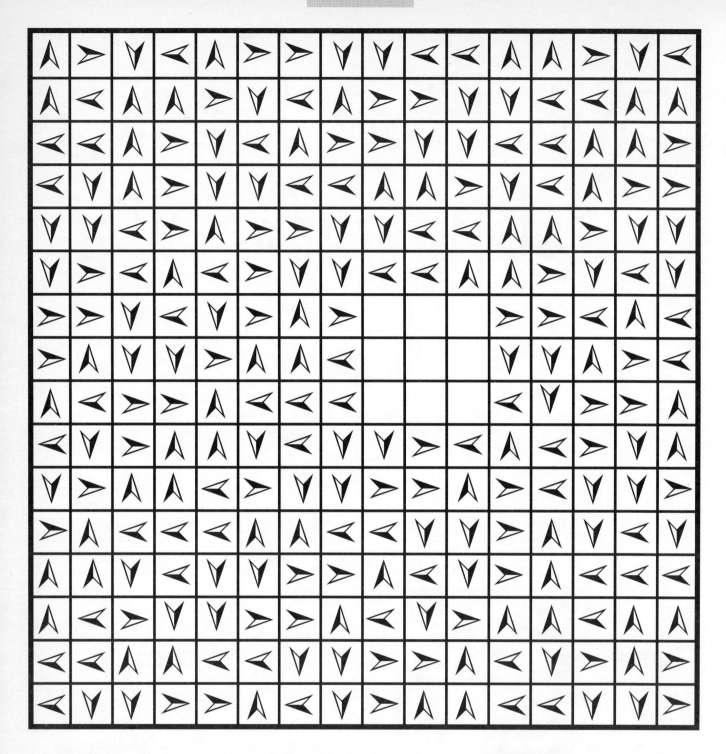

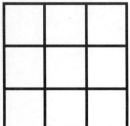

PUZZLE 31

Can you work out the reasoning behind this grid and complete the missing section?

See answer 182

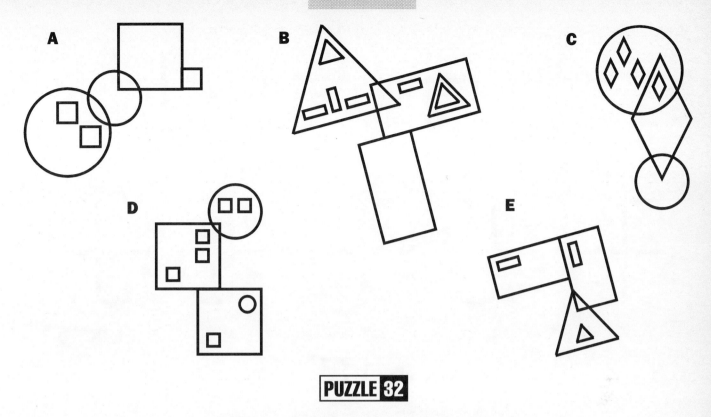

A

B

C

D

E

PUZZLE 32

Can you work out which is the odd diagram out?

See answer 153

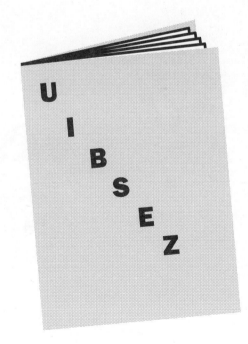

U
I
B
S
E
Z

PUZZLE 33

Can you work out the reasoning behind this code and discover the author of this book?

See answer 123

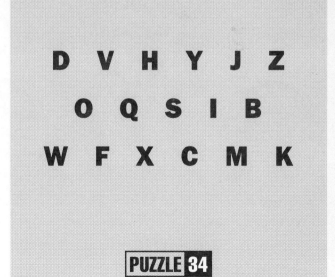

D V H Y J Z
O Q S I B
W F X C M K

PUZZLE 34

This is another anagram in which we have given you only the letters you do NOT need. Find out the missing letters, change their order, and you will have the name of a giant. One letter is used twice. Extra clue: his father also appears in this book.

See answer 171

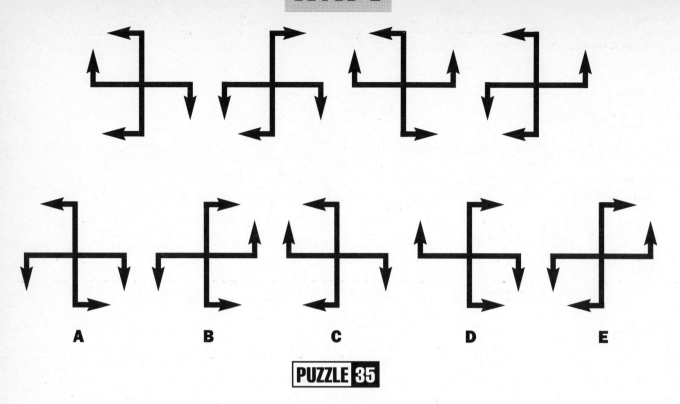

A   **B**   **C**   **D**   **E**

PUZZLE 35

Can you work out which of these symbols comes next in
this sequence?

See answer **104**

654373425

Politiken

41771561

La Stampa

246137

El Pais

34335655

Il Giorno

?

The Independent

PUZZLE 36

Each balloon has been sponsored by a famous newspaper.
The number is somehow linked to the paper's name. What
is the number of *The Independent's* balloon?

See answer **78**

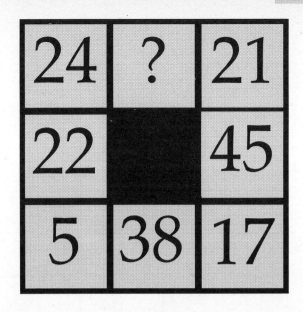

PUZZLE 37

Can you work out the logic behind this square and find the missing number?

See answer 80

PUZZLE 38

Can you work out which symbol is the odd one out?

See answer 155

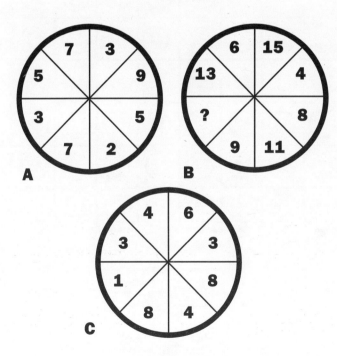

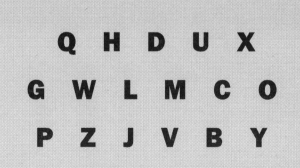

Q H D U X

G W L M C O

P Z J V B Y

PUZZLE 40

This is another anagram in which we haven given you only the letters you do NOT need. Find the missing letters, rearrange them, and you should find the name of the hero of a Gothic novel. The N is used more than once and one other letter is repeated.

See answer 172

PUZZLE 39

Can you replace the question mark with a number?

See answer 111

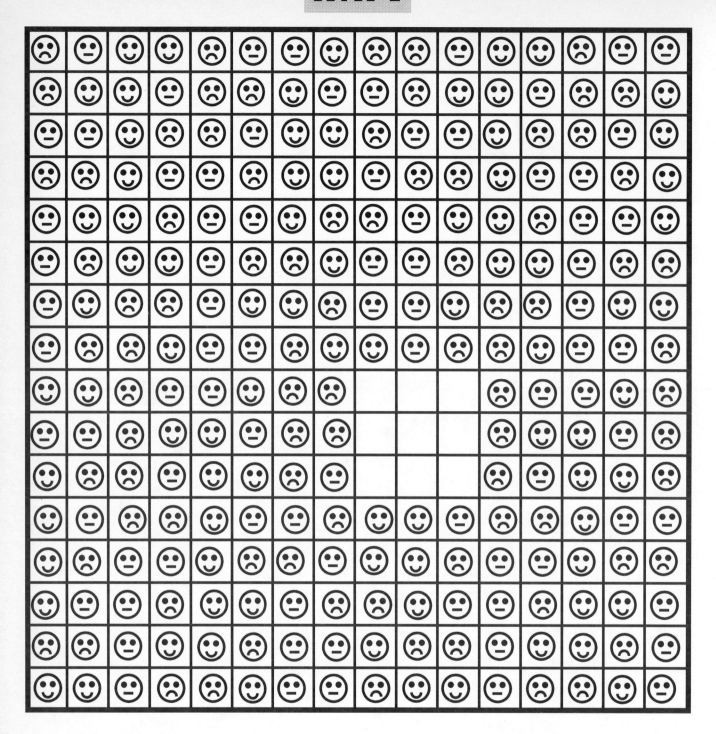

PUZZLE 41

This grid is made up according to a certain pattern. Can you work it out and fill in the missing section?

See answer 42

M N B

A   is to   B   as   C   is to

∞ CC B A BB

D   E   F   G   H

PUZZLE 42

See answer 180

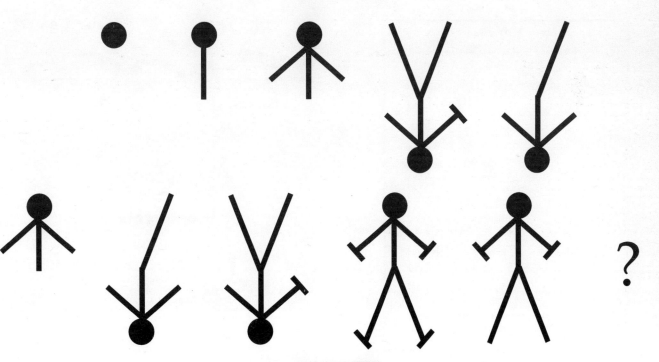

PUZZLE 43

Can you work out what the next matchstick man in this
series should look like?

See answer 53

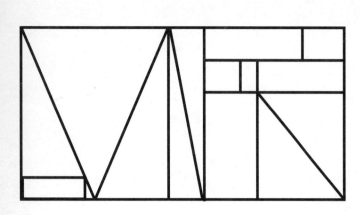

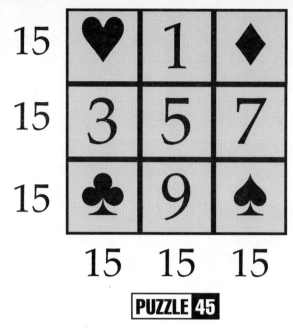

PUZZLE 44

Can you work out how many rectangles can be found
in this diagram altogether?

See answer 56

PUZZLE 45

Can you work out how much each shape is worth?

See answer 45

W V T Z H

PUZZLE 46

Can you unravel the code on the back of the picture to
find the name of its artist.

See answer 102

No. 76 — Schmidt
No. 92 — Perkins
No. 91 — Delacroix
No. 80 — Moreno
No. ? — Pascal

PUZZLE 47

Each car's number is related to its driver's name. Can
you predict which car Pascal will drive?

See answer 79

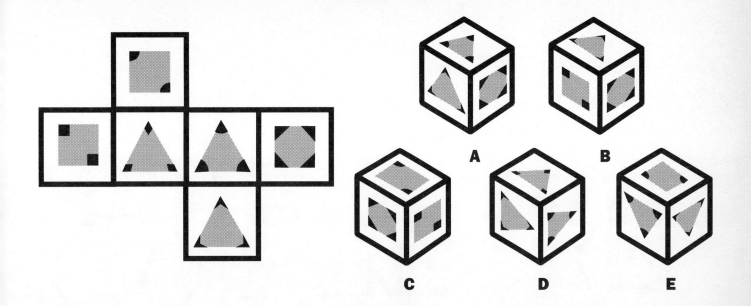

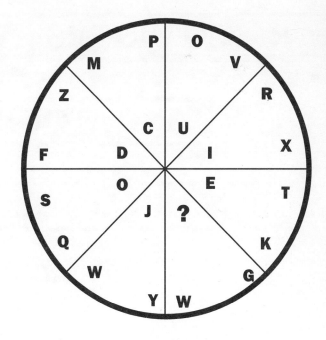

PUZZLE 48

Can you work out which of these cubes cannot be made from the above layout?

See answer 165

RDPNHVEE
FLBFILOAU
AWADNSAGI
ELTSBNOO
PSTAEELTH
IMAMAII

PUZZLE 49

The above are all anagrams of American towns. However, two extra letters have been added to each word. If you collect all the extra letters you will be able to make another place name.

See answer 18

PUZZLE 50

Can you replace the question mark with a letter?

See answer 183

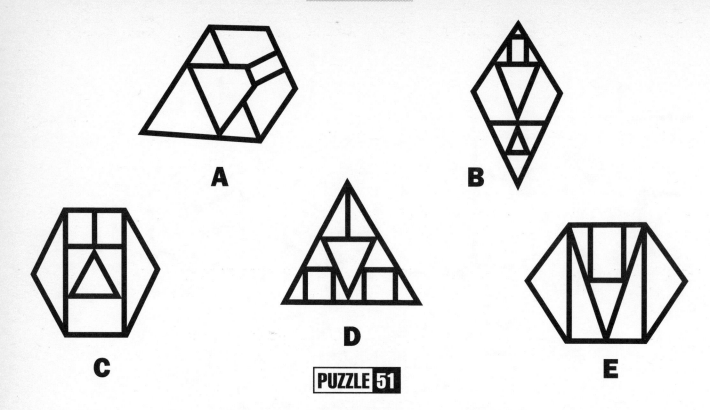

A **B** **C** **D** **E**

PUZZLE 51

Can you work out which shape is the odd one out?

See answer 169

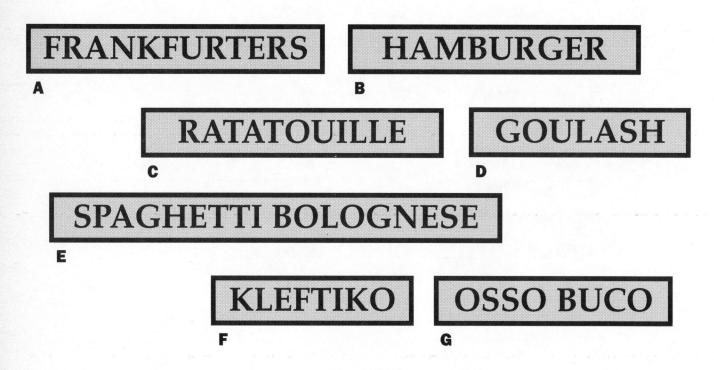

FRANKFURTERS
A

HAMBURGER
B

RATATOUILLE
C

GOULASH
D

SPAGHETTI BOLOGNESE
E

KLEFTIKO
F

OSSO BUCO
G

PUZZLE 52

Can you work out which of these dishes is the odd one out?

See answer 21

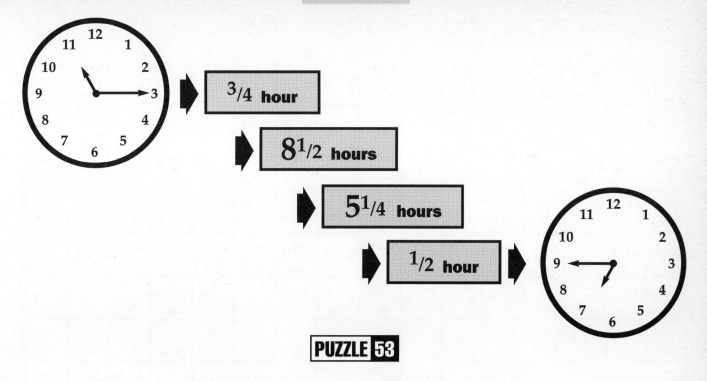

3/4 hour

8 1/2 hours

5 1/4 hours

1/2 hour

PUZZLE 53

Can you work out, using the amounts of time specified,
whether you have to go forward or backward to get from
the top clock to the bottom clock?

See answer 187

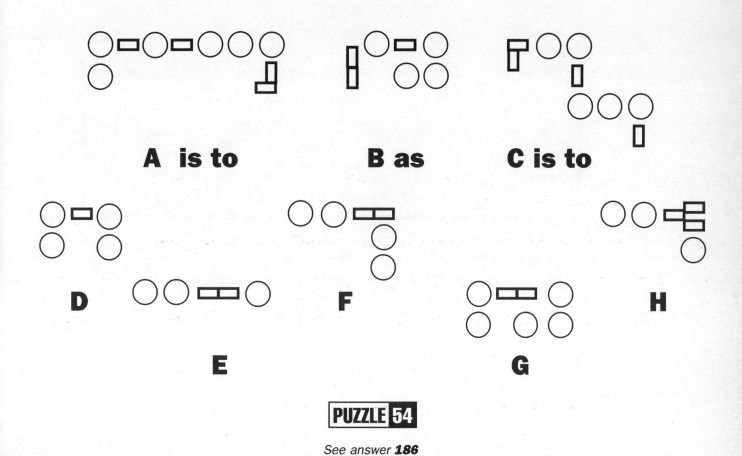

A is to

B as

C is to

D

F

H

E

G

PUZZLE 54

See answer 186

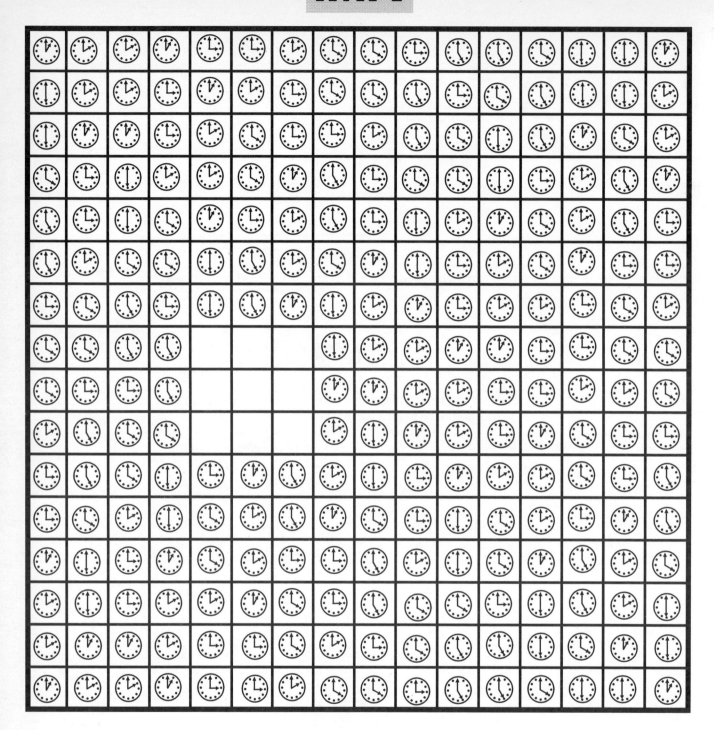

PUZZLE 55

Can you work out which pattern this grid follows and complete the missing section?

See answer 164

PUZZLE 56

Pick one letter from each cloud in order. You should be able to make the names of five composers.

See answer 41

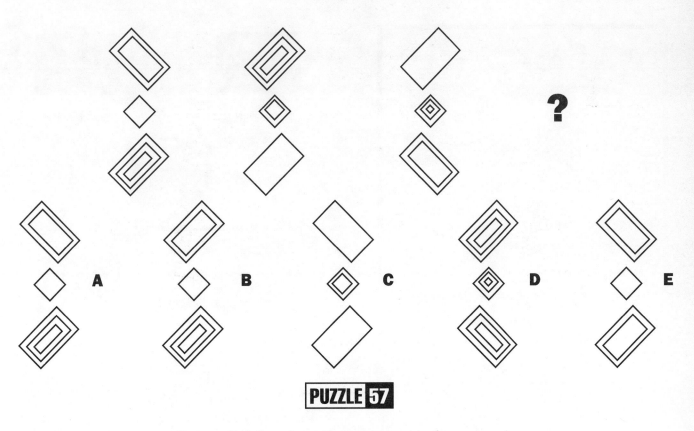

PUZZLE 57

Can you find the column that comes next in the sequence?

See answer 175

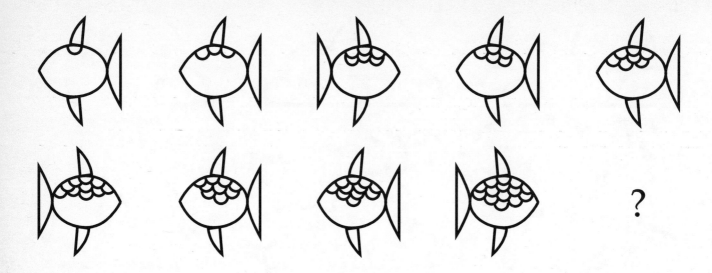

PUZZLE 58

Can you work out what the next fish in this sequence should look like?

See answer 52

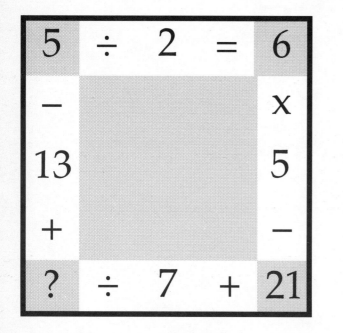

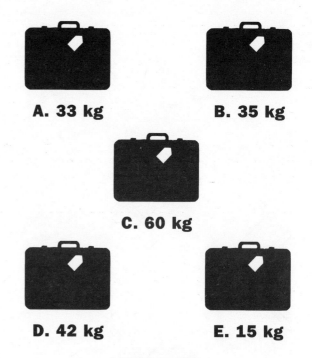

A. 33 kg B. 35 kg

C. 60 kg

D. 42 kg E. 15 kg

PUZZLE 59

Can you work out which number should replace the question mark?

See answer 144

PUZZLE 60

The weight of each suitcase is shown. Which is the odd one out?

See answer 67

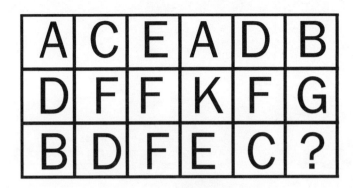

Which letter should replace the question mark?

See answer 160

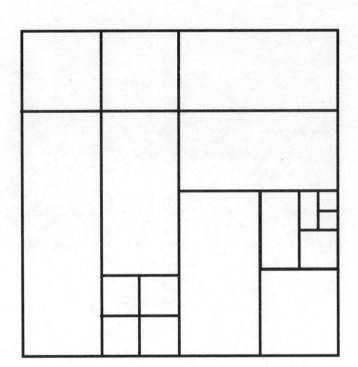

How many squares can you find in this diagram
altogether?

See answer 97

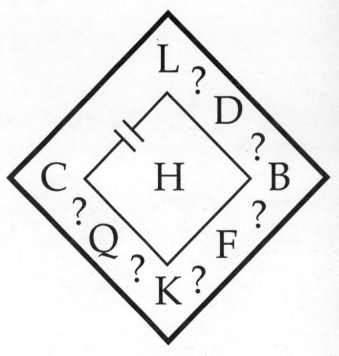

In this diagram the four basic mathematical
signs (+, −, x, ÷) have been missed out.
Can you replace the question marks?

See answer 136

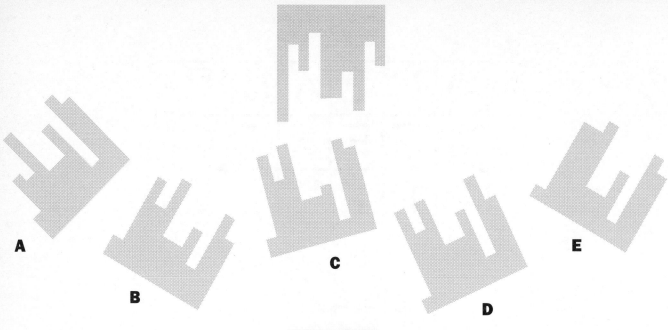

A B C D E

PUZZLE 64

Can you work out which of these shapes would fit together
with the shape above?

*See answer **116***

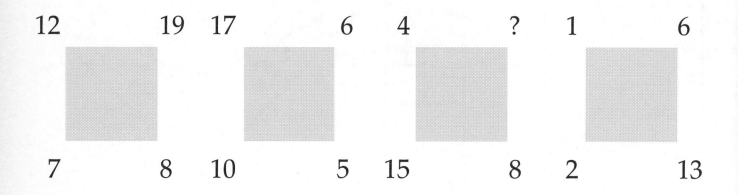

12   19 17   6   4   ?   1   6

7   8 10   5   15   8 2   13

PUZZLE 65

Can you work out the reasoning behind these squares and
replace the question mark with a number?

*See answer **120***

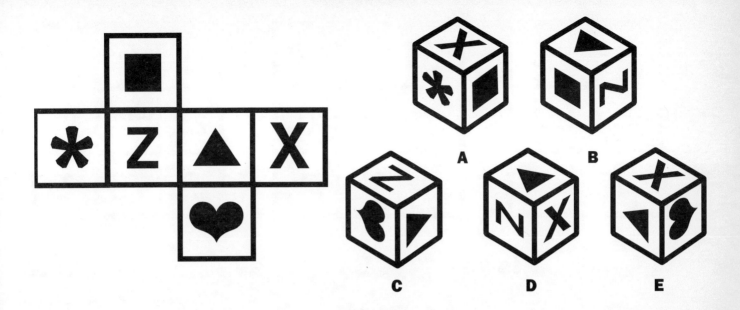

PUZZLE 66

Can you spot the cube that cannot be made from the above layout?

See answer 163

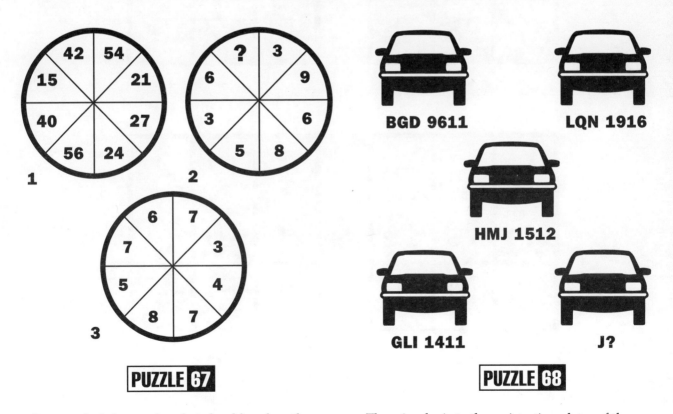

BGD 9611   **LQN 1916**

HMJ 1512

GLI 1411   **J?**

PUZZLE 67

Can you find the number that should replace the question mark?

See answer 121

PUZZLE 68

There is a logic to the registration plates of these cars. What is the plate on the last car?

See answer 77

5	6	9
4	3	2
0	7	1

8	4	12
2	6	0
0	10	4

4	9	6
22	7	11
2	14	1

A   is to   **B**   as   **C**   is to

8	18	12
44	14	22
4	28	2

D

7	7	9
25	5	9
5	17	0

E

7	12	9
25	10	14
5	17	4

F

2	12	4
20	10	14
0	12	4

G

PUZZLE 69

See answer 88

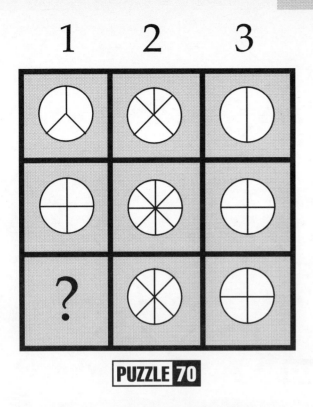

1 2 3

PUZZLE 70

Can you work out the reasoning behind this square and replace the question mark with the correct shape?

See answer 36

A E
F H
I K
L ?

PUZZLE 71

Can you find the letter that comes next in this series?

See answer 64

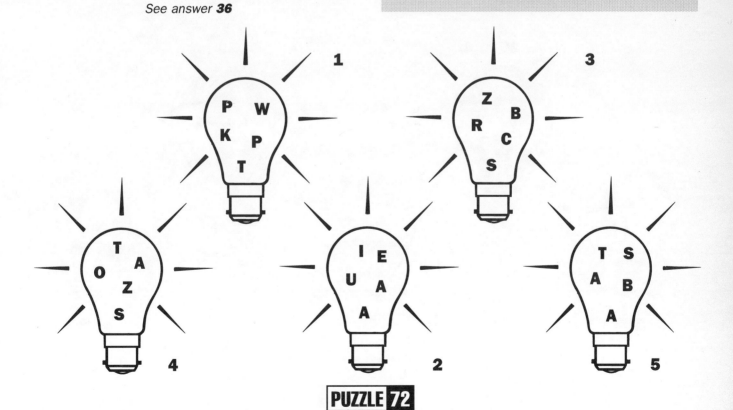

PUZZLE 72

Take one letter from each bulb in order. You should be able to make five five-letter words related to food.

See answer 40

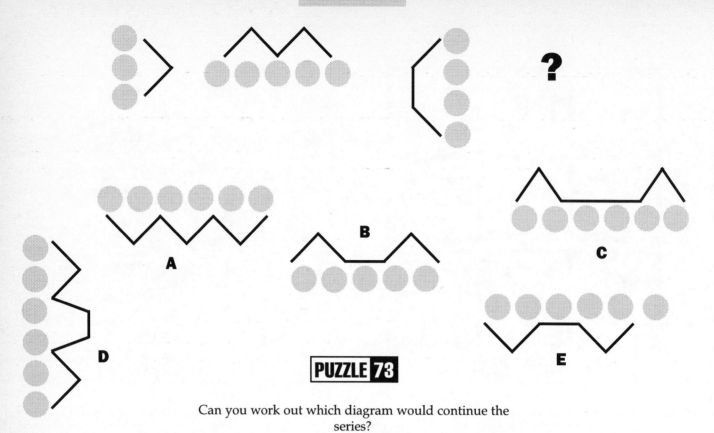

PUZZLE 73

Can you work out which diagram would continue the
series?

See answer 161

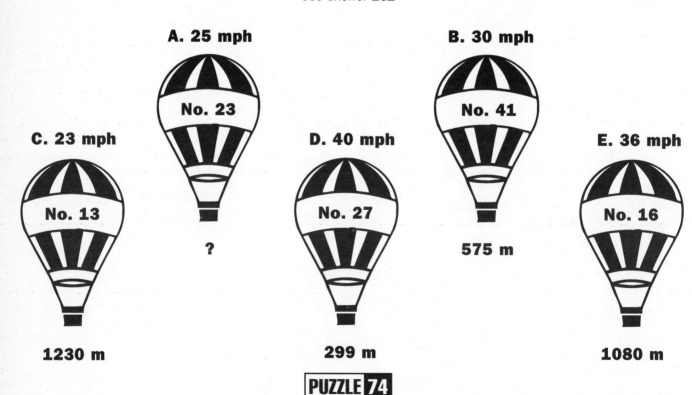

PUZZLE 74

The diagram gives the speed, number and distance covered
for each balloon. Can you work out the distance for A?

See answer 69

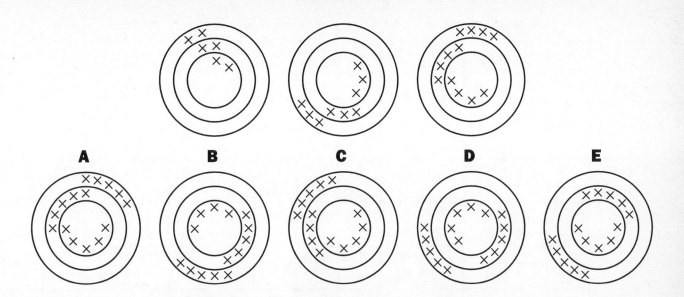

PUZZLE 75

Can you work out which of these symbols
follows the sequence?

See answer 105

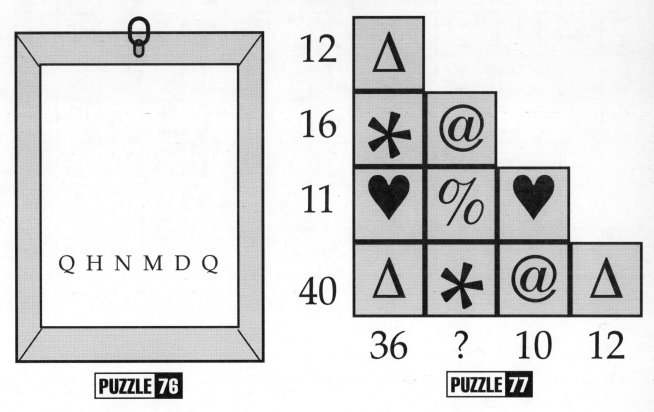

PUZZLE 76

Can you unravel this code and find the
painter of this picture?

See answer 96

PUZZLE 77

Can you work out which number should replace the
question mark in this diagram?

See answer 26

2	2	3	1	1	7	1	4	5	5	2	2	3	1	1	7
5	3	1	1	7	1	4	5	5	2	2	3	1	1	7	1
5	2	3	1	1	7	1	4	5	5	2	2	3	1	1	4
4	2	2	2	2	3	1	1	7	1	4	5	5	2	7	5
1	5	2	5	1	4	5	5	2	2	3	1	1	2	1	5
7	5	5	5	7	2	2	3	1	1	7	1	7	3	4	2
1	4	5	4	1	5	3	1	1	7	1	4	1	1	5	2
1	1	4	1	1	5	2	3	1	1	4	5	4	1	5	3
3	7	1	7	3	4	2	2	2	7	5	5	5	7	2	1
2	1	7	1	2	1	5	5	4	1	5	2	5	1	2	1
2	1	1	1	2	7	1	1	3	2	2	2	2	4	3	7
5	3	1	3	5	5	4	1	7	1	1	3	2	5	1	1
5	2	3	2	2	5	5	4	1	7	1	1	3	5	1	4
			2	5	5	4	1	7	1	1	3	2	2	7	5
			4	1	7	1	1	3	2	2	5	5	4	1	5
			3	2	2	5	5	4	1	7	1	1	3	2	2

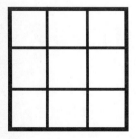

Can you work out the reasoning behind this grid and complete the missing section?

*See answer **135***

130

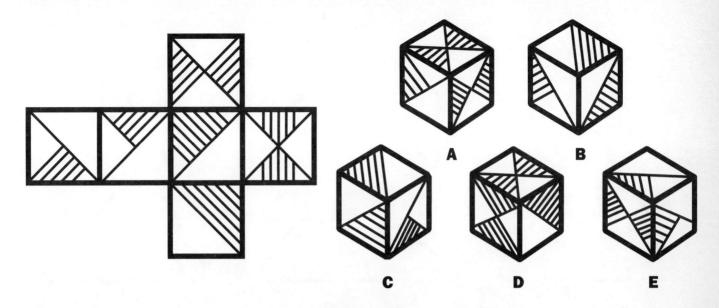

PUZZLE 79

Which of these cubes can be made from the
above layout?

See answer 128

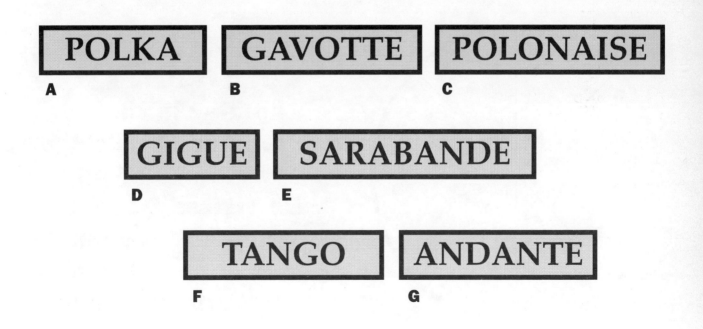

PUZZLE 80

Can you work out which of these musical terms
is the odd one out?

See answer 20

PUZZLE 81

Take one letter from each cloud in order.
You should be able to find five words from around
the world that are in common use.

See answer 50

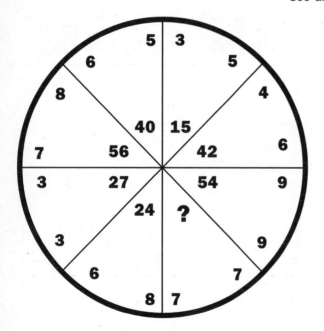

PUZZLE 82

Can you work out the reasoning behind this wheel
and replace the question mark with a number?

See answer 151

Earl left Dallas for a holiday in the UK. He liked Cambridge but not Oxford. He visited Derby but not Nottingham. He went to St Ives but not Polzeath.

Did he like Swansea?

PUZZLE 83

See answer 159

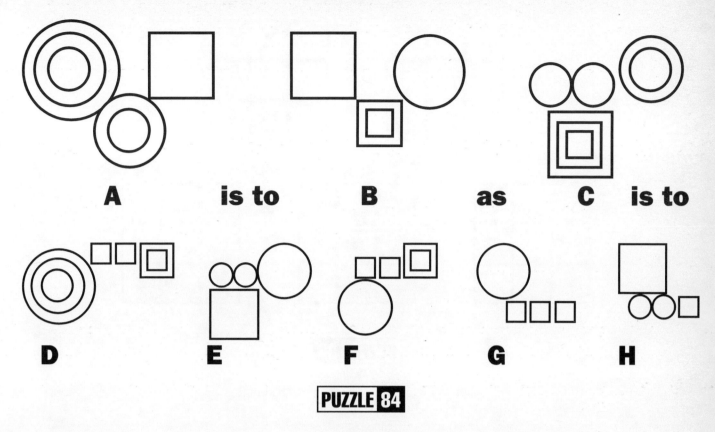

A   **is to**   **B**   **as**   **C**   **is to**

D   **E**   **F**   **G**   **H**

PUZZLE 84

See answer 156

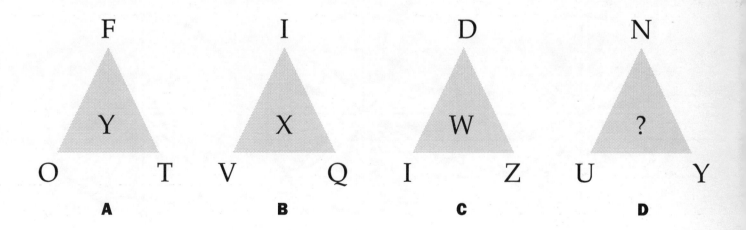

A   **B**   **C**   **D**

PUZZLE 85

Can you work out which letter should replace
the question mark?

See answer 119

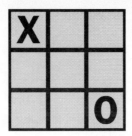
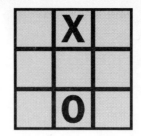

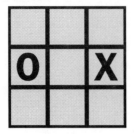
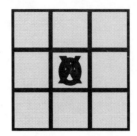
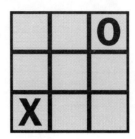

Can you work out what the next grid in this sequence should look like?

See answer **54**

Can you work out what the missing section in the last wheel should look like?

See answer **57**

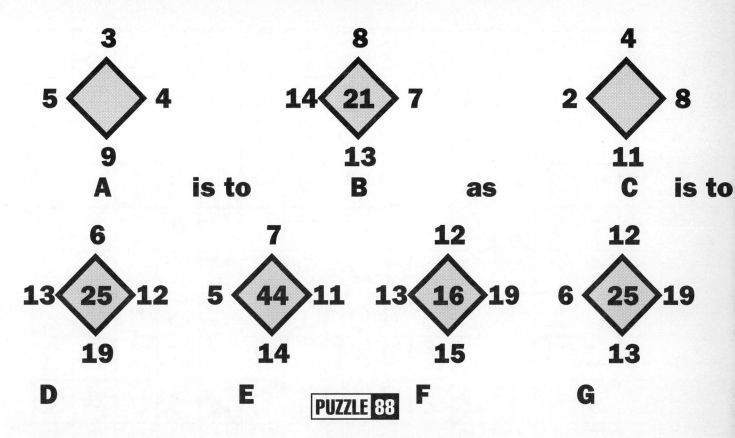

3
5 4
9
A   *is to*

8
14 **21** 7
13
B   *as*

4
2 8
11
C   *is to*

6
13 **25** 12
19
D

7
5 **44** 11
14
E

12
13 **16** 19
15
F

12
6 **25** 19
13
G

PUZZLE 88

See answer 94

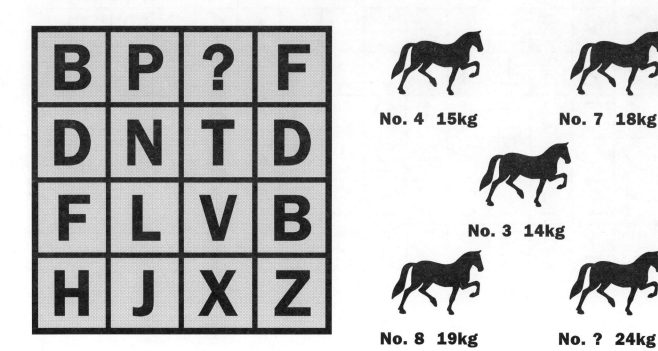

B	P	?	F
D	N	T	D
F	L	V	B
H	J	X	Z

No. 4 15kg   No. 7 18kg

No. 3 14kg

No. 8 19kg   No. ? 24kg

PUZZLE 89

Can you find the letter which completes
this diagram?

See answer 75

PUZZLE 90

Each horse carries a weight handicap.
Can you work out the number of the final horse?

See answer 15

1	2	2	3	4	4	1	2	3	3	4	1	2	2	3	4
3	3	2	1	4	4	3	2	2	1	4	3	3	2	1	4
4	1	2	2	3	4	4	1	2	3	3	4	1	2	2	3
3	2	1	4	4	3	2	2	1	4	3	3	2	1	4	4
3	4	1	2	2	3	4	4	1	2	3	3	4	1	2	2
2	1	4	4	3	2	2	1	4	3	3	2	1	4	4	3
3	3	4	1	2	2	3	4	4	1	2	3	3	4	1	2
1	4	4	3	2	2	1	4	3	3	2	1	4	4	3	2
2	3	3	4	1	2	2	3	4	4	1	2	3	3	4	1
4	4	3	2	2	1	4				1	4	4	3	2	2
1	2	3	3	4	1	2				4	1	2	3	3	4
4	3	2	2	1	4	3				4	4	3	2	2	1
4	1	2	3	3	4	1	2	2	3	4	4	1	2	3	3
3	2	2	1	4	3	3	2	1	4	4	3	2	2	1	4
4	4	1	2	3	3	4	1	2	2	3	4	4	1	2	3
2	2	1	4	3	3	2	1	4	4	3	2	2	1	4	3

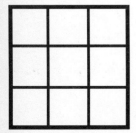

PUZZLE 91

Can you work out the reasoning behind this grid
and complete the missing section?

See answer 51

PUZZLE 92

Pick a letter from each bulb in turn and make the names of five novelists.

See answer 30

NEW YORK
1116

LAS VEGAS
1359

LOS ANGELES
1728

CHICAGO
1233

SAN FRANCISCO

PUZZLE 93

All these cars started from the same place and drove to the cities indicated. The mileages shown on the trip meter seem to make no sense, but the logic comes from the names of the destinations. Can you work out what it is, and the mileage of the last car?

See answer 68

1. M R V N O A E C
2. D O N I G F E I L
3. T V T A L N N A R A A I
4. O O E N H L I N G R A
5. G D I I I V O B O S U N R O

PUZZLE 94

Here are five anagrams of well-known operas. However, two additional letters are hidden in each one, which when put together, make up a new opera. To help you, the first letter of the new opera is a D (not included in any of the anagrams).

See answer 7

137

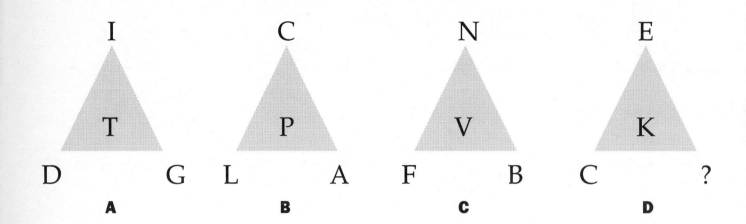

I
C
N
E

T
P
V
K

D   G   L   A   F   B   C   ?

A   B   C   D

PUZZLE 95

Can you find the letter that should replace
the question mark?

See answer 109

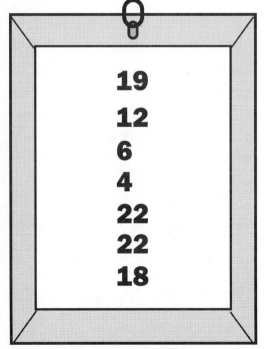

19

12

6

4

22

22

18

PUZZLE 96

Can you work out the reasoning behind this code
and find the artist of this painting?

See answer 87

**Sam took a
holiday in the
United States.
He liked Idaho but
hated Texas.
He enjoyed Hawaii
but not Arkansas.
He loved California
but not Wisconsin.**

Did he like Illinois?

PUZZLE 97

See answer 158

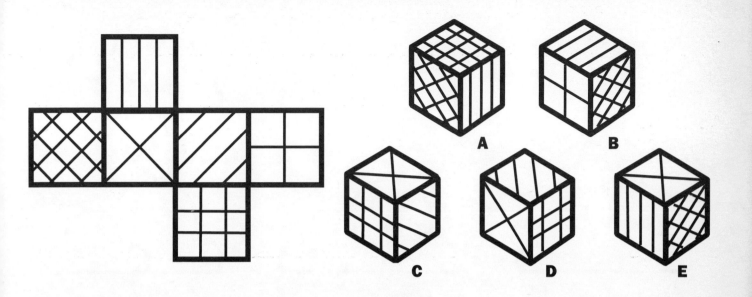

PUZZLE 98

Can you work out which of these cubes cannot be
made from the this layout?

See answer 118

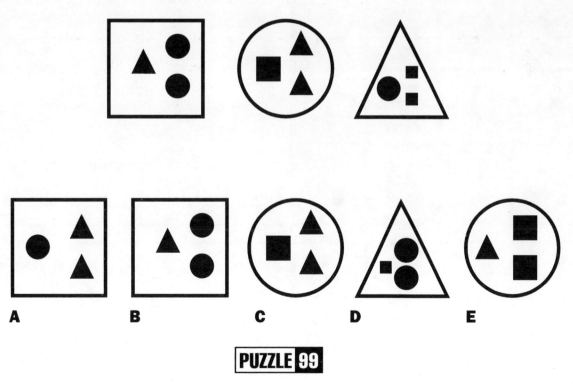

PUZZLE 99

Can you find the shape that would continue the series above?

See answer 150

PUZZLE 100

Take one letter from each cloud in order.
You should be able to make the names of five scientists.

See answer 58

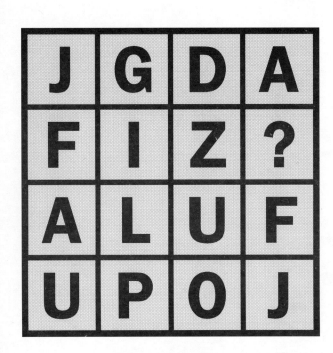

PUZZLE 101

Can you work out which letter should replace the
question mark in this square?

See answer 62

PUZZLE 102

All these bikes took part in an overnight race.
Something really weird happened! The start and finish
times of the bike became mathematically linked. If you
can discover the link you should be able to decide
when bike D finished.

See answer 16

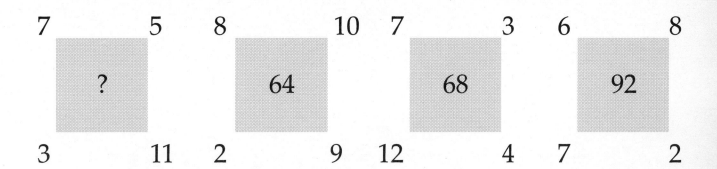

7   5   8   10   7   3   6   8

?   64   68   92

3   11   2   9   12   4   7   2

PUZZLE 103

Can you work out the reasoning behind these squares
and find the missing number?

See answer 32

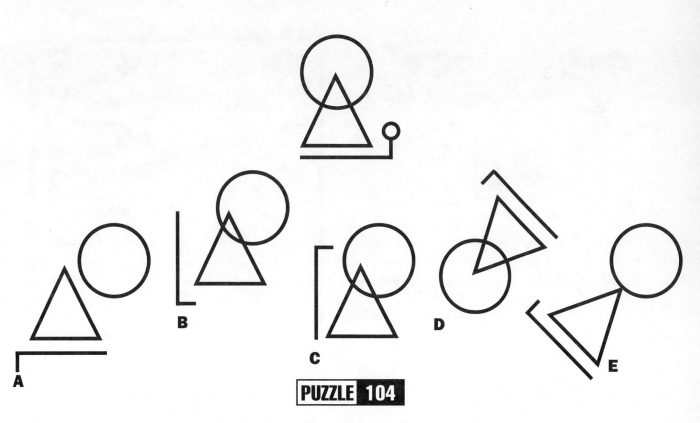

PUZZLE 104

To which of these diagrams could you add a circle to
match the conditions of the above figure?

See answer 148

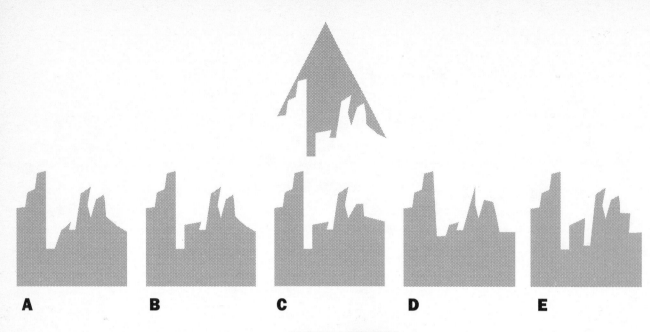

PUZZLE 105

Which of these shapes fits the above to
complete the polygon?

*See answer **174***

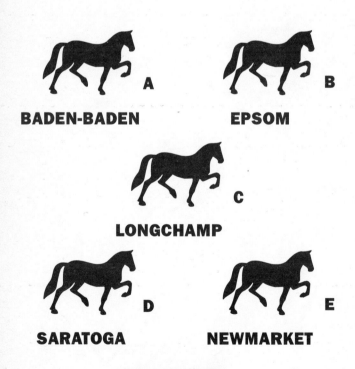

BADEN-BADEN A

EPSOM B

LONGCHAMP C

SARATOGA D

NEWMARKET E

4	x	3	+	8
=				÷
5				2
-				+
?	x	7	÷	11

PUZZLE 106

All these horses are about to race at famous courses
around the world. Which is the odd one out?

*See answer **11***

PUZZLE 107

Can you replace the question mark with a number?

*See answer **143***

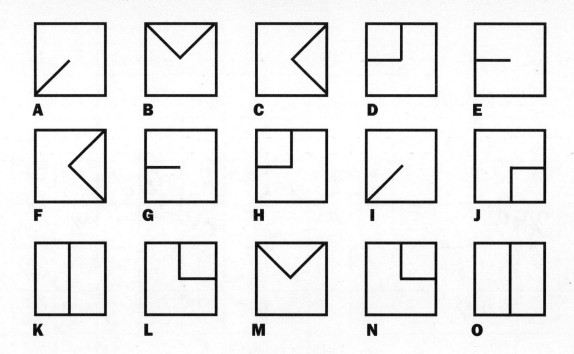

PUZZLE 108

Can you work out which of these squares is
the odd one out?

See answer 103

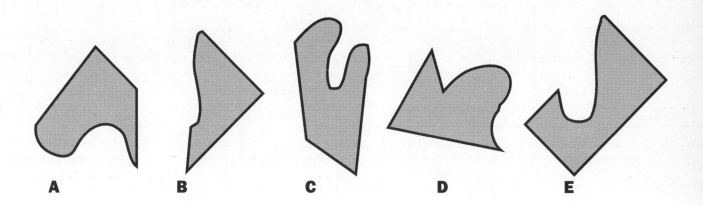

PUZZLE 109

Can you find the odd shape out?

See answer 108

&	&	%	*	%	@	@	%	*	&	&	%	*	%	@	@
*	@	@	%	*	&	&	%	*	%	@	@	%	*	&	&
%	%	&	&	%	*	%	@	@	%	*	&	&	%	*	%
@	*	*	*	%	@	@	%	*	&	&	%	*	%	%	*
@	%	%	%	@				&	&	%	*	%	@	@	%
%	&	@	&	%				&	&	%	*	@	@	@	@
*	&	@	&	*				*	&	&	%	@	%	%	@
%	*	%	*	%	%	@	@	@	%	%	@	%	*	*	%
&	%	*	%	&	*	%	%	*	*	*	@	*	&	&	*
&	@	%	@	&	%	*	%	&	&	%	%	&	&	&	&
*	@	&	@	*	&	&	*	%	@	@	*	&	%	%	&
%	%	&	%	%	@	@	%	*	%	&	&	%	*	*	%
@	*	*	*	%	&	&	*	%	@	@	%	*	%	%	*
@	%	%	@	@	%	*	%	&	&	*	%	@	@	@	%
%	&	&	*	%	@	@	%	*	%	&	&	*	%	@	@
*	%	&	&	*	%	@	@	%	*	%	&	&	*	%	@

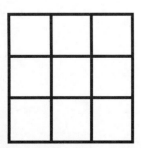

PUZZLE 110

Can you work out the pattern sequence and
fill in the missing section?

See answer 101

144

?	– 5 x		4
÷ 14 +			÷ 6 –
8	= 5 +		1

12
31
23
42
34
53
45
?

PUZZLE 111

Can you work out which number should replace the
question mark?

See answer 152

PUZZLE 112

Can you find the number that comes next
in this series?

See answer 65

FROGGIT
95

BLEASDALE
111

LUDLOW
56

WINTERBOTTOM
146

GRIMBLE
?

PUZZLE 113

Each farmer gets a different tonnage per acre.
Somehow the tons is related to the letters in his name.
How many tons does Grimble get? You need to find
two possible values for each letter.

See answer 61

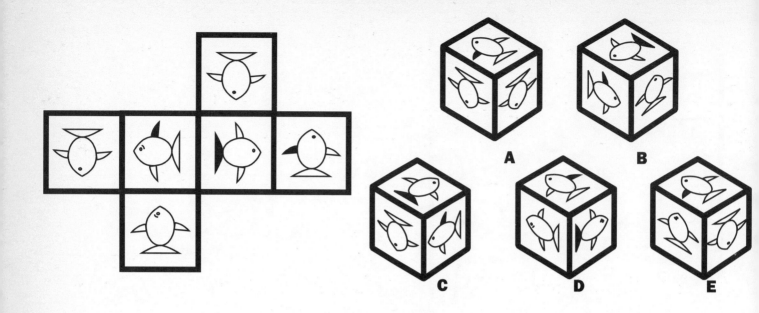

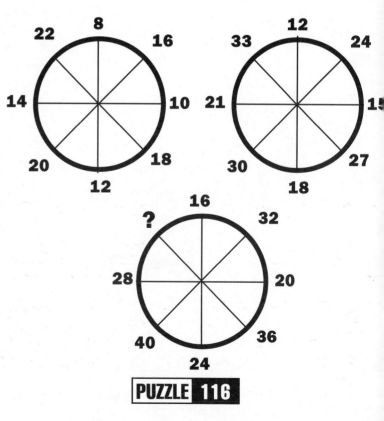

PUZZLE 114

Which cube can be made from this layout?

See answer 114

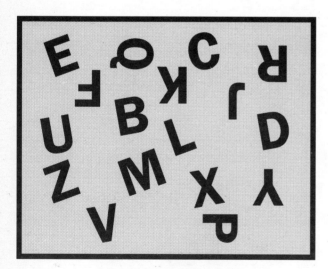

PUZZLE 115

Here is another diagam in which we have supplied the letters you do NOT need to complete the puzzle! When you have decided which letters are missing rearrange them and you will find a city named after a US President. Beware! One letter is used twice.

See answer 166

PUZZLE 116

Can you find work out which number should replace the question mark?

See answer 33

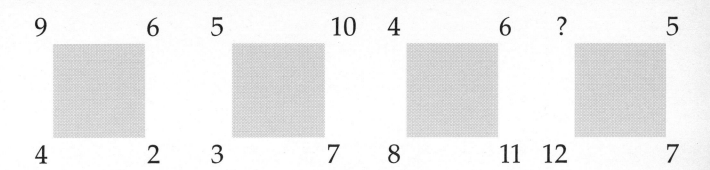

9　　　6　　5　　　10　4　　　6　？　　5

4　　　2　　3　　　7　8　　　11　12　　7

PUZZLE 117

Can you work out the reasoning behind these squares and find the number that should replace the question mark?

*See answer **110***

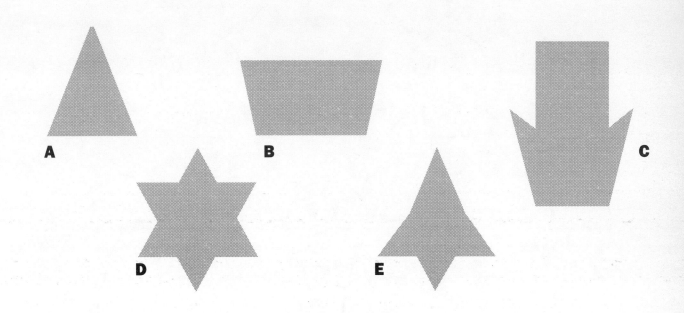

A　　　　B　　　　C

D　　　　E

PUZZLE 118

Can you find the odd shape out?

*See answer **147***

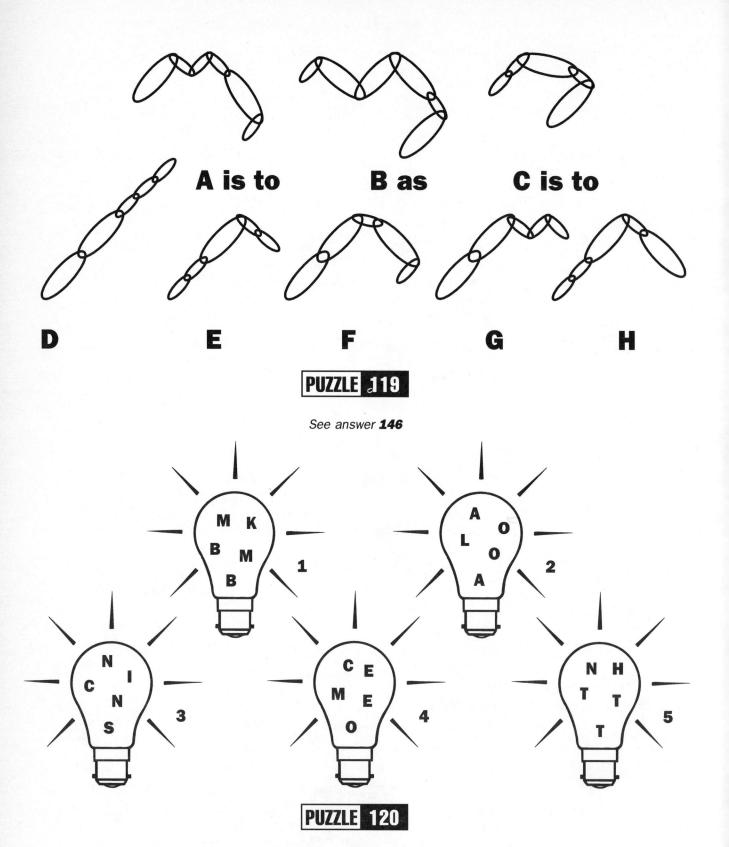

A is to   **B as**   **C is to**

D   **E**   **F**   **G**   **H**

PUZZLE 119

See answer 146

PUZZLE 120

Pick one letter from each bulb in order. You can make the
names of five artists.

See answer 28

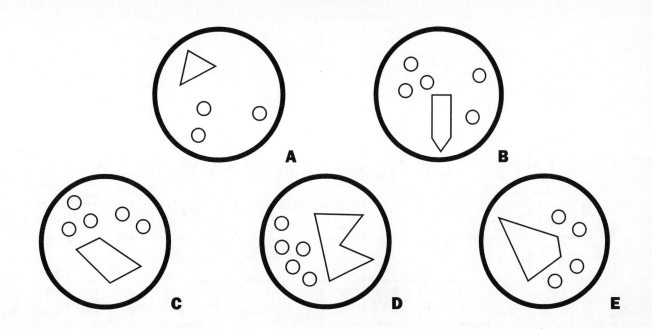

PUZZLE 121

Can you find the odd diagram out?

See answer 124

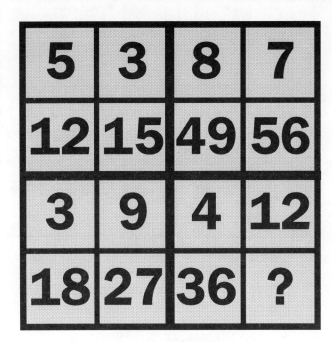

PUZZLE 122

Can you work out the reasoning behind this square and replace the question mark with a number?

See answer 23

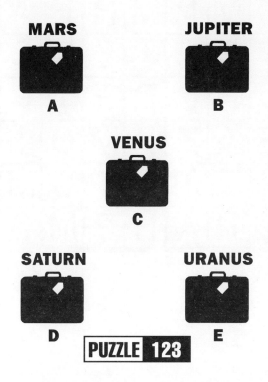

PUZZLE 123

The first interplanetary travellers are about to set off. Whose luggage is going to be put off at the wrong stop?

See answer 49

```
A R C D E T R I O M P A R C D E
R R R T E D C R A H P M O I R T
C D C T R I O M P H E H P M O I
D E T D E T R I O M A R C D E A
H P M O I R T E D P M O I R T R
A R C D E T R I E O M P H E A R
C R A E H P M T E D I R T E D C
D E T R I O R M P H C E A R C D
C D T R I I O M P H E R M I I E
R A E H O P M O I R T P A R R T
O M P M H E A R I D E H O T T R
I R P T E D C R A E H E I E E I
R H C D E T R I O M P A R D D O
E A H P M O I R T E D R T A C M
D E T R I O M P H A R C E R R P
C R A H P M O I R T E D D C A H
```

PUZZLE 124

The phrase ARC DE TRIOMPHE is concealed somewhere in this grid. It occurs in its entirety only once. It is written in straight lines with only one change of direction. Can you find it?

See answer 43

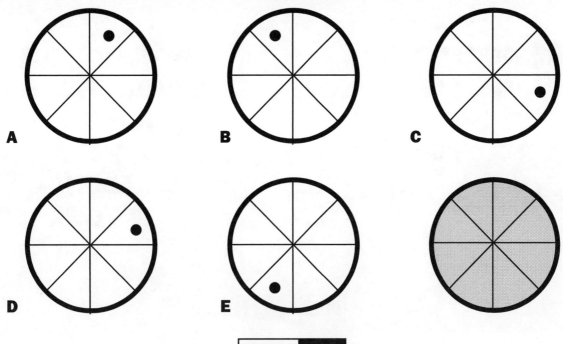

PUZZLE 125

Can you work out what the next wheel in this sequence should look like?

See answer 55

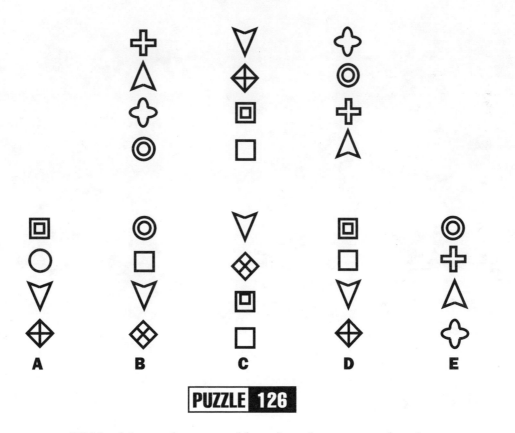

PUZZLE 126

Which of these columns would continue the sequence above?

See answer 130

MINNEAPOLIS
DALLAS
ANDOVER
ROCKFORD
DAVENPORT

INDEPENDENCE
WICHITA FALLS
ATLANTA
CHICAGO
PASADENA
NEW YORK

PUZZLE 127

Which of the names in the right column can be added to the left one? This may seem confusing initially but, despite appearances, it is not an American puzzle and you will find a capital solution.

See answer 139

SOLAR SPRINTER

SILVER STREAK

SKY

SUPER SAVAGE

STEEL SABER

PUZZLE 128

Can you work out which symbol is the odd one out?

See answer 125

PUZZLE 129

All these horses are ready for the off. Which is the odd one out?

See answer 48

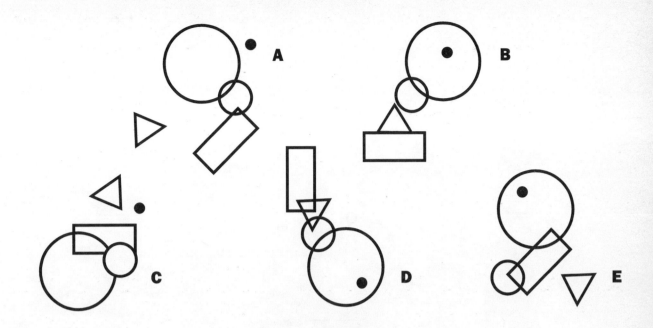

PUZZLE 130

Can you find the odd diagram out?

See answer 142

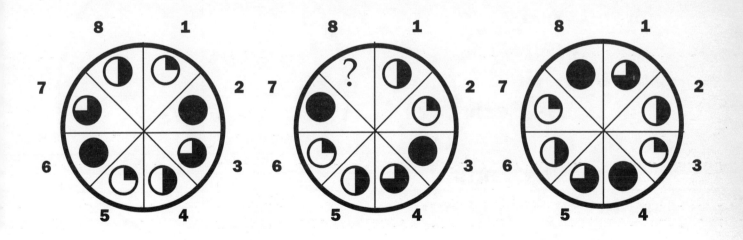

PUZZLE 131

Can you work out which shape should replace the
question mark?

See answer 22

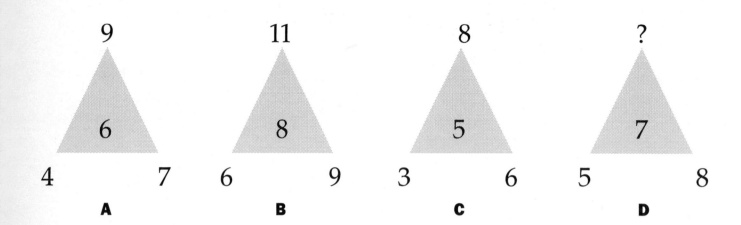

```
    9           11          8           ?
    6            8          5           7
  4     7      6     9    3     6     5     8
    A            B          C           D
```

PUZZLE 132

Can you work out the logic behind these triangles and
replace the question mark with a number?

See answer 100

**Stephie goes on
holiday around
Europe.
She likes Hamburg
but hates Berlin.
She likes Strasbourg
but avoids Paris.
She loves Barcelona
but hates Madrid.**

Does she like London?

PUZZLE 133

See answer 157

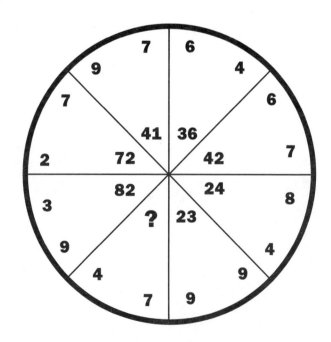

PUZZLE 134

Can you work out which number should replace the
question mark?

See answer 13

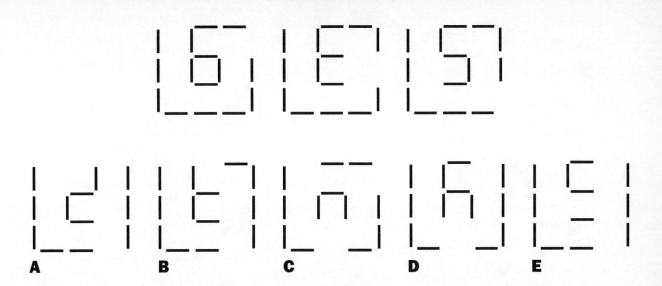

A   B   C   D   E

PUZZLE 135

Can you work out which of these diagrams would
continue the series?

See answer 141

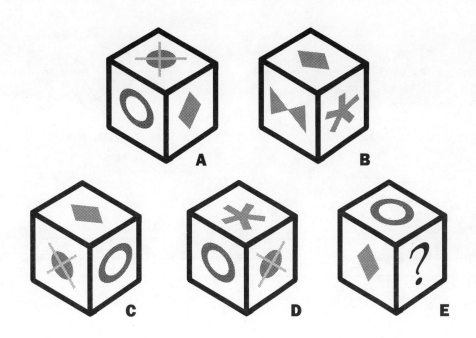

PUZZLE 136

Which of these shapes should replace the
question mark?

See answer 29

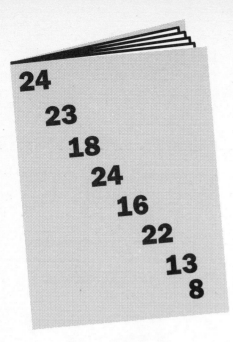

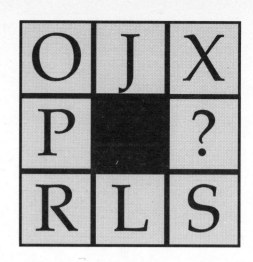

PUZZLE 137

Can you unravel the code on this book to find its famous author?

See answer 1

PUZZLE 138

Can you unravel the logic behind this square and find the missing letter?

See answer 81

A

No. 220
Denver

B

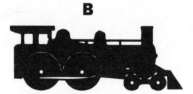

No. 47
Kansas City

C

No. 25
Galveston

D

No. 363
Lafayette

E

No. 428
a) **Portland**
b) **Chicago**
c) **Nashville**
d) **Buffalo**

PUZZLE 139

The number of each train and its destination are in some way related. Can you work out where train No. 428 is bound for?

See answer 47

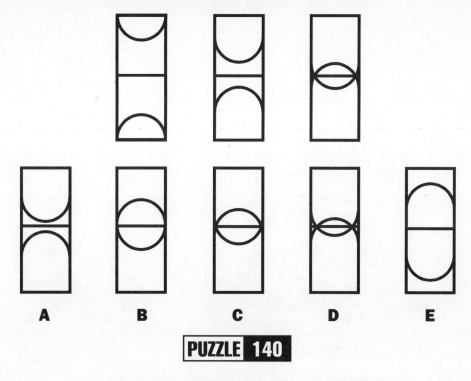

PUZZLE 140

Can you work out which of these symbols follows
the sequence above?

See answer 113

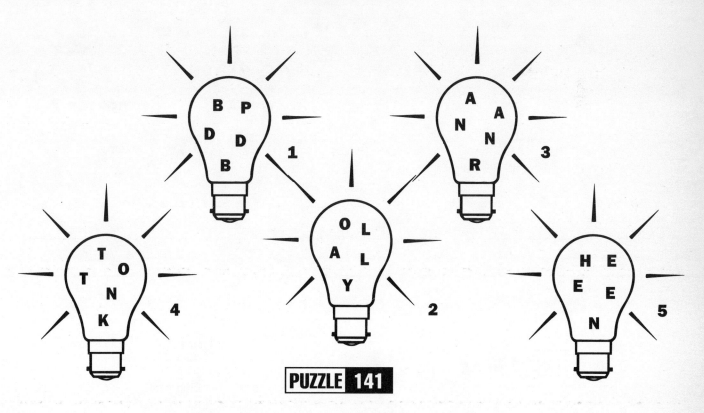

PUZZLE 141

Take one letter from each of these bulbs in order.
You will be able to make the names of five poets.

See answer 19

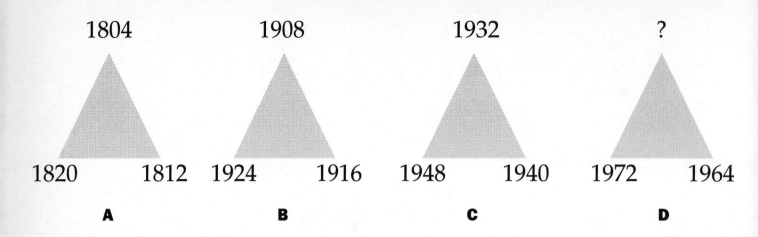

1804   1908   1932   ?

1820   1812   1924   1916   1948   1940   1972   1964

A   B   C   D

PUZZLE 142

Can you work out the reasoning behind these triangles and replace the question mark with a number?

See answer 34

No. 10   **No. 2**

Arrives 2.15   Arrives 3.02

No. 30

Arrives 2.45

No. 8   **No. ?**

Arrives 3.08   Arrives 2.30

3 4 6 8 9 12 15 16 ?

PUZZLE 143

Can you find the number that comes next in this series?

See answer 66

PUZZLE 144

Five cyclists are taking part in a race. The number of each rider and its arrival time are in some way related. Can you work out the number of the rider who arrives at 2.30?

See answer 3

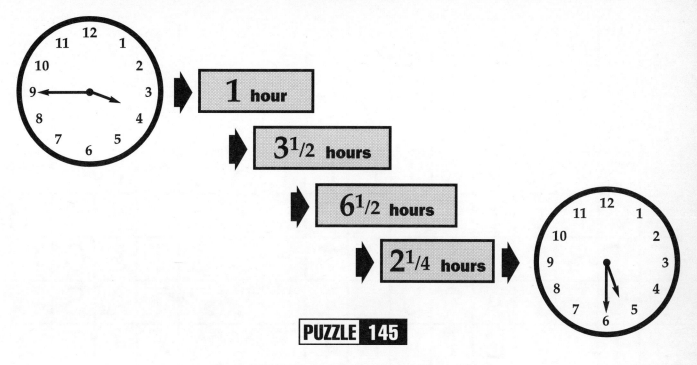

PUZZLE 145

Can you work out, using the amounts of time specified, whether you have to go forward or backward to get from the time on the top clock to the bottom clock?

See answer 162

PUZZLE 146

Can you work out which letter should replace the question mark in this square?

See answer 31

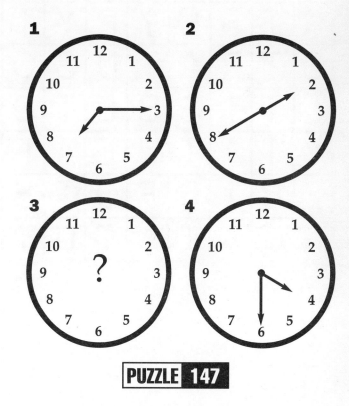

PUZZLE 147

The following clock faces are in some way related. Can you work out what the time on clock No. 3 should be?

See answer 5

S	T	A	T	U	E	O	R	T	S	T	A	T	U	E	S
S	R	E	B	I	L	F	O	E	U	T	A	T	A	T	D
L	S	T	A	T	U	L	I	B	E	R	T	O	F	F	A
I	L	I	B	E	R	T	E	L	I	B	E	R	L	O	T
B	O	F	L	I	B	U	E	O	S	T	A	I	F	S	U
E	T	S	T	A	T	U	E	O	F	S	B	T	S	O	F
R	O	F	L	A	S	U	F	T	L	E	T	T	A	S	L
T	I	C	T	B	T	L	R	I	T	Y	A	S	T	T	I
Y	U	S	E	A	I	S	B	Y	T	T	A	T	U	A	B
E	L	I	T	B	B	E	E	S	T	A	T	U	E	T	E
R	T	S	E	Y	R	Y	T	R	E	B	L	F	O	U	R
S	T	R	A	T	U	S	O	F	L	I	B	E	R	T	Y
L	T	I	S	B	E	T	O	F	S	T	A	T	U	E	O
Y	T	A	T	U	E	A	F	O	T	R	E	B	I	L	F
E	B	I	L	F	O	T	S	T	A	T	U	E	O	E	L
R	T	S	T	A	T	U	T	S	F	O	T	R	E	B	I

PUZZLE 148

The phrase STATUE OF LIBERTY is concealed in this grid. It occurs only once in its entirety. Can you find it? It is written in straight lines with only one change of direction.

*See answer **98***

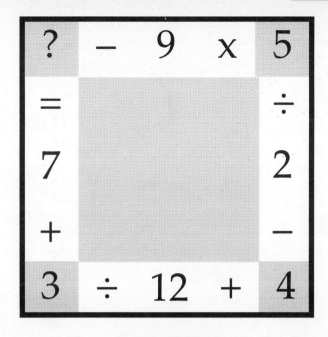

PUZZLE 149

Can you work out which number should replace the question mark in this square?

See answer 138

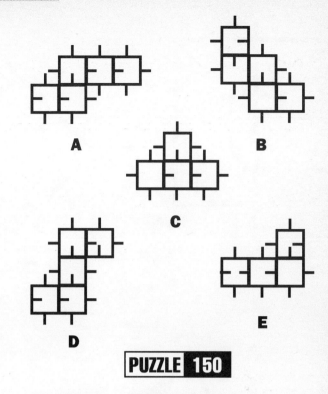

PUZZLE 150

Can you work out which diagram is the odd one out?

See answer 140

A. No. 6 (873) 4372

B. No. 10 (?) 6356

C. No. 4 (1093) 5238

D. No. 14 (454) 3786

E. No. 3 (1262) 9870

PUZZLE 151

Each tractor gathers potatoes over a certain acreage (shown in brackets). The weight of potatoes in kilos is shown under each tractor. There is a relationship between the number of the tractor, the acreage and the weight gathered. What weight should tractor B show?

See answer 39

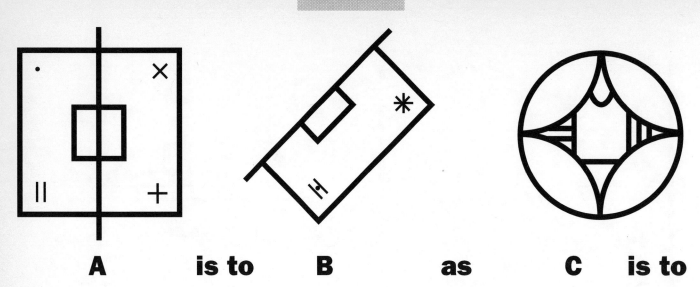

A   **is to**   **B**   **as**   **C**   **is to**

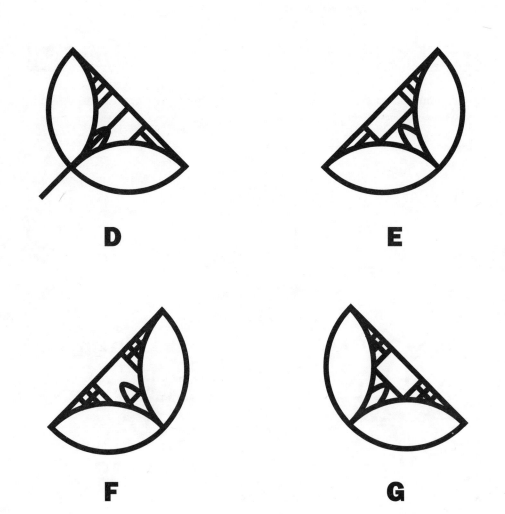

D   **E**

F   **G**

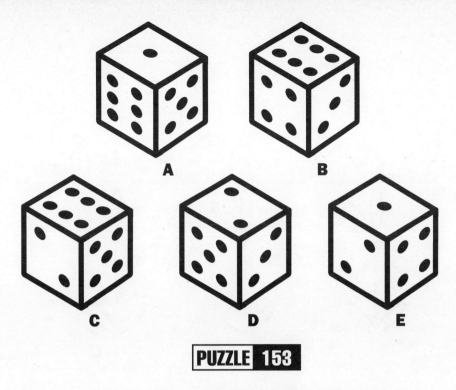

PUZZLE 153

Can you work out which of these cubes is not the same
as the others?

See answer 2

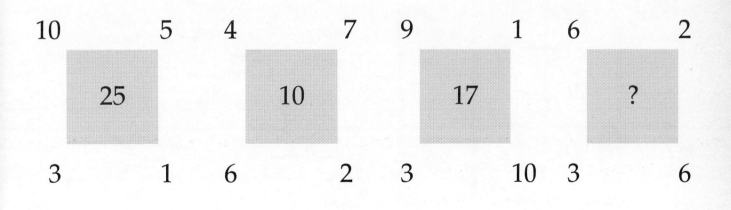

PUZZLE 154

Can you unravel the logic behind these squares and find
the missing number?

See answer 71

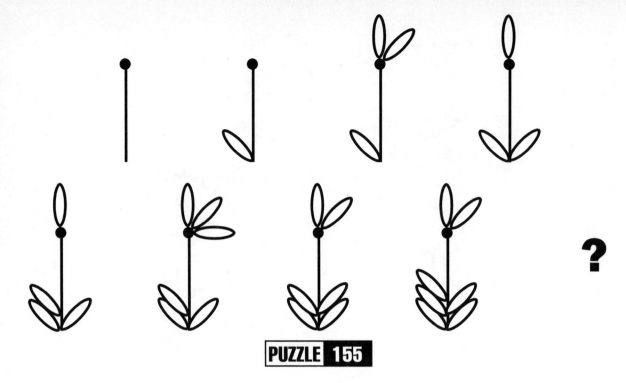

Can you work out what the next flower in this series should look like?

See answer 95

1536	48	96	3
384	192	24	12
768	96	48	6
192	?	12	24

PUZZLE 156

Can you find the missing number in this square?

See answer 10

No. 9
Takes 1 hr 35

No. 10
Takes 1 hr 43

No. 11
Takes 1 hr 52

No. 14
Takes 2 hr 27

No. ?
Takes 2 hr 33

PUZZLE 157

Five cyclists are taking part in a race. The number of each rider and his cycling time are related to each other. Can you work out the number of the last cyclist?

See answer 38

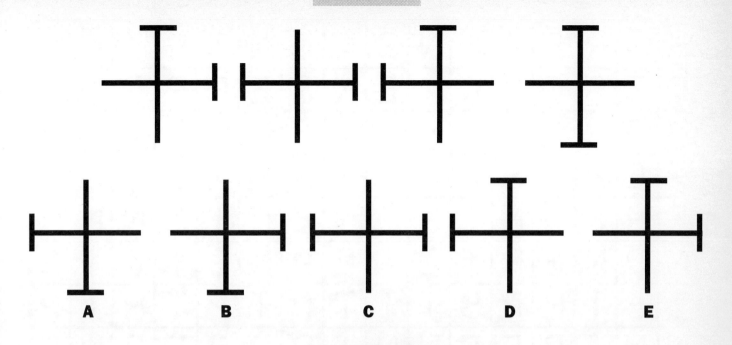

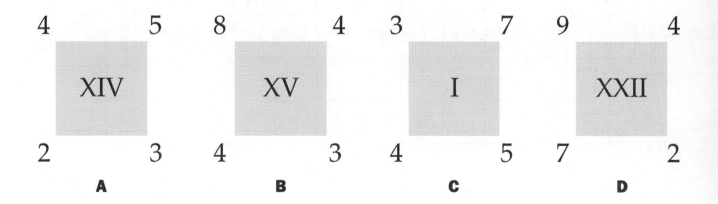

PUZZLE 158

Can you work out which of these symbols would continue the series?

See answer 134

4		5	8		4	3		7	9		4
	XIV			XV			I			XXII	
2		3	4		3	4		5	7		2
	A			**B**			**C**			**D**	

PUZZLE 159

Which of these squares does not follow the same rule as the others?

See answer 74

S	E	R	E	P	E	N	S	T	I	N	E	R	E	S	E
E	E	S	E	N	R	P	E	N	S	E	R	P	E	N	T
R	S	R	S	E	I	S	R	T	E	R	P	E	N	T	I
P	E	P	P	S	E	T	P	I	N	E	N	E	S	S	S
E	R	E	S	N	T	N	N	N	E	R	I	N	N	N	E
N	P	N	E	R	T	E	T	E	P	N	S	E	E	I	R
T	E	T	R	P	S	I	I	T	P	T	P	T	R	T	P
N	N	I	P	E	E	N	N	T	R	R	S	E	P	N	E
E	T	N	E	N	T	E	E	E	E	S	E	T	E	E	N
I	N	E	N	T	R	S	E	S	R	E	T	S	N	P	T
S	E	R	T	P	E	N	T	I	N	E	T	S	T	R	I
S	E	R	N	P	E	N	T	I	N	E	E	N	I	E	T
E	S	R	E	I	S	E	R	P	E	N	T	I	N	S	E
S	E	T	E	N	N	I	T	N	E	P	R	E	S	T	E
R	S	E	N	E	I	T	N	I	P	R	E	S	E	S	T
S	E	R	P	E	N	S	N	I	T	N	E	P	R	E	S

PUZZLE 160

The word SERPENTINE is hidden somewhere in this grid. It occurs in its entirety only once. Can you find it? It may be spelt in any direction but is all in one line.

See answer 59

166

PUZZLE 161

Pick one letter from each cloud in order. You should be able to make the names of five Roman emperors.

See answer 63

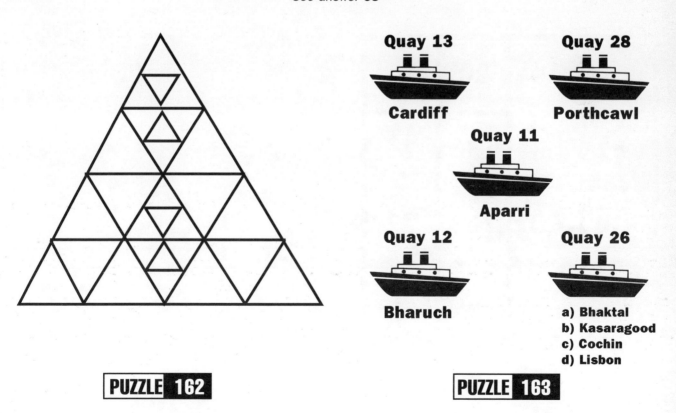

PUZZLE 162

PUZZLE 163

Can you work out how many triangles there are in this diagram altogether?

See answer 99

The number of the quay and the ship's destination are in some way related. Can you work out which harbour the ship on Quay 26 is bound for?

See answer 4

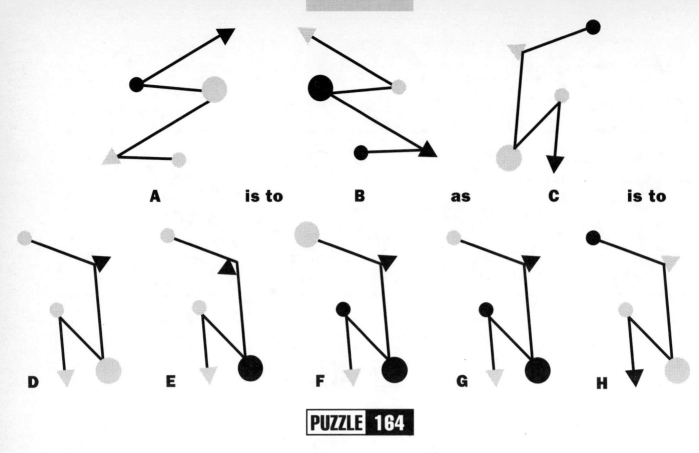

A   is to   **B**   as   **C**   is to

PUZZLE 164

See answer 112

16	10	20	14
8	140	134	28
14	70	268	22
7	?	38	44

PUZZLE 165

Can you find the number to replace the question mark?

See answer 27

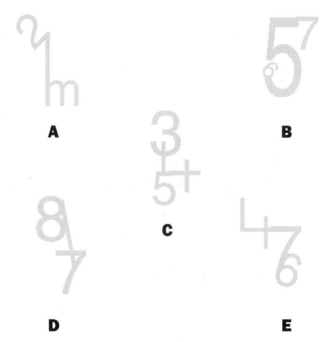

A

B

C

D

E

PUZZLE 166

Can you find the odd figure out?

See answer 132

PUZZLE 167

Can you find the shape that should replace the question
mark in the last circle?

See answer 8

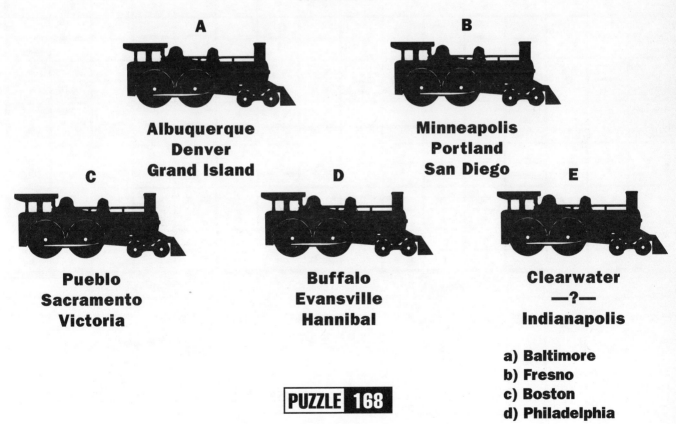

A

**Albuquerque
Denver
Grand Island**

B

**Minneapolis
Portland
San Diego**

C

**Pueblo
Sacramento
Victoria**

D

**Buffalo
Evansville
Hannibal**

E

**Clearwater
—?—
Indianapolis**

a) Baltimore
b) Fresno
c) Boston
d) Philadelphia

PUZZLE 168

These trains pass three American towns on their route. Can
you find the missing town of the last train?
See answer 37

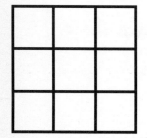

PUZZLE 169

This grid follows a certain pattern. Can you work out which signs complete the missing grid?

See answer 70

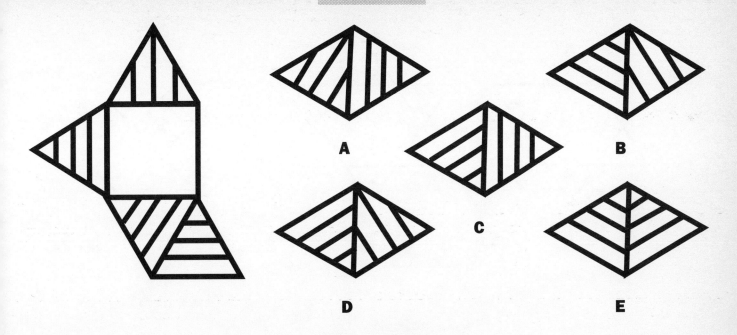

A

B

C

D

E

PUZZLE 170

Can you work out which two pyramids cannot be made
from the above layout?

See answer 168

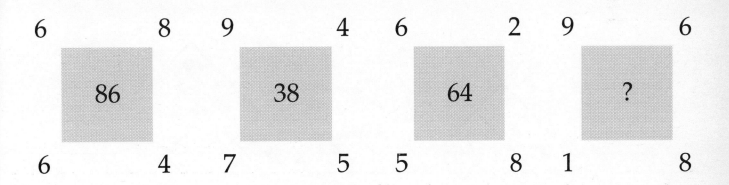

PUZZLE 171

Can you work out the reasoning behind these squares and
replace the question mark with a number?

See answer 72

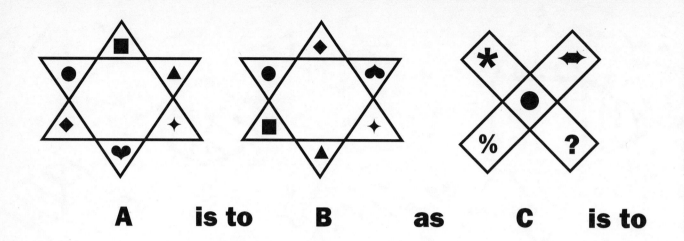

A   is to   **B**   as   **C**   is to

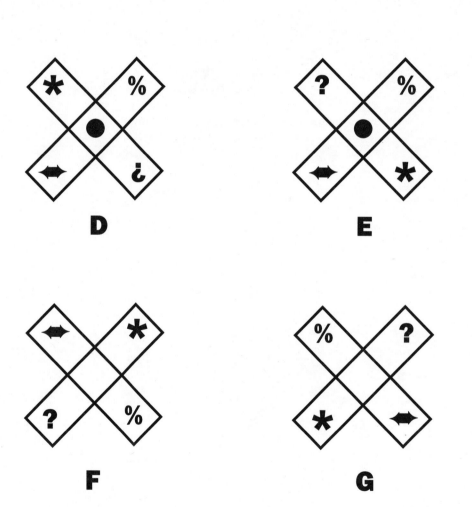

D

E

F

G

See answer 83

PUZZLE 173

Take one letter from each cloud in order. You should be able to make the names of five playwrights.

See answer 25

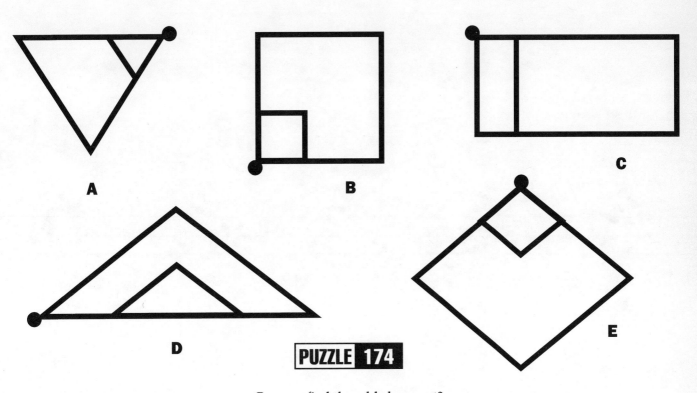

PUZZLE 174

Can you find the odd shape out?

See answer 133

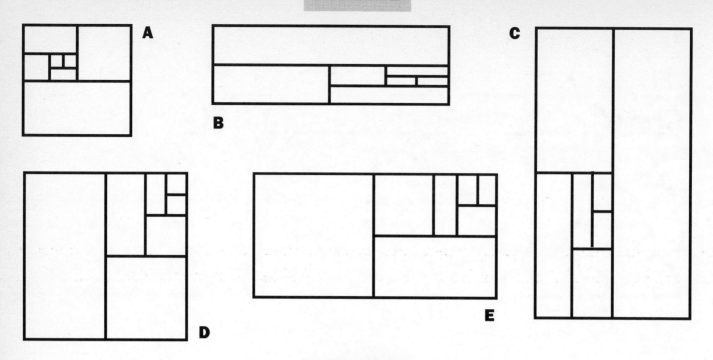

PUZZLE 175

Can you work out which of these diagrams is the odd
one out?

See answer 107

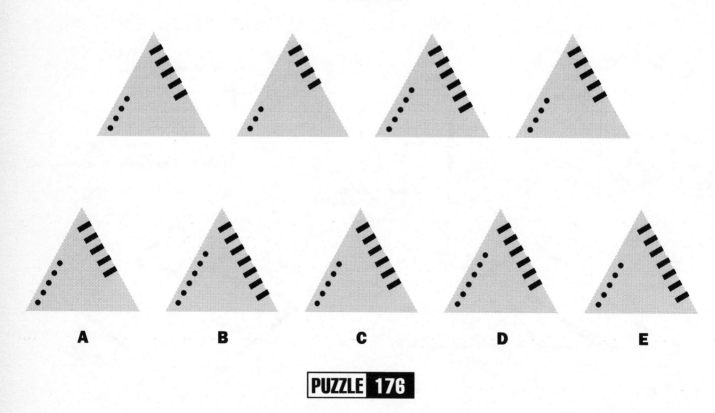

PUZZLE 176

Can you find the symbol that would continue
the sequence above?

See answer 126

PUZZLE 177

Can you work out what the next symbol in this sequence should look like?

See answer 44

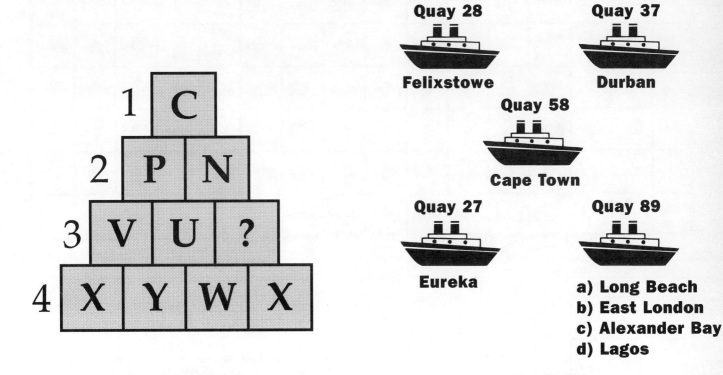

Quay 28 — Felixstowe

Quay 37 — Durban

Quay 58 — Cape Town

Quay 27 — Eureka

Quay 89 —
a) Long Beach
b) East London
c) Alexander Bay
d) Lagos

1	C	
2	P	N
3	V	U	?
4	X	Y	W	X

PUZZLE 178

Can you find the letter which completes this diagram?

See answer 14

PUZZLE 179

Can you work out where the boat leaving from Quay 89 is bound for?

See answer 24

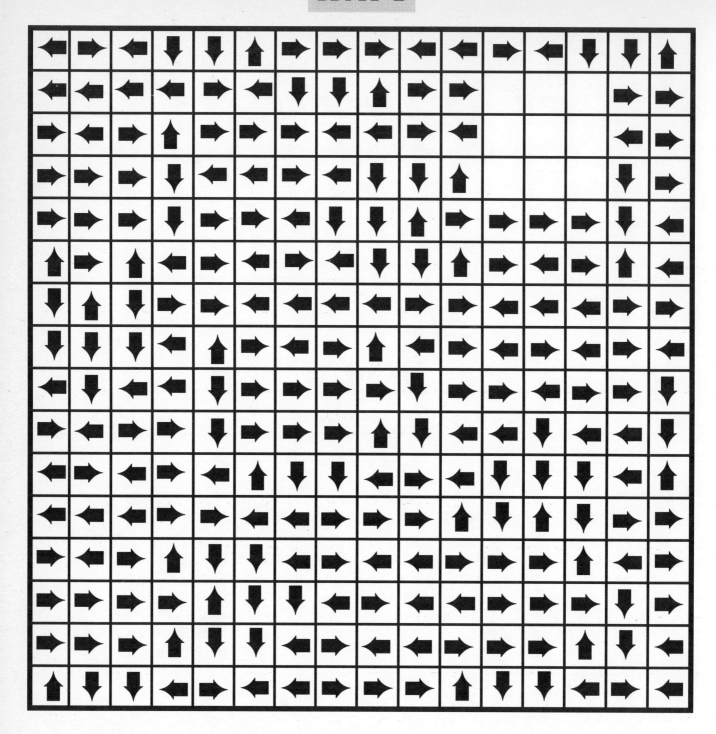

PUZZLE 180

This grid is made up according to a pattern. Can you work it out and complete the missing section?

See answer 12

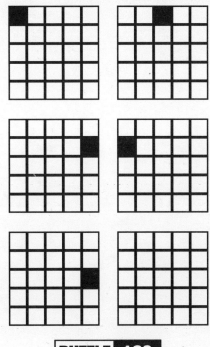

11 13 17 25 32 37 47 ?

PUZZLE 181

Can you work out which number comes next in this series?

See answer 82

PUZZLE 182

Can you work out where the shaded square in the last diagram should be?

See answer 129

Die Zeit

Boston Globe

Daily Mail

France Soir

Ethnos

PUZZLE 183

Each balloon has been sponsored by a famous newspaper and given a registration number based on the paper's name. What number should the *Ethnos* balloon bear?

See answer 17

4
XXVIII
8   16
A

5
XL
10   25
B

2
XVI
4   8
C

3
XVIII
6   9
D

PUZZLE 184

Can you work out which triangle does not follow the same
rule as the others?

*See answer **73***

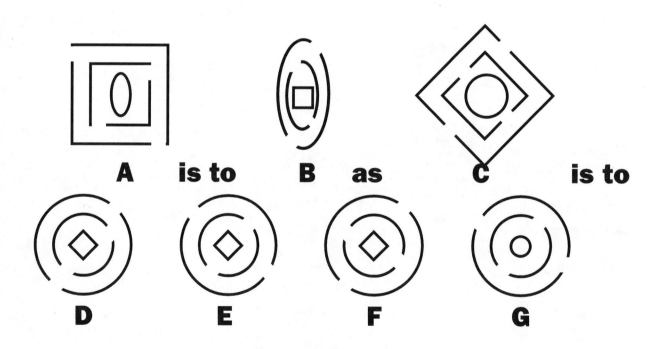

A   **is to**   **B**   **as**   **C**   **is to**

D   **E**   **F**   **G**

PUZZLE 185

*See answer **89***

A   B   C   D   E

PUZZLE 186

Can you find the odd diagram out?

See answer 127

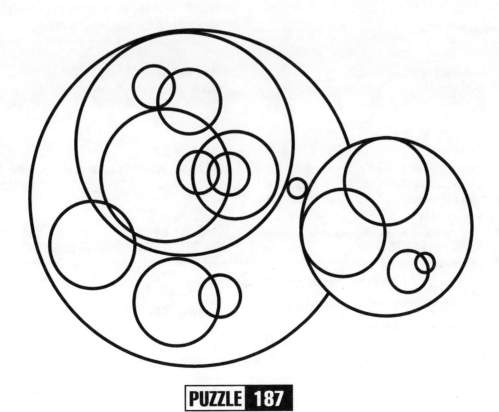

PUZZLE 187

How many circles can you find in this diagram altogether?

See answer 76

Answer 1
C. Dickens. The code is based on the number alphabet reversed, i.e. Z = 1, A = 26, etc.

Answer 2
C.

Answer 3
20. Multiply hours by minutes and divide by 3 to get the number of the rider.

Answer 4
D. Multiply digits. The resulting product gives the alphabetical position of the first letter of the place name.

Answer 5
9.05. The minute hand goes forward 25 minutes, the hour hand back by 5 hours.

Answer 6
E. Fold the top half onto the bottom half and turn the shape 45° anti-clockwise.

Answer 7
Carmen, Fidelio, La Traviata, Lohengrin, Boris Godunov. The additional opera is Don Giovanni.

Answer 8
 The symbols are determined by the number of sides, as follows: circle 1, L-shape 2, triangle 3, square 4, pentagon 5, hexagon 6. Starting at 1 and moving in a clockwise direction skip 1 shape, then 2, repeat. When you have reached the 8th segment continue with the 1st segment in the 2nd circle, and continue in the same order in this and the subsequent circle.

Answer 9
The shapes form two series which go from top to bottom of succeeding squares. The squares and circles alternate. The sequence of shading is: quarter, half, three-quarters, fully shaded.

Answer 10
384. Starting at the top right hand corner work through the square in a vertical boustrophedon, multiplying by 4 and dividing by 2 alternately.

Answer 11
D. They are all in alphabetical order except for D.

Answer 12
It starts at the top left and works inward in an anti-clockwise spiral.

Answer 13
18. Multiply the numbers in the outer section, reverse the product and put in the middle of the next section.

Answer 14
T. Based on the number alphabet backwards, add together two consecutive squares in the same row. Convert the sum to a new letter and put in the row above in the square that is directly above the two consecutive squares.

Answer 15
No. 2. Take the first digit of the weight from the second to arrive at new number.

Answer 16
3.13. Start time A minus Finish A = Finish B. Start time B minus Finish B = Finish C, etc.

Answer 17
142334. It works on a number code. 1 is letters A–E inclusive, 2 F–J, 3 K–O, 4 P–T, 5 U–Y and 6 Z.

Answer 18
Denver, Buffalo, Saginaw, Boston, Seattle, Miami. The extra city is Philadelphia.

Answer 19
Blake, Byron, Dante, Donne, Plath.

Answer 20
G. It is a term for tempo, while the others are types of dances.

Answer 21
Ratatouille. It is the only vegetarian dish.

Answer 22
The sequence is:

The symbol moves from section 1 in the first circle to section 1 in the second circle, then to section 1 in the third circle, and then to section 2 in the first circle etc.

Answer 23
48. In each box of four numbers, multiply the top two numbers, put the product in the bottom right box, then subtract the top right number from the bottom right one and put the difference in the bottom left box.

Answer 24
C. Take the first digit from the second. The resulting digit gives the alphabetic number of the initial letter of the answer.

Answer 25
Brecht, Coward, Dryden, Pinter, Racine.

Answer 26
21. △ = 12, ✱ = 9, ♡ = 3, % = 5, @ = 7.

Answer 27
76. Starting at the bottom left hand corner, work through the square in a clockwise spiral, multiplying by 2 and subtracting 6, alternately.

Answer 28
Bacon, Bosch, Klimt, Manet, Monet.

Answer 29

Answer 30
Camus, Defoe, Dumas, Verne, Wells.

Answer 31
G. Starting at the bottom left corner, work through the alphabet in an anti-clockwise spiral. Miss 1 letter, then 2 letters, 1 letter, etc., going back to the start of the alphabet after reaching Z.

Answer 32
92. Multiply the numbers on the diagonally opposite corners of each square and add the products. Put the sum in the third square along.

Answer 33
44. The numbers increase clockwise first missing one spoke, then two at the fourth step. Each circle increases by a different amount (2, 3, 4).

Answer 34
1956. The numbers represent the leap years clockwise around the triangles starting at the apex. Miss one leap year each time.

Answer 35
Tiramisu. This is a dessert; the others are all main courses.

Answer 36
Add the number of segments in column 1 to the number of segments in column 3. Draw this number of segments in to column 2.

Answer 37
Fresno. Skip two letters in the alphabet each time.

Answer 38
15. Take the minutes in the hours, add the minutes and divide by 10. Ignore the remainder.

Answer 39
987. The tractor number is divided into the weight to give the acreage. The weights have been mixed up.

Answer 40
Kebab, Pasta, Pizza, Tacos, Wurst.

Answer 41
Bartok, Boulez, Chopin, Delius, Mahler.

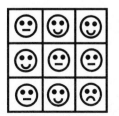

Answer 42
The faces pattern sequence is smiley, smiley, straight, sad, sad, smiley, straight, straight, sad, etc. Start at the bottom left and work in a horizontal boustrophedon.

Answer 43

A	R	C	D	E	T	R	I	O	M	P	A	R	C	D	E
R	R	R	T	E	D	C	R	A	H	P	M	O	I	R	T
C	D	C	T	R	I	O	M	P	H	E	H	P	M	O	I
D	E	T	D	E	T	R	I	O	M	A	R	C	D	E	A
H	P	M	O	I	R	T	E	D	P	M	O	I	R	T	R
A	R	C	D	E	T	R	I	E	O	M	P	H	E	A	R
C	R	A	E	H	P	M	T	E	D	I	R	T	E	D	C
D	E	T	R	I	O	R	M	P	H	C	E	A	R	C	D
C	D	T	R	I	I	O	M	P	H	E	R	M	I	I	E
R	A	E	H	O	P	M	O	I	R	T	P	A	R	R	T
O	M	P	M	H	E	A	R	I	D	E	H	O	T	T	R
I	R	P	T	E	D	C	R	A	E	H	E	I	E	E	I
R	H	C	D	E	T	R	I	O	M	P	A	R	D	D	O
E	A	H	P	M	O	I	R	T	E	D	R	T	A	C	M
D	E	T	R	I	O	M	P	H	A	R	C	E	R	R	P
C	R	A	H	P	M	O	I	R	T	E	D	D	C	A	H

Answer 44

The symbol turns 180° clockwise, 135° anti-clockwise, 90° clockwise, 45° anti-clockwise.

Answer 45

$\heartsuit$ = 8, $\clubsuit$ = 4, $\diamondsuit$ = 6, $\spadesuit$ = 2.

Answer 46

Idaho, Iowa, Maine, Texas, Utah. The dummy letters are K and L.

Answer 47

C. Add the digits to get the alphabetic number of the town's initial letter.

Answer 48

Sky Fly. The name contains no vowels.

Answer 49

C. The others are all in the correct order if you start from Earth and travel away from the sun.

Answer 50

Bodega, Bonsai, Ersatz, Hombre, Kitsch.

3	3	2
2	3	4
3	2	1

Answer 51

The pattern sequence is 1, 2, 2, 3, 4, 4, 1, 2, 3, 3, 4. Start at the top left and work in a horizontal boustrophedon.

Answer 52
The pattern is +2 scales, +3 scales, –1 scale. A fish with an even number of scales faces the other way.

Answer 53
The pattern is +1 limb, +2, +3, –2, –1, +1, +2, +3, etc. A figure with an uneven number of limbs is turned upside down.

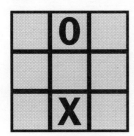

Answer 54
Starting at opposite ends the symbols move alternately 1 and 2 steps to the other end of the grid in a boustrophedon.

Answer 55
Starting with a vertical line reflect the dot first against that line and then each following line in a clockwise direction.

Answer 56
23.

Answer 57
The corresponding sections in each wheel should contain a black section in each compartment.

Answer 58
Brunel, Darwin, Edison, Pascal, Planck.

Answer 59 – See page 184

Answer 60
D. All the others are cities, Kansas is a state (Kansas City actually straddles the Missouri-Kansas border).

Answer 61
61. Letters are worth the value based on alphabetical position (A=1, etc.). However, alternate letters are worth the value based on the reversed alphabet (A=26, etc.).

Answer 62
C. Starting at the top right hand corner, work through the alphabet, missing 1, 2, 3, 4, 5, 4, 3, 2, 1, 2, etc. letters each time, in a vertical boustrophedon.

Answer 63
Gallus, Jovian, Julian, Trajan, Valens.

Answer 64
M. These are all the letters with straight sides only.

Answer 65
64. Take each digit individually. The pattern is 1, 2, 3, 1, then 2, 3, 4, 2, then 3, 4, 5, 3, and finally 4, 5, 6, 4.

Answer 66
18. These are all the numbers that can be divided by either 3 or 4.

Answer 67
B. The digits of all the others add up to 6.

Answer 68
1980. Vowels = 243, Consonants = 126

Answer 69
576. Multiply No. by speed, put the product as the distance for the next balloon.

Answer 70
The pattern is:

+ + − − − ÷ ÷ X X X

Start at the top left and work clockwise in an inward spiral.

Answer 71
6. In each square, multiply the top and bottom left together, then multiply the top and bottom right. Subtract this second product from the first and put this number in the middle.

Answer 59

S	E	R	E	P	E	N	S	T	I	N	E	R	E	S	E
E	E	S	E	N	R	P	E	N	S	E	R	P	E	N	T
R	S	R	S	E	I	S	R	T	E	R	P	E	N	T	I
P	E	P	P	S	E	T	P	I	N	E	N	E	S	S	S
E	R	E	S	N	T	N	N	N	E	R	I	N	N	N	E
N	P	N	E	R	T	E	T	E	P	N	S	E	E	I	R
T	E	T	R	P	S	I	I	T	P	T	P	T	R	T	P
N	N	I	P	E	E	N	N	T	R	R	S	E	P	N	E
E	T	N	E	N	T	E	E	E	E	S	E	T	E	E	N
I	N	E	N	T	R	S	E	S	R	E	T	S	N	P	T
S	E	R	T	P	E	N	T	I	N	E	T	S	T	R	I
S	E	R	N	P	E	N	T	I	N	E	E	N	I	E	T
E	S	R	E	I	S	E	R	P	E	N	T	I	N	S	E
S	E	T	E	N	N	I	T	N	E	P	R	E	S	T	E
R	S	E	N	E	I	T	N	I	P	R	E	S	E	S	T
S	E	R	P	E	N	S	N	I	T	N	E	P	R	E	S

Answer 72

75. In each square, multiply the top and bottom left numbers, then the top and bottom right. Add these two products, reverse the digits of this sum and place it in the middle.

Answer 73

C. Divide the left number by 2, place this number at the apex, then square it and put this number at the right. Finally, add all three numbers together and put the sum as a roman numeral in the middle. In triangle C, the right number should be 4 and the middle number should be X.

Answer 74

B. In each square multiply the two top numbers, then the two bottom ones. Subtract the latter product from the former, translate the difference into Roman numerals and put it in the middle. Square B should be XX (20).

Answer 75

R. Starting on the top left hand corner, work through the alphabet, missing a letter each time, in a vertical boustrophedon.

Answer 76
17.

Answer 77
JOL 1714. Go 5 forward and 3 back in the alphabet. The numbers continue from the alphabetic position of the letter.

Answer 78
35226252257. The numbers are in code from the newspaper titles. A–C = 1, D–F = 2, G–I = 3, J–L = 4, M–O = 5, P–R = 6 S–U = 7, V–X = 8, Y–Z = 9.

Answer 79
No. 52. Add together the value of the letters based on their alphabet position.

Answer 80
29. Add together the corner squares of each row or column in a clockwise direction. Put the sum in the middle of the next row or column.

Answer 81
F. This is based on the number alphabet backwards. Add together the corner squares of each row or column and put the sum in the middle square of the opposite row or column.

Answer 82
58. Add the digits of the last number and move on by that number.

Answer 83
D. Reflect the shape along a horizontal line, then move each sign one segment clockwise.

Answer 84
QUS 2321. Go forward by 4 and back by 2 in the alphabet, then continue with numbers taken from the letters' alphabetical position.

Answer 85
No 201. Add together the values of the letters based on their reversed alphabetical position, (A = 26, Z = 1).

Answer 86
E. The shape has been folded along a horizontal line. A shaded piece covers an unshaded one.

Answer 87
Picasso. Based on the letters' position in the alphabet, 3 has been added to each value.

Answer 88
G. Add 3 to odd numbers, subtract 2 from even numbers.

Answer 89
E. The outer shape changes to the inner shape, the openings rotate through 90° clockwise.

Answer 90
84. Multiply the hours of A by the minutes of B to get the tonnage of C, then B hours by C minutes to get D, C hours by D minutes to get E, D hours by E minutes to get A, and E hours by A minutes to get the tonnage of B.

Answer 91
I. It is based on the number alphabet backwards. Add the top and bottom rows together and put the sum in the middle.

Answer 92
It should have two dots. Add together the corner squares of each row or column and put the sum in the middle square of the opposite row or column.

Answer 93
E. Based on the position of the letters in the alphabet, multiply column one by column three and place the product in the middle column.

Answer 94
D. Add consecutive clockwise corners of the diamond and place the sum on the corresponding second corner. Add the four numbers together and place the sum in the middle.

Answer 95
Add one leaf. Add two petals. Deduct 1 petal and add 1 leaf. Repeat.

Answer 98

S	T	A	T	U	E	O	R	T	S	T	A	T	U	E	S
S	R	E	B	I	L	F	O	E	U	T	A	T	A	T	D
L	S	T	A	T	U	L	I	B	E	R	T	O	F	F	A
I	L	I	B	E	R	T	E	L	I	B	E	R	L	O	T
B	O	F	L	I	B	U	E	O	S	T	A	I	F	S	U
E	T	S	T	A	T	U	E	O	F	S	B	T	S	O	F
R	O	F	L	A	S	U	F	T	L	E	T	T	A	S	L
T	I	C	T	B	T	L	R	I	T	Y	A	S	T	T	I
Y	U	S	E	A	I	S	B	Y	T	T	A	T	U	A	B
E	L	I	T	B	B	E	E	S	T	A	T	U	E	T	E
R	T	S	E	Y	R	Y	T	R	E	B	L	F	O	U	R
S	T	R	A	T	U	S	O	F	L	I	B	E	R	T	Y
L	T	I	S	B	E	T	O	F	S	T	A	T	U	E	O
Y	T	A	T	U	E	A	F	O	T	R	E	B	I	L	F
E	B	I	L	F	O	T	S	T	A	T	U	E	O	E	L
R	T	S	T	A	T	U	T	S	F	O	T	R	E	B	I

Answer 96
Renoir. The letters in this code come one before in the alphabet, with the artist's name reversed.

Answer 97
16.

Answer 98 – See above

Answer 99
39.

Answer 100
10. Add 2 to each value, place sum in corresponding position in next triangle, then subtract 3, add 2 again.

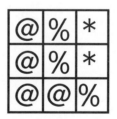

Answer 101
The pattern sequence is @, @, %, *, %, &, &, *, %. It starts at the top right and works inwards in an anti-clockwise spiral.

Answer 102
Degas. Each letter is the same number of letters from the end of the alphabet as the letter in the artist's name is from the beginning.

Answer 103
J. All of the others have a matching partner.

Answer 104
D. Alternate between rotating the pattern 90° anti-clockwise, and swapping direction of each individual arrow.

Answer 105
A. Each ring contains one cross more than the previous example, and the first and last cross in each adjacent circle are level.

Answer 106
G. The top and bottom elements swap position, the smaller central element becomes smaller still and all three elements move inside the larger central shape.

Answer 107
E. Each shape is divided into smaller ones by alternating between adding horizontal and vertical lines (or vice versa) except in 'E' where 2 vertical lines are added in succession.

Answer 108
E. All elements consist of 3 straight lines except 'E' which consists of 4 straight lines.

Answer 109
C. Convert each letter to its value based on its position in the alphabet. The values on each corner of a triangle added together result in the new letter in the middle.

Answer 110
9. The numbers rotate clockwise and increase by 1 each time.

Answer 111
12. Add together the values in the same segments in wheels 1 and 3 and put the answer in the opposite segment in wheel 2.

Answer 112
G. The figures are vertical images of each other but with shaded and unshaded elements becoming unshaded and shaded respectively.

Answer 113
B. Each arch moves closer to its opposite end by an equal amount each time.

Answer 114
B.

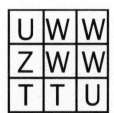

Answer 115
The pattern sequence is:

Z R T T U W W Z Z S

Start at the bottom right and work up in a horizontal boustrophedon.

Answer 116
B.

Answer 117
F. A curve turns into a straight line and a straight line into a curve.

Answer 118
A.

Answer 119
V. The letters are based on the number alphabet backwards (Z = 1, A = 26, etc). The values on the bottom corners and the value in the middle added together result in the value on the apex.

Answer 120
3. The numbers rotate anti-clockwise from one square to the next and decrease by 2 each time.

Answer 121
9. Multiply the values in the same segments in wheels 2 and 3 and put the answer in the next segment in wheel 1, going clockwise.

Answer 122
N. Going from the top to the bottom of one domino piece, then to the top of the next piece, etc., alternately move on five letters and three back.

Answer 123
T. Hardy. Each letter in this code follows that of the author, e.g. 'U' comes after 'T' in the alphabet.

LEVEL 2 — ANSWERS

Answer 124

C. The number of small circles equals the number of edges of the shape, except for 'C' where there is one more circle than edges.

Answer 125

E. All the others consist of 3 consecutive letters in the alphabet.

Answer 126

B. Deduct one dot and one line, add two dots and two lines, repeat.

Answer 127

E. All the others contain two stars for every half moon.

Answer 128

C.

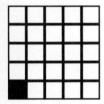

Answer 129

The shaded square moves around the square in a horizontal boustrophedon, starting at the top left hand corner. It advances by 2 squares, then 3, then 4, etc.

Answer 130

D. Each column of elements alternates and moves up two rows.

Answer 131

J. Austen. Each number is double the letters' alphabetical position.

Answer 132

E. All the other elements consist of 3 consecutive numbers.

Answer 133

D. The circle in all other elements intercepts an edge in both the small and large shape outline.

Answer 134

A. Each small bar moves one place anti-clockwise in alternate shapes, so that they are either 90° or 180° apart.

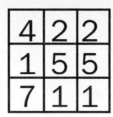

Answer 135

The pattern sequence is 7, 1, 1, 3, 2, 2, 5, 5, 4, 1. It starts at the top right and works in an anti-clockwise spiral.

Answer 136

+ ÷ − X − +. The letters are based on their alphabetic position, so the sum would read:
L(12) **+** D(4) **÷** B(2) **−** F(6) **X** K(11) **−** Q(17) **+** C(3) = H(8).

Answer 137

39. Multiply Top and Left numbers and subtract Right. Swap totals diagonally.

Answer 138

13.

Answer 139

Independence. The initials can be rearranged to form the name Madrid.

Answer 140

B. It is the only figure that does not have three boxes in one row.

Answer 141

B. Working in an anti-clockwise spiral pattern, in the first square there are eight lines, one missing, seven lines, one missing, etc. The number of lines before the first break decreases by one with each square.

Answer 142

E. It is the only one where the small and large circles do not overlap.

Answer 143

3.

Answer 144

4.

Answer 145

B. It is the only figure which, with an additional line, has a triangle adjoining the rectangle which overlaps the square.

Answer 146
F. The small and large elements become large and small respectively.

Answer 147
A. It is the only one to have an odd number of lines.

Answer 148
D. It is the only one to which a circle can be added where the triangle overlaps the circle and a right angled line runs parallel to the whole of one side of the triangle.

Answer 149
B.

Answer 150
B. Each time the square becomes the circle, the triangle the square and the circle the triangle.

Answer 151
21. Multiply each number by the number on the opposite side of the wheel on the same side of the spoke and put the product in that segment next to the centre.

Answer 152
2.

Answer 153
C. It is the only one to have an odd number of one element.

Answer 154
D. A circle becomes a square, a line a circle and a square a line, all in the same size and position as original.

Answer 155
D. All the others are symmetrical.

Answer 156
F. The circles and squares become squares and circles respectively. The largest element loses all internal elements.

Answer 157
No. She hates capital cities.

Answer 158
No. Illinois had an S in it.

Answer 159
Yes. Swansea had no O in it.

Answer 160
D. **Use alphanumeric values.** The letters are added in horizontal pairs and the totals put in the middle .

Answer 161
E. Add two circles and two lines, take away one of each, repeat. The pattern is also rotated by 90° anti-clockwise each time.

Answer 162
Forward, back, forward, back.

Answer 163

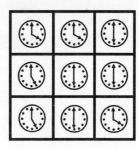

D.

Answer 164
The pattern sequence is: 1.00, 2.00, 2.00, 1.00, 3.00, 3.00, 2.00, 4.00, 4.00. 3.00, 5.00, 5.00, 4.00, 6.00, 6.00. Starting at the bottom left work upwards in a vertical boustrophedon.

Answer 165
E.

Answer 166
Washington.

Answer 167
C.

Answer 168
D and **E**.

Answer 169
B. It consists of 14 straight lines, the rest of 13.

Answer 170
C. It is the only one which does not have half as many 'step' lines as there are triangles.

Answer 171
Pantagruel.

Answer 172
Frankenstein.

Answer 173
E. A square becomes a circle, a circle a triangle and a triangle a square of similar proportions and positions.

Answer 174
B.

Answer 175
A. Each shape increases by one of the same until there are three and it then becomes one. The image is reflected after a shape with two elements.

Answer 176
Excalibur.

Answer 177
Nostradamus.

Answer 178
H. Longer rectangles and arrows swap shading. Smaller rectangles and arrows interchange shape and shading. The pattern is then flipped vertically.

Answer 179
B. It is the only one with the same number of vertical and horizontal lines.

Answer 180
E. Two letters following the first example, facing the correct direction, run into each other.

Answer 181
D.

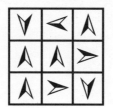

Answer 182
The pattern sequence is as follows.

Start at the bottom left and work in a clockwise spiral.

Answer 183
B. Based on the number alphabet backwards, add the values of the two letters on the outer edge of each segment and place the sum into the opposite segment on the inside.

Answer 184
− X + − ÷ +. $9 - 3 \times 4 + 19 - 8 \div 5 + 4 = 11$.

Answer 185
B. The others all have an equal number of straight lines and curves.

Answer 186
F. Circles and rectangles interchange except for strings of 3 circles which disappear.

Answer 187
Back, back, forward, back.

YOUR PUZZLE NOTES

YOUR PUZZLE NOTES

START

FINISH

FINISH

START

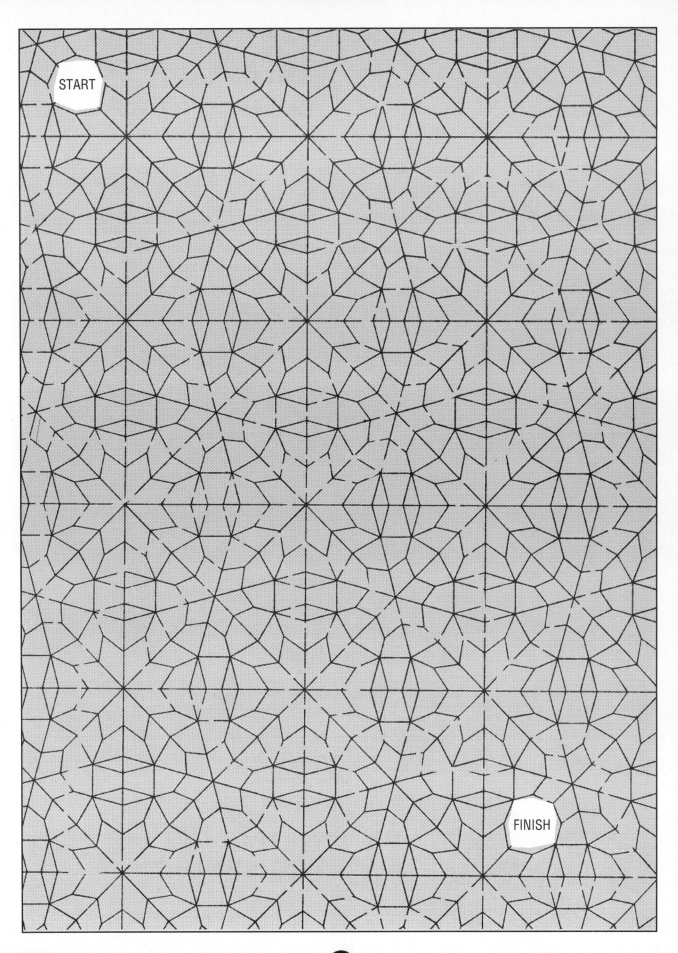

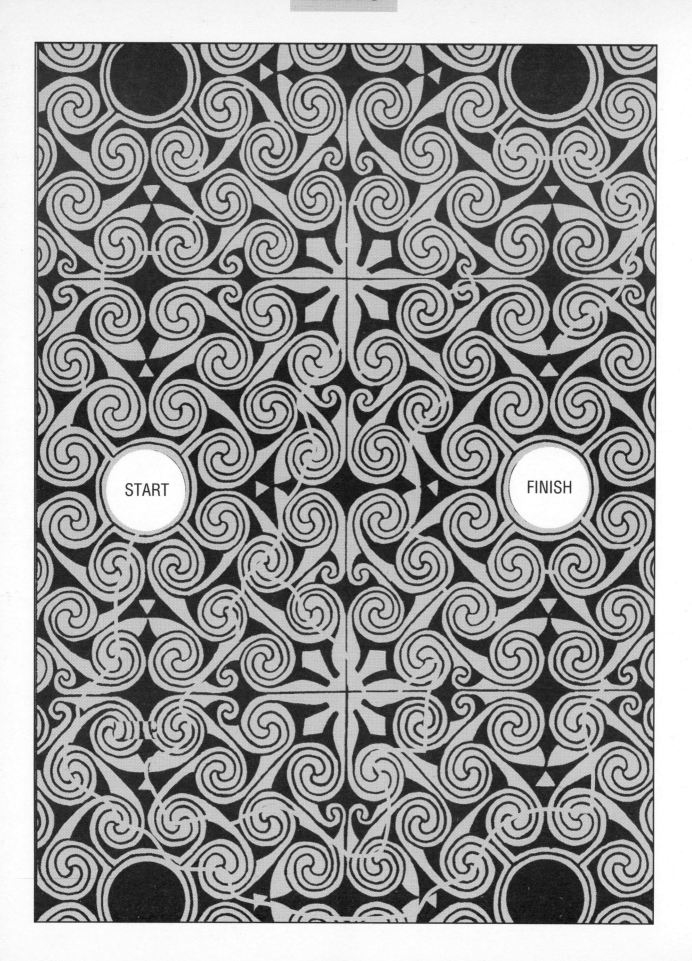

START

FINISH

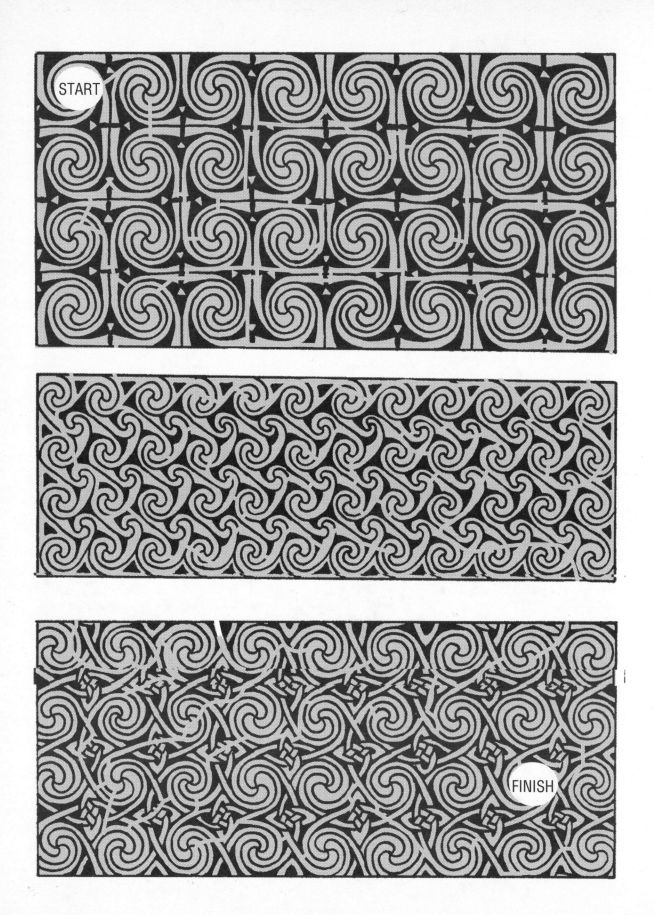

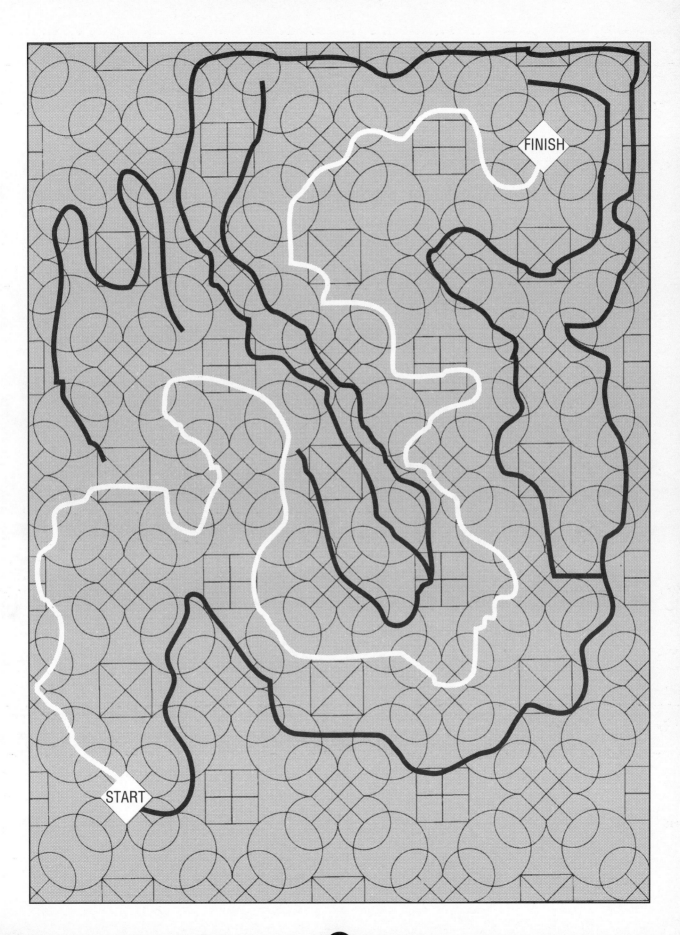

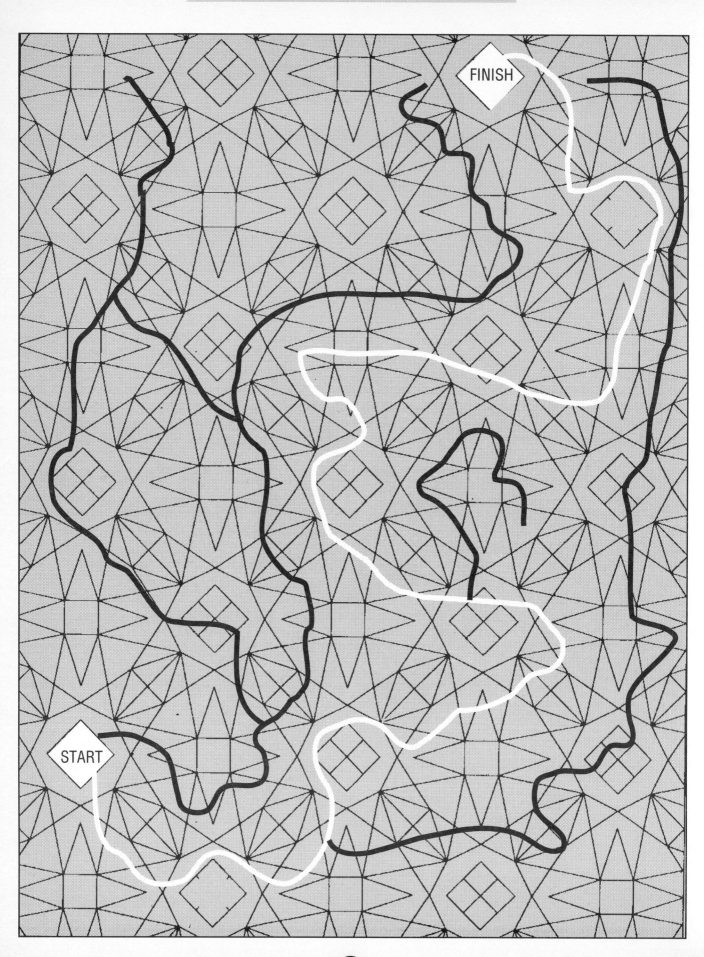

FINISH

START

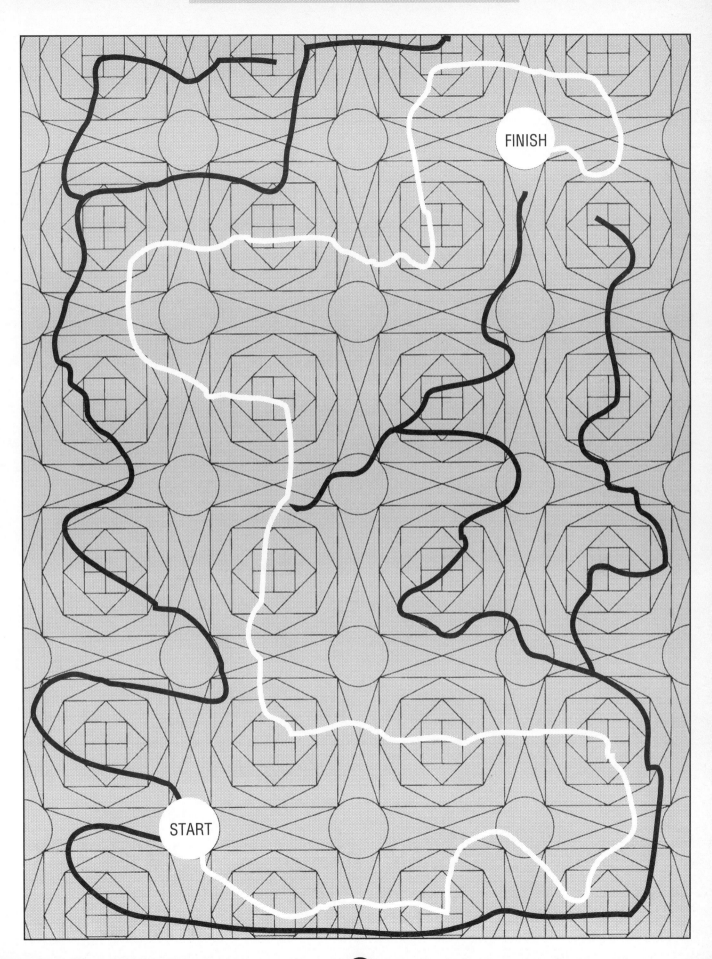

FINISH

START

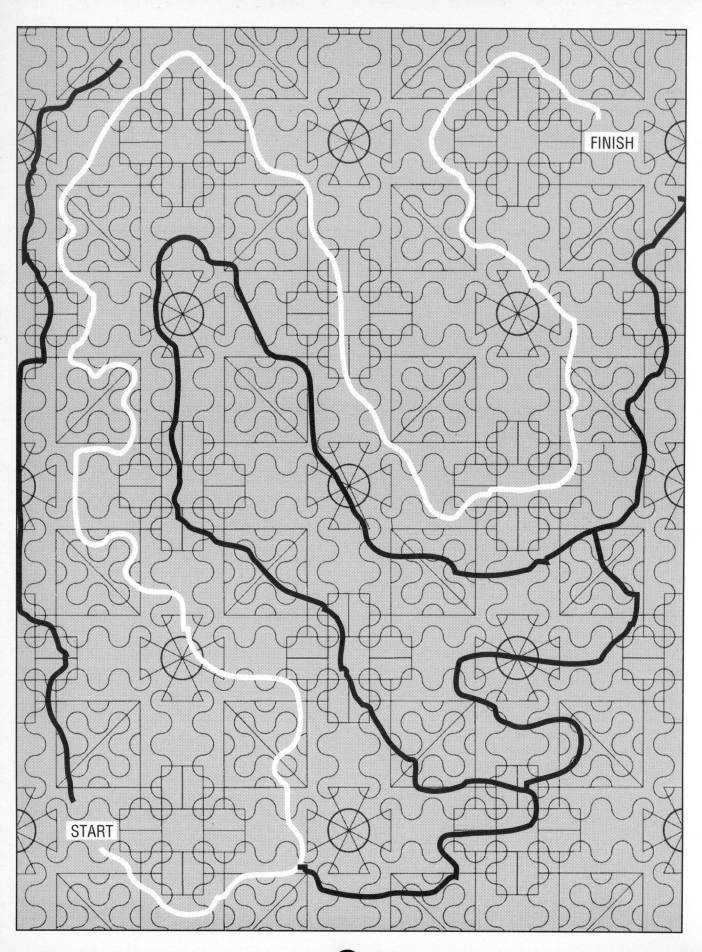

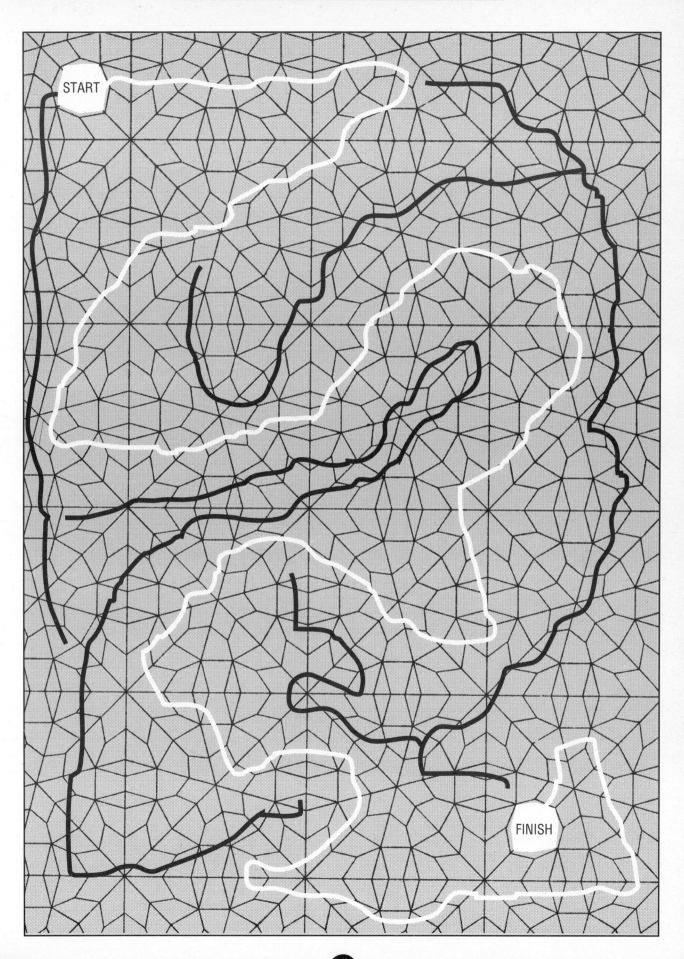

START

FINISH

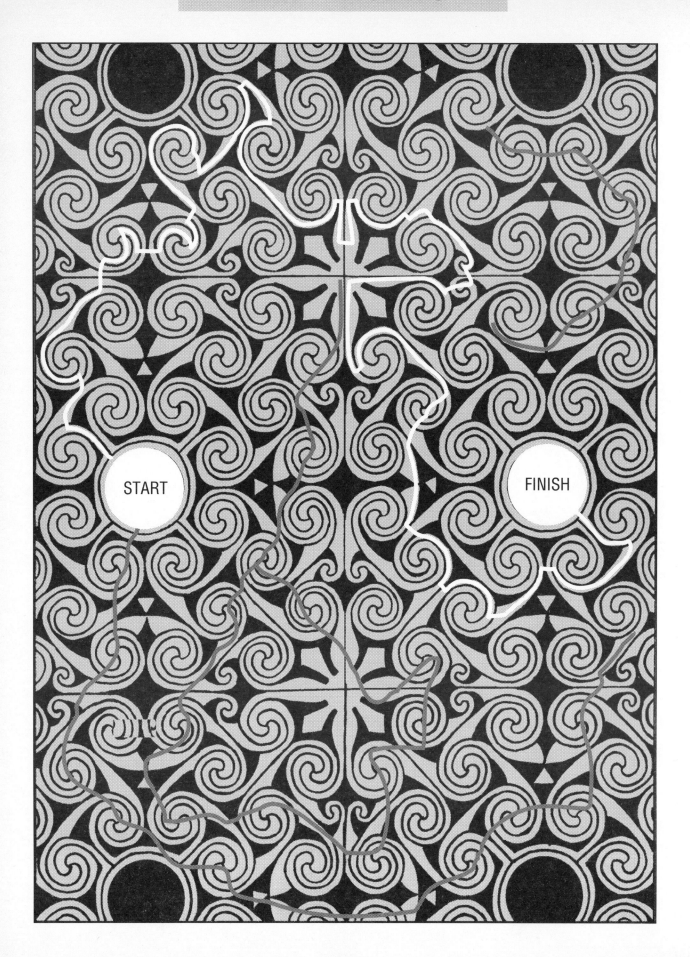

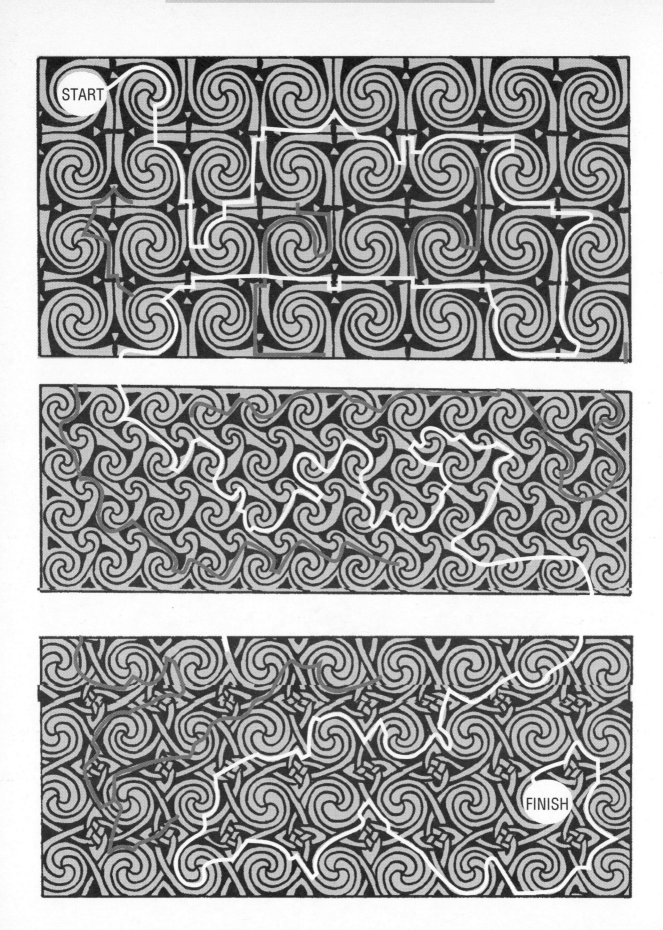

PUZZLE 1

Take a letter from each cloud in turn. You will find the surnames of five film actors plus one extra name.
Who is it?

See answer 23

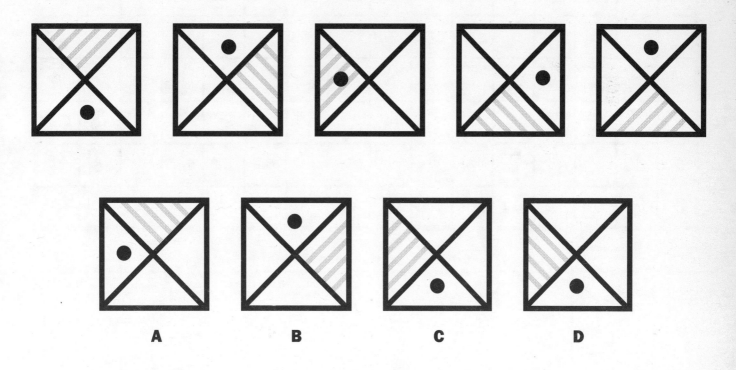

PUZZLE 2

Can you work out which symbol follows the series?

See answer 70

LEVEL 3

See answer **4**

PUZZLE 3

Can you work out the reasoning behind this grid and complete the missing section?

PUZZLE 4

Take a letter from each cloud in the given order. You will find the names of five composers and one extra name. Who is it?

See answer 72

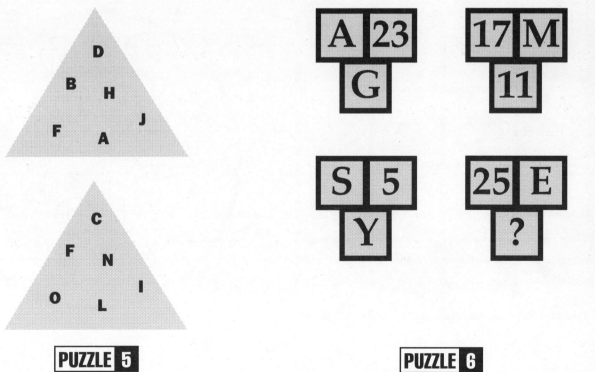

PUZZLE 5

Can you work out which are the two odd letters out in these triangles?

See answer 127

PUZZLE 6

Can you work out what should replace the question mark?

See answer 81

PUZZLE **7**

S4	E3	SW2	E8	E3	E3	SE3	SW1	SW6	S6	S1	W2
SE4	S2	SE5	S2	NE1	S6	SE3	SE4	W5	SW2	S1	W11
NE1	E5	N2	E2	W1	SE3	S1	W5	S4	E2	NE1	W4
NE2	S3	W2	N3	E6	NW1	NW2	W5	N1	E2	S3	W7
E2	SW1	NE4	SW1	S2	S2	W5	W1	W4	SE1	✳	W1
E3	NE4	E7	SW2	E2	N2	SE2	N4	N1	N4	N5	S2
E6	N1	E9	NE2	NE1	NE3	NE1	NW6	W5	N4	W10	N2
NE3	N5	NE6	E4	W2	W2	E3	W1	W4	E1	NW3	W11

This diagram represents a treasure map. You are allowed to stop on each square only once (though you may cross a square as often as you like). When you stop on a square you must follow the instructions you find there. The first one or two letters stand for points of the compass (N = North, S = South, etc.), the number for the number of steps you have to take. The finishing point is the square with the asterisk.
Can you find the starting point? There is one complication. You will find that you never land on some of the squares at all. If you cross out those squares on which you have landed you will see that those on which you have not form a two-figure number.
What is it?

See answer 33

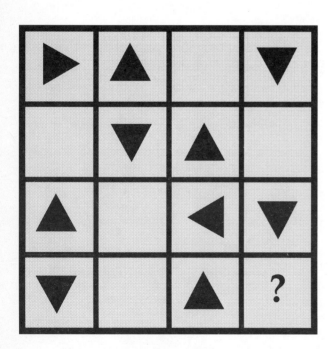

PUZZLE **8**

Can you work out the reasoning behind this diagram and fill in the last square?

See answer 2

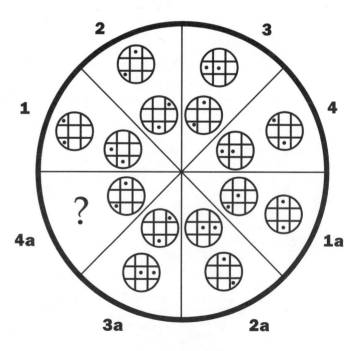

PUZZLE **9**

Can you work out what the missing symbol should look like?

See answer 8

PUZZLE 10

Joshua Shrimp had been at sea for forty years and in that time he had been right around the globe many times. **However, he had always spent his nights in bed and on dry land.**

How?

See answer 66

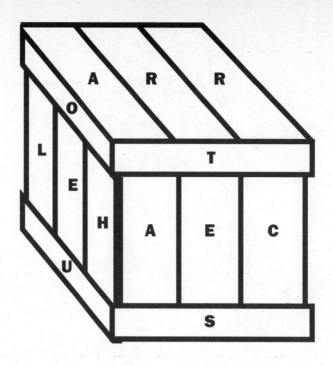

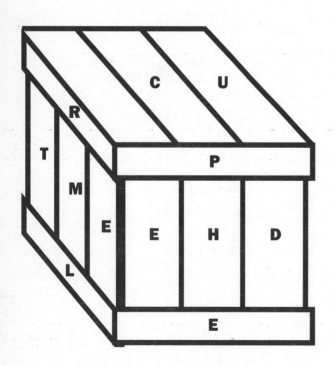

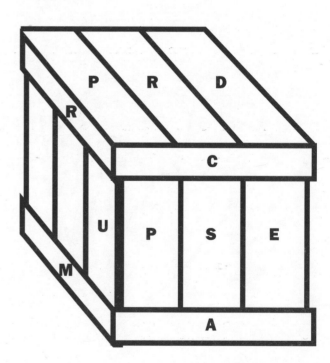

PUZZLE 11

These letters, when joined together correctly, make up a
novel and its author. Can you spot it?

See answer 85

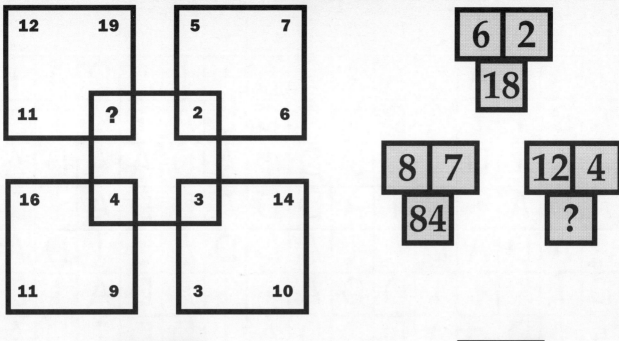

PUZZLE 12

Can you find the number that should replace the question mark?

See answer 155

PUZZLE 13

Can you work out which number should replace the question mark?

See answer 84

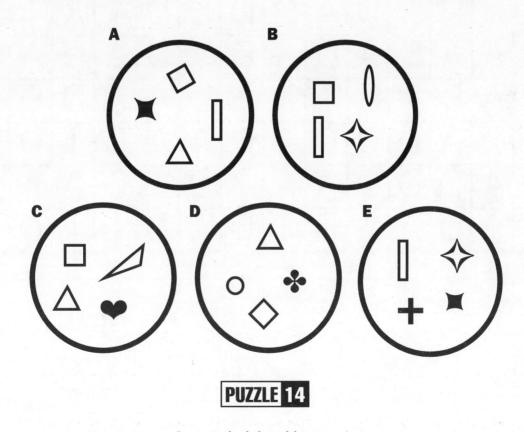

PUZZLE 14

Can you find the odd one out?

See answer 110

```
I D I A I D D A I A I I D A I D
D I A I A D A A D A I I A D A I
A A D I I A D D A D D A I D I A
I A A I D I D D D I A D A A D A
D A D A I D I A D D A D D A I D
I A A D A D A I A D D A D I D A
A D I I I I D D A I I A D A I D
D A I D D A D D D A I D D I D A
D A D A D D A D D A A D A A D I
I A D D A I A D D A A D D A D I
D A A D A D A D D D D I A I D I
A D A A D A D A D A D A D A D A
I A A D A A I A I D A A D D A D
D I D A D D I A A D I D D A
I D A D D D A A I D I D A A I A
A I A D A A D I D A D I I D I D
```

PUZZLE 15

In this grid the word AIDA, written without a change of direction, appears twice. It can be written forwards and backwards in a horizontal, vertical or diagonal direction. Can you spot it both times?

See answer 18

216

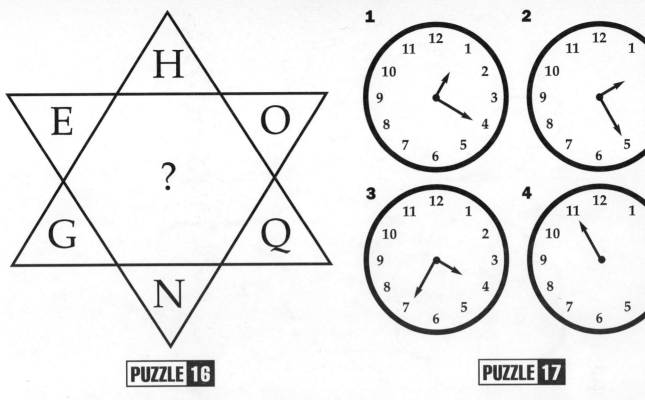

PUZZLE 16

Can you unravel the reasoning behind this star and fill in the missing letter?

See answer 86

PUZZLE 17

Can you work out what number the missing hour hand on clock 4 should point at?

See answer 10

A

Boston – Nashville

B

Chicago – Vancouver

C

Houston – Toronto

D

Cleveland – Richmond

E

Augusta – ?
a) Washington
b) Milwaukee
c) Ottawa
d) Galveston

PUZZLE 18

Can you unravel the logic behind the starting point and destination of each of these cars and find out where car E is going?

See answer 55

PUZZLE 19

Pick one letter from each flower in the order shown. You
will get the names of five statesmen. Who are they?

See answer 105

218

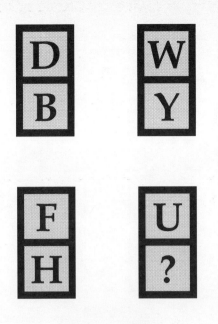

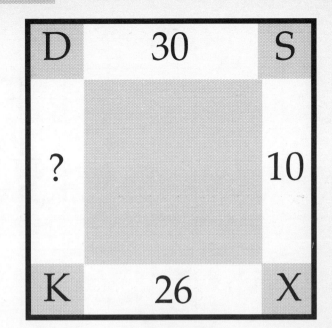

PUZZLE 20

Can you unravel the reasoning behind these domino pieces and find the missing letter?

See answer 93

PUZZLE 21

Can you work out which number should replace the question mark?

See answer 1

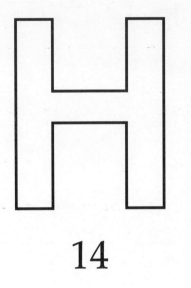

14

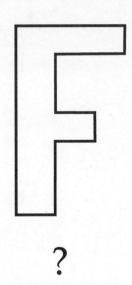

?

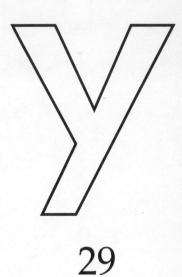

29

PUZZLE 22

Can you work out which number fits underneath letter A?

See answer 104

		2	7	3	8	4	9		2	7	3	8	4	9
9	9								2	7	3	8	4	9
4	4	3	8	4	9									
8	8	7				2	7	3	8	4	9			
3	3	2		4	9									
7	7			8	7	3	8	4	9				2	
2	2			3	2								7	
				7									3	
				2									8	2
													4	7
9													9	3
4														8
8					9	4	8	3	7	2				4
3					9	4	8	3	7	2				9
7		9	4	8	3	7	2							
2					9	4	8	3	7	2				

PUZZLE 23

The numbers in this grid occur in the following order:
9, 4, 8, 3, 7, 2 and run in an anti-clockwise spiral
starting at the top right. It is complicated by the addition
of spaces and repeats according to a pattern.
Can you complete the missing section?

See answer 30

Bill and his brother, Tom, were at the airport seeing their elderly mother off on holiday.

Suddenly Bill saw a man in the crowd.

"Here, Tom, do you see who that is?"

"I don't believe it!", gasped Tom. "It's Phil!"

He was quite right. But how did they both recognize Phil?

Neither brother had ever seen him before.

See answer 56

Can you work out the reasoning behind this grid and complete the missing section?

See answer 14

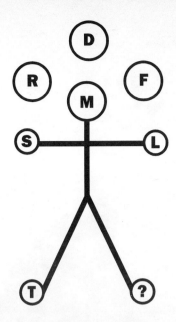

PUZZLE 26

Can you unravel the reasoning behind this juggler and find the missing letter?

See answer **83**

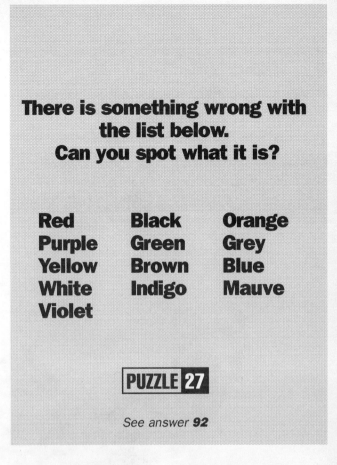

**There is something wrong with the list below.
Can you spot what it is?**

Red	Black	Orange
Purple	Green	Grey
Yellow	Brown	Blue
White	Indigo	Mauve
Violet		

PUZZLE 27

See answer **92**

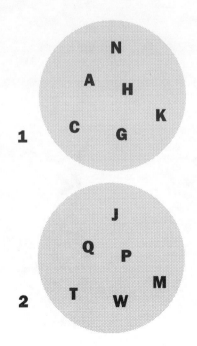

PUZZLE 28

Can you work out which letter does not belong in the second circle?

See answer **138**

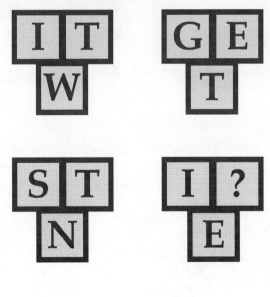

PUZZLE 29

Can you work out which letter fits the square with the question mark?

See answer **94**

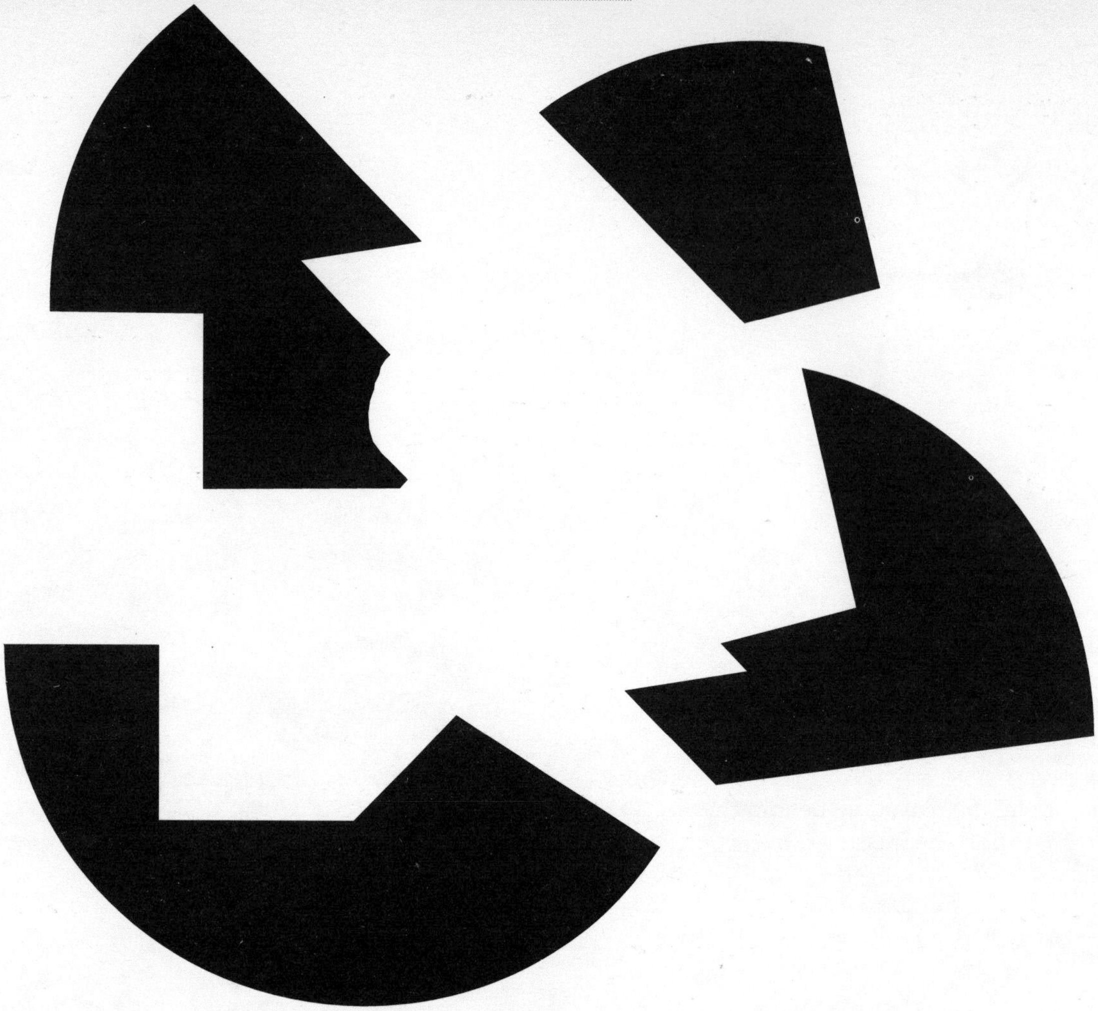

A **B** **C** **D**

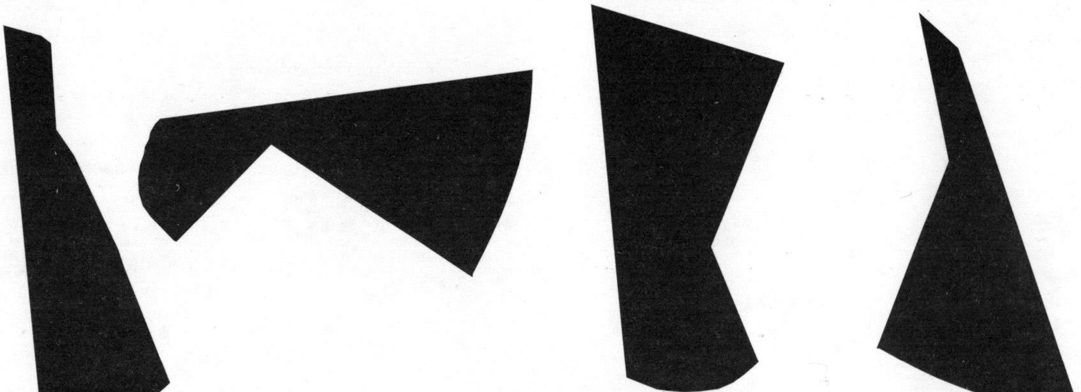

PUZZLE 30

The four pieces, top, when fitted together correctly, form a circle. However, one has gone missing. Can you find which one it is?

See answer ***22***

PUZZLE 31

PUZZLE 32

Can you unravel the reasoning behind this square and complete the missing square?

See answer 5

Can you find the missing number in this wheel?

See answer 11

PUZZLE 33

Take a letter from each cloud in turn. You should find the names of five painters and one extra name. What is it?

See answer 28

PUZZLE 34

Can you work out which is the odd one out?

See answer **75**

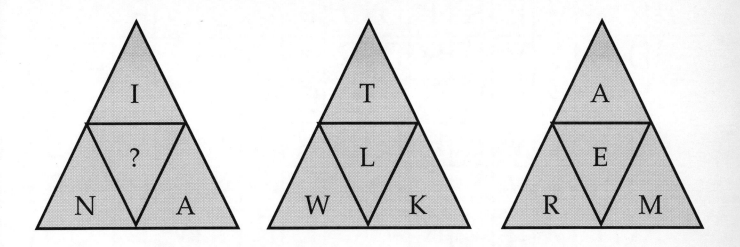

PUZZLE 35

Can you unravel the logic behind these diagrams and find
the missing letter?

See answer 97

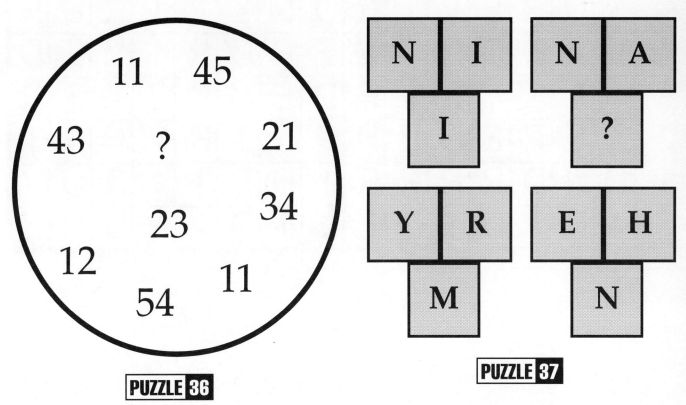

PUZZLE 36

Can you work out what the missing number is?

See answer 115

PUZZLE 37

Can you find the letter that should replace
the question mark?

See answer 102

LEVEL 3

```
D R I V E R I D V E R D D R I V
R D R I V E R D R I V E R V E R
I V E R D V E R D D R I V E R V
V D R I V E R D E R C I E V V E
E D R I V E E R V D I V E R D R
D R I V E V R V D E R I V E R D
V D E R I D I V E R D R I V E R
D R I R V E R D R I D R D V D E
D R R V I D R E V E R D R I V E
D A D R I V E D R I V D R I V E
I R D R E V I R D R E V I R D R
V E R D D R I V E R D R I V E D
V I V I V E V R D E V D E V I R
E R E R E D E D R R I R V E R I
R D R D R R R R I D R I I R D V
I I D I D I D E V I D V R D R E
```

PUZZLE 38

In this grid the name VERDI appears in its entirety only once in a straight line. Can you spot it? However, there is also another word hidden which involves one change of direction. What is it? It might have been one of the composer's famous last words.

See answer 24

228

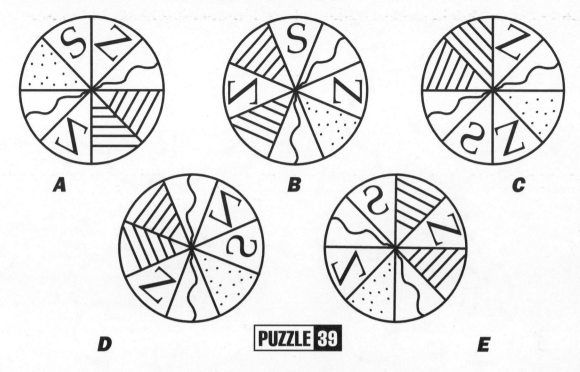

A **B** **C**

D **PUZZLE 39** **E**

Can you work out which is the odd diagram out?

See answer 82

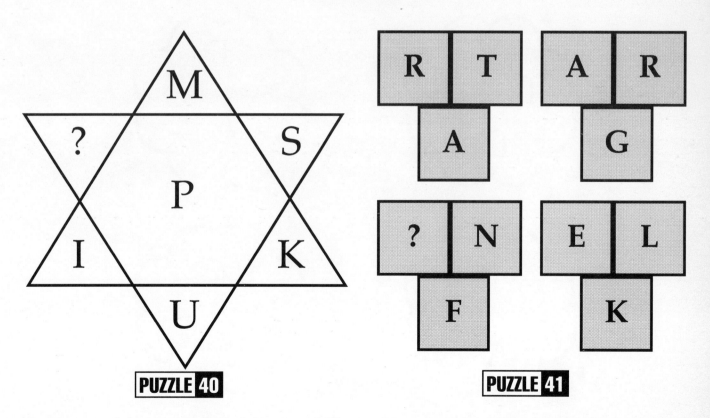

PUZZLE 40

Can you unravel the reasoning behind this star and fill in the missing letter?

See answer 91

PUZZLE 41

Can you work out which letter fits in the square with the question mark?

See answer 106

PUZZLE 42

Pick one letter from each flower in the order shown. You will get the names of five actors.

See answer 76

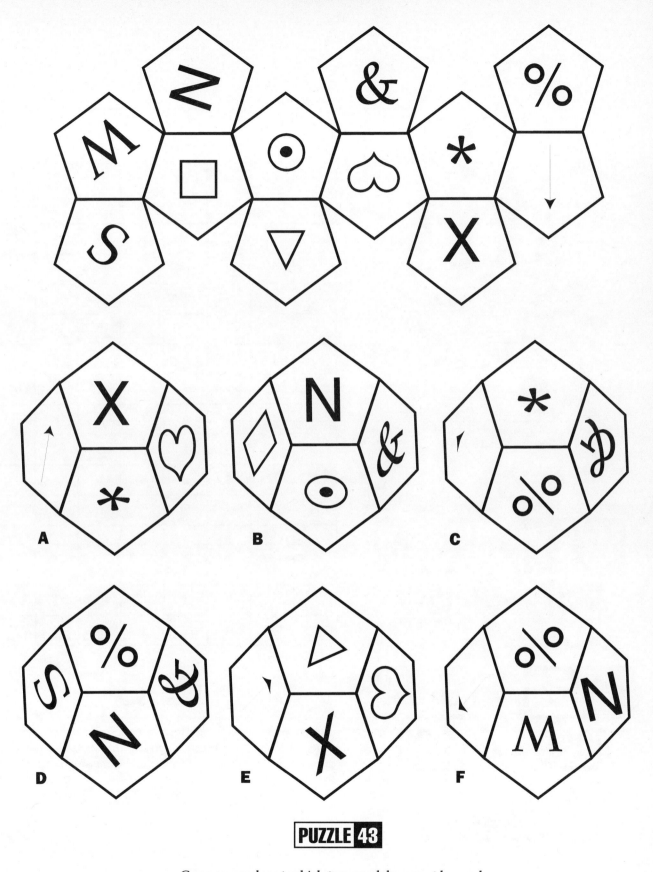

PUZZLE 43

Can you work out which two models cannot be made
from the above layout?

See answer 78

PUZZLE 44

Can you spot which are the odd letters out in these triangles?

See answer 135

6	G	B	6	2	G	F	5
5	D	3	9	D	I	3	4
1	F	7	H	A	7	1	H
9	E	4	C	2	5	C	E
2	A	6	G	8	I	F	8
8	I	5			B	1	4
3	B	1			H	9	E
7	H	9	E	4	C	2	A
4	C	2	A	6	G	8	I
6	G	8	I	5	D	3	B
A	D	3	B	1	F	7	H
H	5	7	H	9	E	4	C
6	2	F	C	2	A	6	G
8	D	I	4	8	I	5	D
A	B	7	1	G	B	1	F
F	5	9	C	E	3	9	E

PUZZLE 45

This grid follows the pattern: 5, 6, 4, 7, 3, 8, 2, 9, 1, with the letters (in their positions in the alphabet) alternately replacing numbers. Can you fill the missing section?

See answer 35

PUZZLE 46

Can you work out which number should go into the square with the question mark?

See answer 108

PUZZLE 47

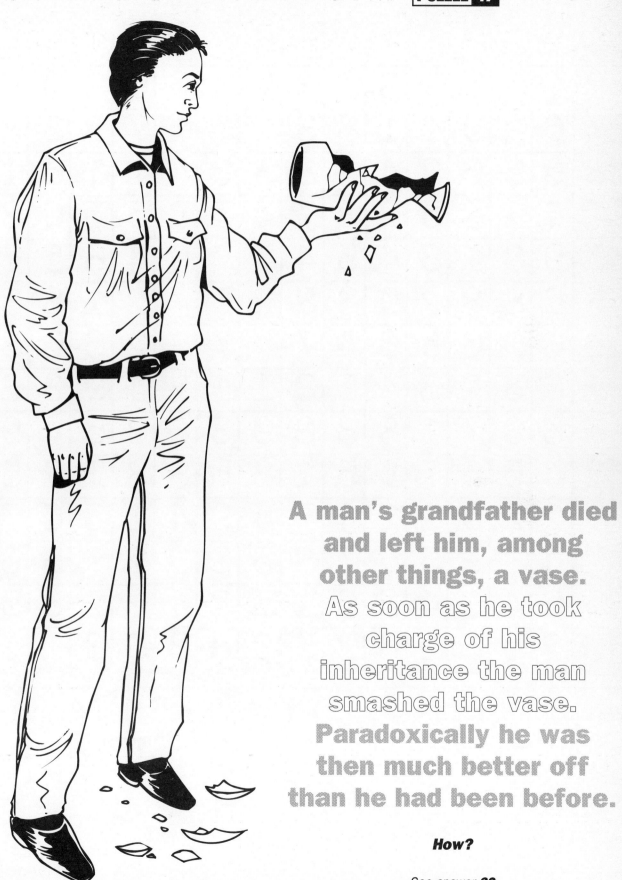

A man's grandfather died and left him, among other things, a vase. As soon as he took charge of his inheritance the man smashed the vase. Paradoxically he was then much better off than he had been before.

How?

See answer 32

233

LEVEL 3

5	3	6	4	4	3	5	7	5	7	9	2	2	5	8	3
9	8	9	6	1	5	8	6	6	8	3	7	6	7	4	4
2	1	5	7	8	3	1	3	5	1	6	6	8	9	8	6
7	6	2	9	1	1	8	3	1	5	1	7	5	3	4	1
8	5	6	6	2	4	4	8	3	8	4	7	1	6	1	8
7	6	2	2	5	2	3	7	4	5	8	5	7	6	3	1
7	9	3	1	8	4	5	4	7	7	9	4	8	5	6	3
3	6	8	8	2	9	8	8	2	5	7	2	1	8	3	5
5	6	9	6	5	3	4	7	4	7	4	2	6	6	5	5
1	6	3	2	3	4	5	8	1	1	2	4	9	3	2	7
5	8	9	7	1	8	3	6	9	3	6	3	5	4	9	4
8	4	5	6	7	1	5	1	8	5	8	3	1	2	5	7
7	2	2	9	2	2	4	7	4	9	4	1	8	6	7	8
2	4	3	9	5	6	7	8	5	8	3	2	7	5	6	1
5	9	4	3	4	2	6	1	7	3	4	9	2	6	9	1
3	2	5	8	1	3	2	5	3	8	3	5	3	1	2	7

PUZZLE 48

Look at this grid carefully and you will find pairs
of numbers that add up to 10, in a either horizontal,
vertical or diagonal direction.
How many can you spot?

See answer 47

234

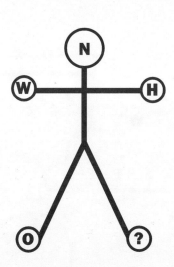

PUZZLE 49

Can you replace the question mark with a letter?

*See answer **87***

PUZZLE 50

Can you find the missing number on the domino piece? You will find the answer in Japan.

*See answer **113***

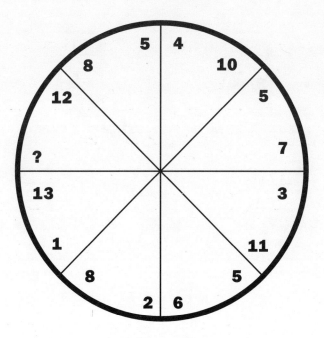

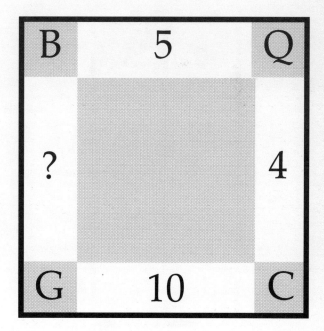

PUZZLE 51

Can you work out the reasoning behind this wheel and fill in the missing number?

*See answer **25***

PUZZLE 52

Can you replace the question mark with a number?

*See answer **6***

PUZZLE 53

Pick one letter from each cloud in the order shown.
You will find the names of five playwrights plus
one extra name. Who is it?

See answer 41

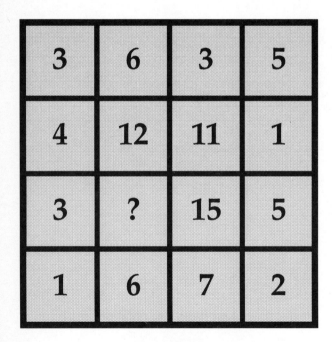

PUZZLE 54

Can you unravel the reasoning behind this square and
replace the question mark with a number?

See answer 7

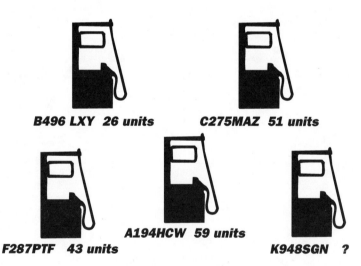

B496 LXY 26 units   C275MAZ 51 units

F287PTF 43 units   A194HCW 59 units   K948SGN ?

PUZZLE 55

Each of the cars was filled with petrol.
Can you unravel the connection between the
registration mark and amount of petrol and work out
what amount the last car was filled with?

A) 30 units   B) 72 units
C) 36 units   D) 78 units

See answer 40

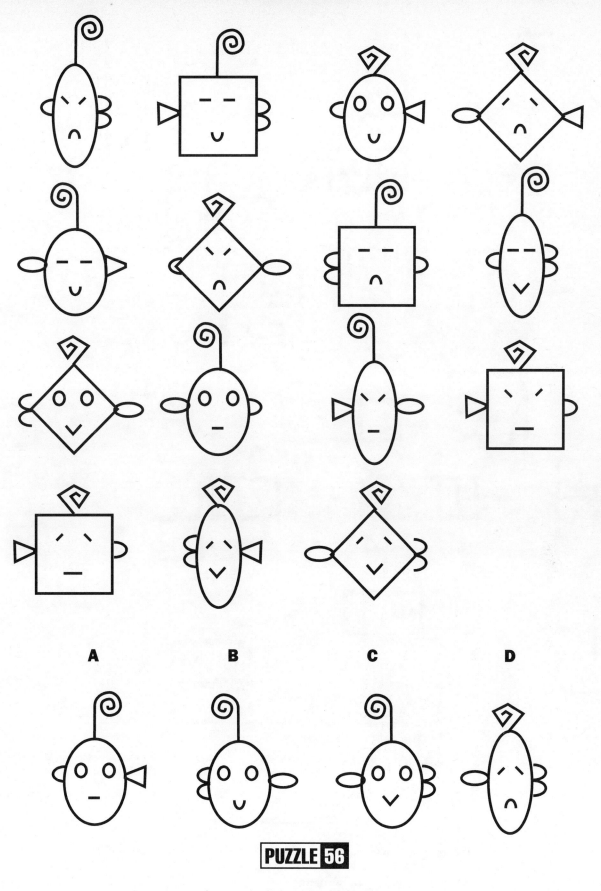

PUZZLE 56

Can you work out which face would fit the missing space?

*See answer **88***

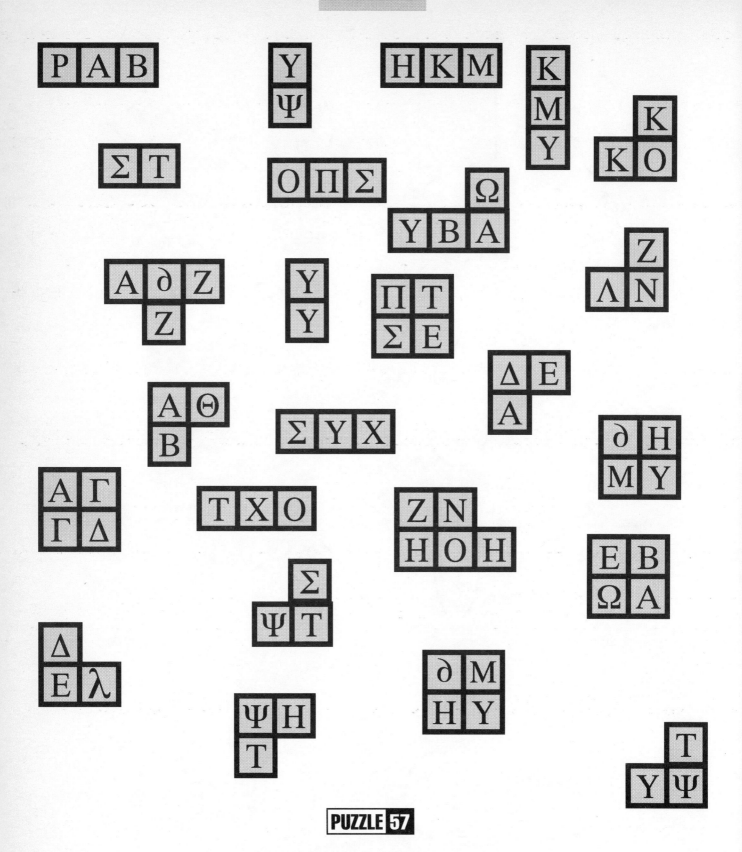

PUZZLE 57

These tiles when placed in the right order will form
a square in which each horizontal line is
identical with one vertical line.
Can you successfully form the square?

See answer **80**

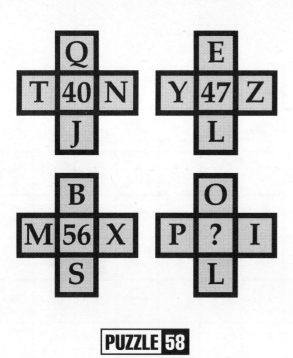

PUZZLE 58

Find a number to replace the question mark.

See answer 16

PUZZLE 59

Can you work out which is the missing letter on the last domino piece?

See answer 120

PUZZLE 60

This diagram represents a treasure map.
You are allowed to stop on each square only once
(though you may cross a square as often as you like).
When you stop on a square you must follow
the instructions you find there. The first one or two
letters stand for the points of the compass
(N = North, S = South, etc).
What the last letter stands for is for you to find out.
The finishing point is the square with the asterisk.
Can you work out where the starting point is?

See answer 13

SEV	SEU	SU	SEY	SWY	EX	SP	SP
SS	*	WY	SEV	EX	WW	SWT	WS
SES	SS	WX	NWX	SQ	NY	SQ	SWT
ET	SX	NEY	SEV	SU	SWW	WW	SR
SS	ET	SV	NWY	WV	NX	WY	SWT
SU	NEU	NEY	ST	NEW	NX	NW	NWU
NEV	NEW	SV	SEY	SV	NT	NX	NU
NX	NT	NT	EX	SWX	NX	NWY	SY
NX	NEX	NY	SY	NWY	SWX	NY	WY
NT	NEW	EW	NV	NEW	EY	SWY	NT
SEY	NV	NT	NEY	NU	NWX	NV	NWT
NX	NR	NEW	NO	NO	NWV	WY	WU

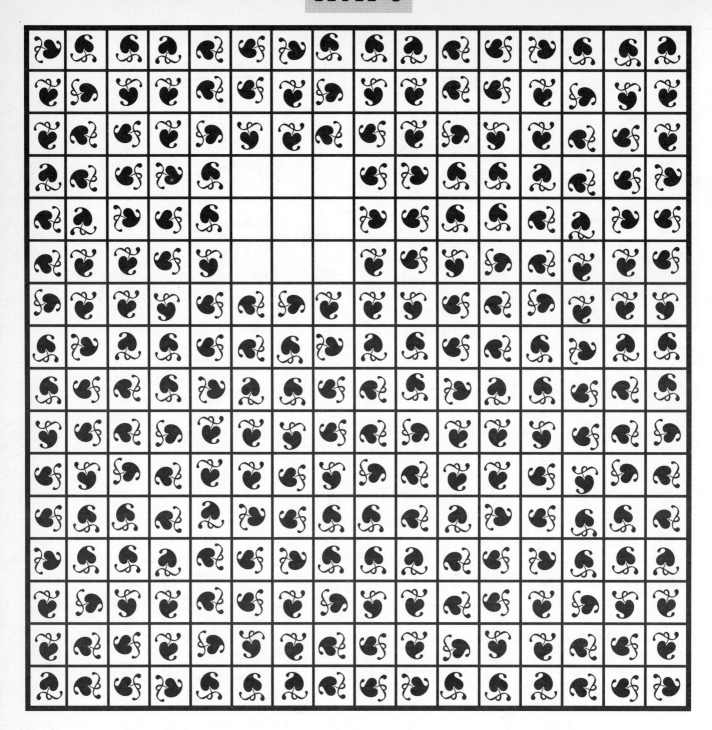

PUZZLE 61

Can you work out the reasoning behind this grid and fill in the missing section?

See answer 114

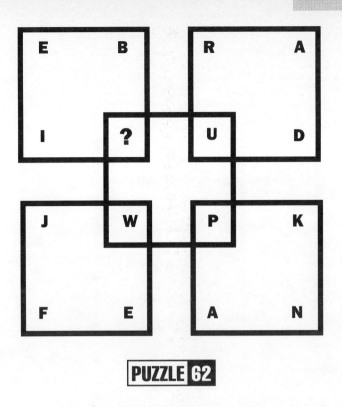

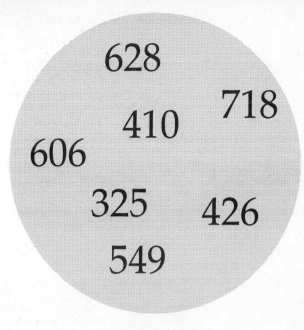

PUZZLE 62

Can you unravel the reasoning behind this diagram and find the missing letter?

See answer **153**

PUZZLE 63

Can you find the odd number out?

See answer **124**

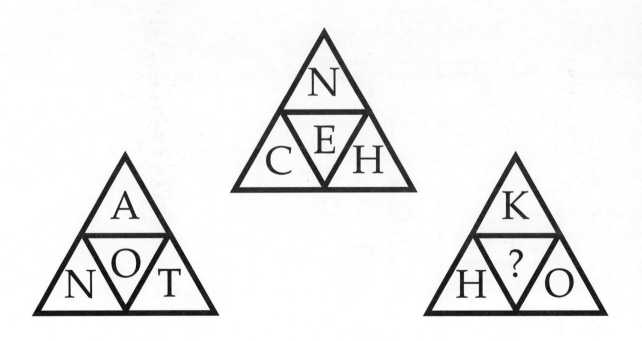

PUZZLE 64

Can you find the missing letter?

See answer **156**

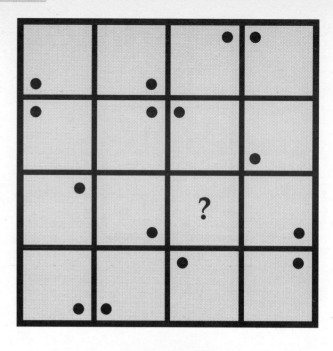

PUZZLE 65

Can you unravel the pattern of this wheel and find the missing element?

See answer 15

PUZZLE 66

Can you work out what the square with the question mark should look like?

See answer 12

PUZZLE 67

Can you unravel the reasoning behind these diagrams and find the missing letter?

See answer 134

PUZZLE 68

Can you work out which is the odd letter out in these triangles?

See answer 144

A man working the night shift received a telephone call and rushed home instantly.

His informant was right –

his wife was in bed with a stranger!

However, he seemed more surprised than angry

and even went so far as to bring them both breakfast in bed.

What had happened?

See answer 21

PUZZLE 70

The above pieces, put together correctly, form a disc.
However, two extra pieces got mixed up with them which
are not part of the disc. Can you find them?

See answer 38

5	0	5	6	4	3	5	0	5	6	4	3
1	8	7	1	8	7	1	8	7	1	8	7
6	4	3	5	0	5	6	4	3	5	0	5
5	3	4	1	5	6	5	4	4	0	5	6
7	7	8	8	2	1	8	7	8	8	1	1
3	5	0	4	6	6	3	5	0	4	6	5
4	6	5	3	6	0	5	6	5	3	5	0
8	1	1	8	7	8	8	2	1	7	7	8
0	5	6	5	3	4	0	5	6	5	3	4
5	0	5	6	4	3	5	0	5	6	4	3
1	8	7	1	8	7	1	8	7	1	8	7
6	4	3	5	0	5	6	4	3	5	0	5

PUZZLE 71

This grid follows the pattern: 6, 1, 5, 0, 8, 4, 3, 7, 5.
As a complication you will find some numbers have
increased by one. If you highlight these numbers
you will discover a letter. Which one is it?

See answer 52

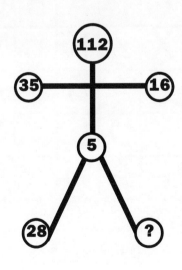

PUZZLE 72

Can you unravel the reasoning behind this diagram
and find the missing number?

See answer 99

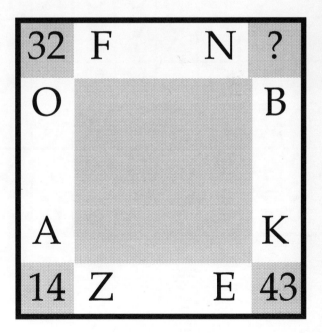

PUZZLE 73

Can you replace the question mark with a number?

See answer 37

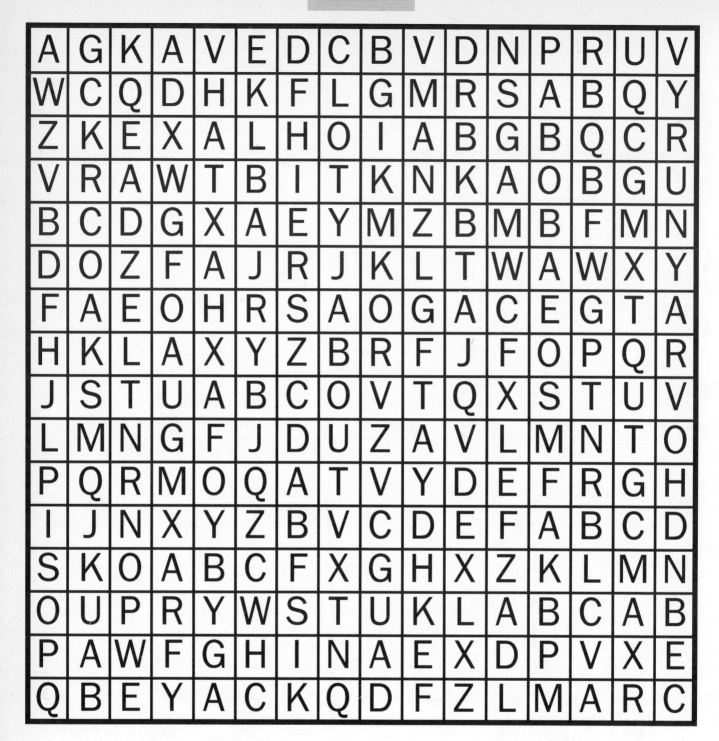

PUZZLE 74

Look at the above grid carefully. You will find pairs of
letters from the alphabet, with one letter missed out
between them (i.e. AC, DF, etc). The pairs can be in a
horizontal, vertical or diagonal direction.
How many can you spot?

*See answer **54***

PUZZLE 75

PUZZLE 76

Can you work out the logic behind these clockfaces and fill in the missing hands on clock No. 4? Both hands will point precisely in the same direction.

See answer 27

Can you find the letter that would replace the question mark?

See answer 137

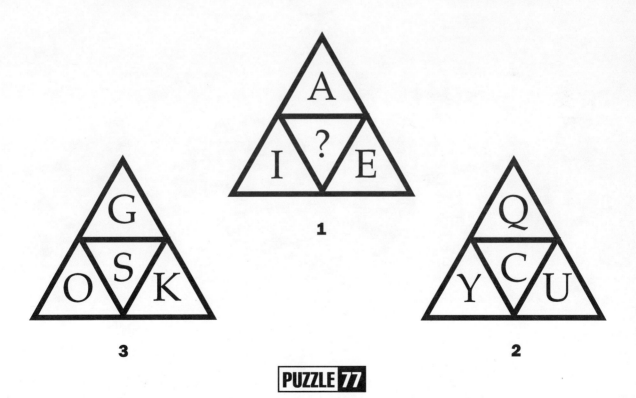

PUZZLE 77

Can you unravel the logic behind these diagrams and find the missing letter?

See answer 109

PUZZLE 78

The above pieces make up a disc when put together correctly. However, one piece is missing. Which is it?

See answer 3

AMSTERDAM

ROTTERDAM

IJMUIDEN

SCHEVENINGEN

EINDHOVEN

NIJMEGEN

PUTTEN

ARNHEM

BREDA

PUZZLE 79

Which of the towns in the right hand box should fill the blank space in the left? The answer is a long way from the Netherlands.

See answer 100

A   **B**   **C**   **D**

PUZZLE 80

Can you work out which diagram would follow the series above?

See answer 111

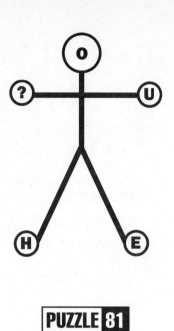

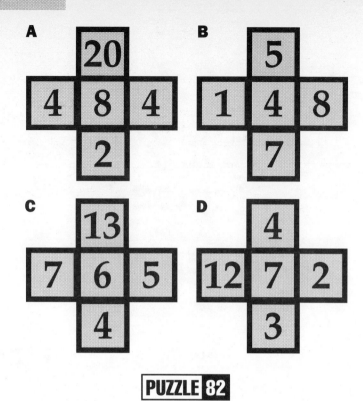

PUZZLE 81

Can you work out which is the missing letter?

See answer 107

PUZZLE 82

Can you work out which is the odd diagram out?

See answer 139

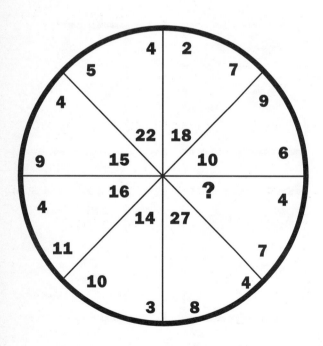

PUZZLE 83

Can you find the missing number?

See answer 36

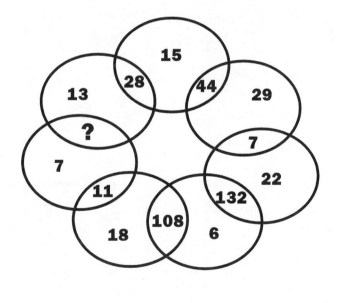

PUZZLE 84

Can you unravel the reasoning behind this diagram and find the missing number?

See answer 74

PUZZLE 85

Nauseating little Jimmy Toobright was having a biology lesson.

Feeling bored, he put up his hand and told the teacher,

"I know something that has legs, a chest and a back but no head. What is it?"

The teacher was, as usual, furious at being stuck for an answer.

What was Jimmy thinking of?

See answer 17

G	A	R	A	R	D	D	E	P	G	A	R	D	I	E	U
E	G	E	R	A	D	G	R	A	E	P	E	G	D	I	G
R	D	A	D	R	D	E	D	R	R	A	D	E	R	E	E
A	E	R	A	G	E	R	I	D	G	E	R	R	A	U	R
R	P	R	D	E	P	P	E	G	E	R	A	A	P	D	A
D	E	E	D	R	A	A	U	A	R	D	U	R	E	E	R
G	U	I	R	A	R	D	I	E	U	I	E	D	E	E	D
G	E	R	A	R	D	E	G	E	P	A	R	D	P	E	R
D	R	A	R	E	G	P	G	E	R	A	R	I	I	E	U
D	D	D	P	G	I	A	D	D	E	P	A	E	A	I	D
E	R	E	E	E	D	R	R	D	I	E	U	U	R	G	A
P	A	P	D	R	R	D	G	E	R	A	R	D	G	D	E
A	R	A	D	A	A	I	G	E	R	A	R	D	D	E	P
R	E	R	R	R	P	E	G	D	U	A	E	I	D	R	A
D	G	G	A	D	E	G	E	R	A	R	D	D	E	P	A
I	E	E	R	D	D	D	R	A	R	E	G	E	I	D	R

PUZZLE 86

In this grid the name of the actor Gerard Depardieu appears only once in its entirety. It is written in a horizontal, vertical or diagonal direction with two changes of direction. Can you spot it?

See answer 59

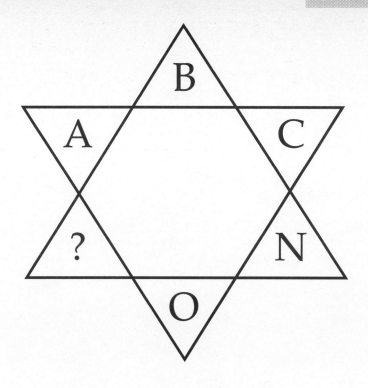

1	1	5	2	1	8	4	3
1	4	4	1	8	3	5	1
1	4	2	2	5	6	7	1
1	4	2	3	3	1	1	2
1	4	2	3	7	7	3	4
4	4	2	4	8	2	2	7
3	1	2	3	7	2	8	8
8	7	4	3	7	2	8	5
1	5	3	7	7	2	8	5
5	3	2	8	2	2	8	5
2	1	7	4	5	8	8	5
7	8	4	2	1	1	5	5

PUZZLE 87

Can you unravel the reasoning behind this star and find the missing letter?

See answer 101

PUZZLE 88

This grid follows the pattern: 3, 1, 4, 1, 5, 8, 2, 7. As a complication you will find some numbers have been increased by one. If you highlight these numbers you will discover a letter. Which one is it?

See answer 60

A. Bruno Velvet

7 hrs 20 min

B. Isaac Checkers

8 hrs 26 min

C. Damien Wallis

9 hrs 20 min

D. Samuel Blackborough

9 hrs 40 min

E. Arthur Hastings

a) 8 hrs 20 min
b) 8 hrs 26 min
c) 9 hrs 20 min
d) 7 hrs 14 min

PUZZLE 89

Each racing driver takes a different length of time to complete the race. Can you unravel the connection between the name of the driver and the time and work out how long Arthur Hastings took? (Clue: The values are based on vowels and consonants).

See answer 61

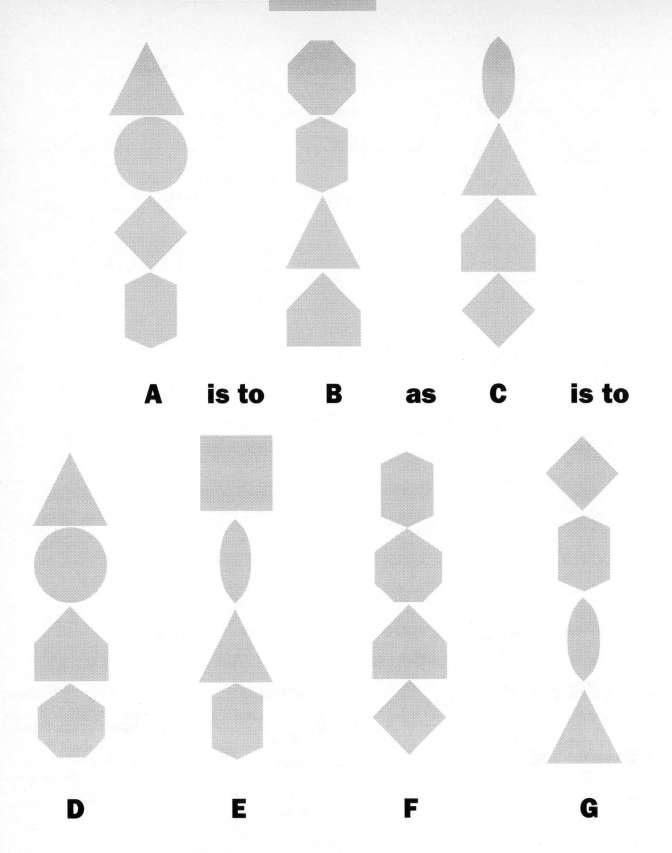

A **is to** **B** **as** **C** **is to**

D **E** **F** **G**

*See answer **98***

PUZZLE 91

E3	S6	E3	SE3	E3	SW1	SW1	SW1
S6	N1	SE4	NW1	W2	S1	S5	W4
E4	S2	W2	S3	S1	E2	W4	SW4
E2	N1	SW2	SE2	SE1	W5	S4	S1
E2	W1	S1	N2	N4	S2	N2	N3
N4	SW1	E5	N2	NW1	W1	N1	N2
NE6	SE1	NW1	SE1	SE1	N3	NW5	*
E1	NE1	E5	NE1	N3	NW4	W3	N1

This diagram represents a treasure map. You are allowed to stop on each square only once (though you may cross a square as often as you like). When you stop on a square you must follow the instructions you find there. The first one or two letters stand for points of the compass (N = North, S = South, etc), the figure for the number of steps you have to take. The finishing point is the square with the asterisk.

Can you find the starting point? There is one complication. You will find that you never land on some of the squares at all. If you cross out those squares on which you have landed you will see that those on which you have not form a letter.

Which one is it?

See answer 49

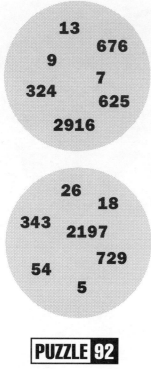

PUZZLE 92

Can you work out which is the odd number out in each circle?

See answer 132

PUZZLE 93

Can you unravel the reasoning behind these diagrams and find the missing shape?

See answer 141

PUZZLE 94

These pieces, when fitted together correctly, form a square.
However, two are not needed. Can you work out which
ones they are?

See answer 64

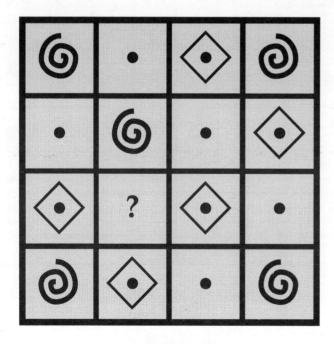

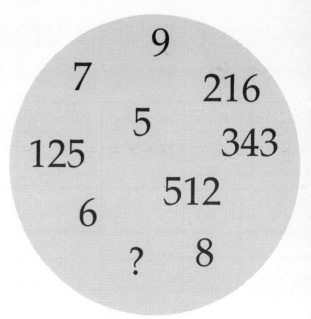

PUZZLE 95

Take a letter from each cloud in turn. You will find the names of five scientists plus one extra name. Who is it?

See answer 46

PUZZLE 96

Can you work out which shape should replace the question mark in this square?

See answer 20

PUZZLE 97

Can you work out which number is missing from this circle?

See answer 126

18	3	16	7	10	3	14	15	2	13	7	6	12	19	2	8
16	5	12	10	14	7	9	19	12	6	13	3	8	7	7	6
16	18	3	16	12	14	7	4	13	12	15	9	14	5	13	4
12	8	8	3	7	11	6	8	5	11	9	13	11	7	6	12
15	8	11	19	10	10	7	14	4	12	5	7	16	13	9	15
13	14	11	4	3	10	17	9	18	7	3	6	12	5	14	19
11	4	9	11	18	4	18	12	9	12	14	15	14	17	2	6
17	5	4	18	3	17	6	8	19	17	4	15	8	11	12	15
4	6	8	19	15	11	19	12	12	13	11	8	4	3	14	3
13	5	1	19	6	8	15	2	17	13	7	15	11	14	17	12
9	1	2	13	4	6	5	8	19	12	9	8	17	7	15	4
5	12	2	18	11	8	15	6	3	4	2	1	4	6	16	12
17	18	9	12	5	13	2	8	6	16	10	14	3	4	12	11
8	6	13	16	5	11	12	8	9	14	7	3	8	9	13	6
5	6	19	1	7	8	15	4	5	15	3	6	15	8	8	11
9	18	2	4	3	1	19	8	13	16	12	18	14	19	2	12

PUZZLE 98

In this grid there are hidden pairs of numbers which add up to 20. They can appear in a horizontal, vertical or diagonal direction. How many can you spot?

See answer 63

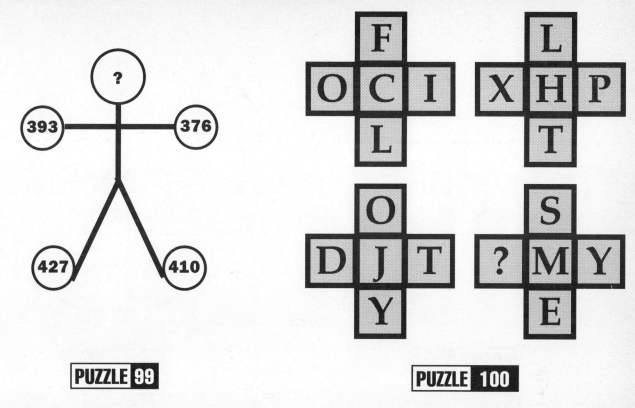

PUZZLE 99

Can you find the number that fits into the man's head?

See answer 125

PUZZLE 100

Can you replace the question mark with a letter?

See answer 143

32

41

?

PUZZLE 101

Can you find the number that fits below the 7?

See answer 90

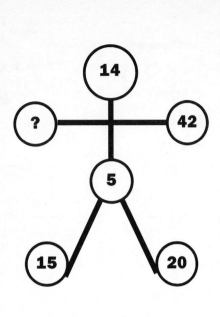

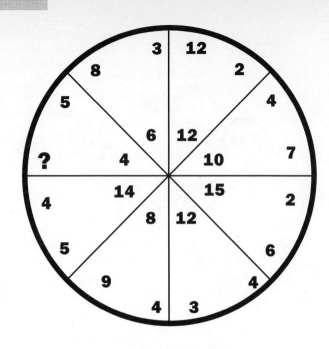

PUZZLE 102

Can you unravel the logic behind this diagram and find the missing number?

See answer 129

PUZZLE 103

Can you unravel the reasoning behind this wheel and replace the question mark with a number?

See answer 44

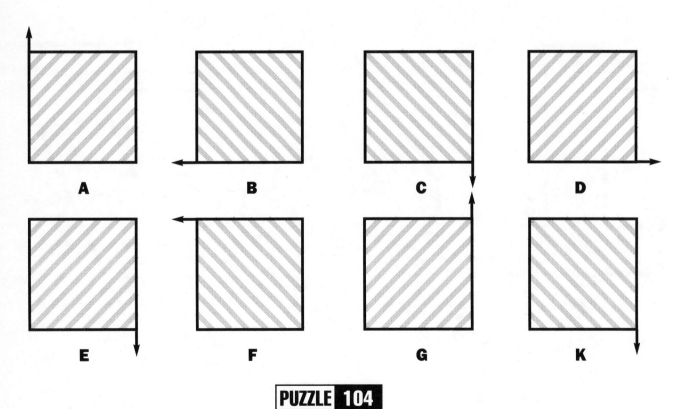

PUZZLE 104

Can you work out which diagram is the odd one out?

See answer 136

Fred was often inquisitive about the world outside.

Each day he gazed wistfully through the glass at a world he could never know.

Then, one day, the unthinkable happened.

Some boys playing outside accidentally broke the glass.

Instantly Fred regretted his curiosity.

Why?

See answer 9

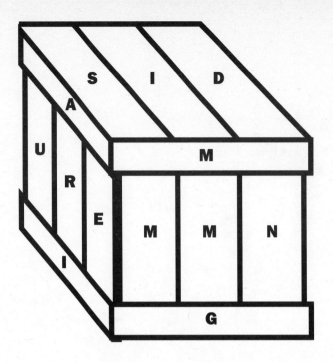

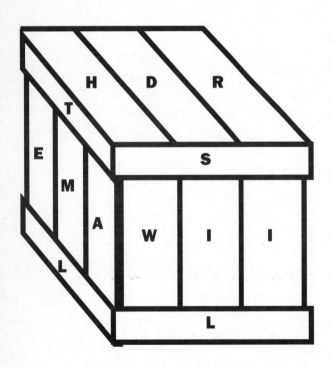

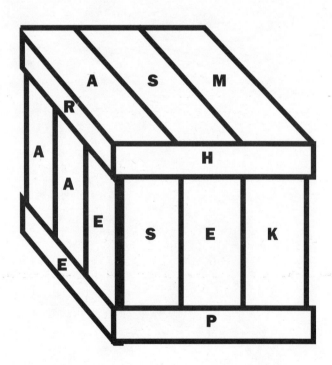

PUZZLE 106

A well known work of literature and its author are
concealed in these crates. What are they?

See answer 117

C

D

G

A

E

F

B

PUZZLE 107

These pieces, when fitted together correctly, make up a
square. However, one piece is not needed. Can you work
out which one it is?

See answer 69

Ω	Σ	Σ	Σ	Σ	Σ	Ω	Σ	Ω	Ω	Σ	Φ	Ω	Σ	Σ	Φ
Σ	Φ	Ω	Φ	Ω	Ω	Σ	Ω	Σ	Σ	Φ	Ω	Σ	Σ	Φ	Σ
Φ	Ω	Φ	Ω	Ω	Φ	Σ	Σ	Ω	Σ	Ω	Φ	Ω	Σ	Σ	Ω
Ω	Σ	Ω	Σ	Φ	Σ	Φ	Ω	Σ	Σ	Φ	Ω	Σ	Φ	Ω	Σ
Σ	Σ	Σ	Σ	Φ	Φ				Σ	Ω	Ω	Φ	Ω	Σ	Ω
Σ	Φ	Σ	Φ	Σ	Σ				Σ	Ω	Σ	Σ	Φ	Ω	Σ
Φ	Ω	Σ	Σ	Σ	Ω				Ω	Σ	Σ	Φ	Ω	Σ	Φ
Ω	Σ	Ω	Φ	Σ	Σ	Ω	Φ	Σ	Ω	Φ	Σ	Σ	Ω	Φ	Φ
Ω	Ω	Φ	Σ	Σ	Ω	Φ	Σ	Ω	Φ	Σ	Σ	Ω	Σ	Σ	Φ
Ω	Σ	Φ	Ω	Σ	Σ	Φ	Ω	Σ	Ω	Φ	Ω	Σ	Σ	Σ	Ω
Σ	Φ	Ω	Σ	Σ	Φ	Σ	Σ	Ω	Φ	Σ	Σ	Ω	Σ	Ω	Σ
Σ	Ω	Φ	Ω	Σ	Σ	Ω	Ω	Σ	Σ	Ω	Σ	Ω	Ω	Σ	Σ
Σ	Φ	Ω	Σ	Φ	Ω	Σ	Σ	Φ	Ω	Ω	Ω	Σ	Φ	Σ	Φ
Σ	Ω	Ω	Φ	Ω	Σ	Ω	Φ	Σ	Σ	Ω	Σ	Φ	Ω	Φ	Ω
Σ	Ω	Σ	Σ	Φ	Ω	Σ	Σ	Σ	Φ	Σ	Ω	Σ	Ω	Σ
Ω	Σ	Σ	Φ	Ω	Σ	Φ	Φ	Σ	Φ	Σ	Ω	Σ	Ω	Σ	Φ

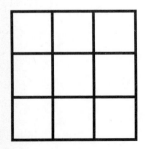

PUZZLE 108

This grid follows a certain pattern. Can you work it out
and complete the missing section?

See answer 103

264

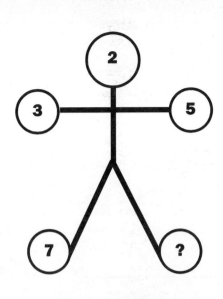

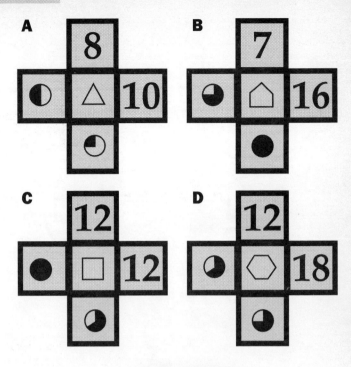

A **B** **C** **D**

PUZZLE 109

Can you work out which number would replace the question mark?

See answer 133

PUZZLE 110

Can you spot the odd one out?

See answer 148

PUZZLE 111

Which letter is the odd one out?

See answer 39

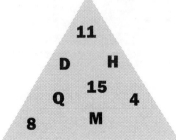

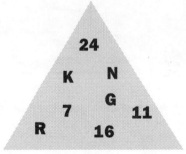

PUZZLE 112

Can you find the odd number and letter in these triangles?

See answer 147

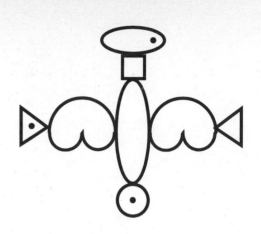

A   is to   B   as   C   is to

D

E

F

G

S7	E1	E1	SE3	W3	W1	S7	S4
E7	E2	E3	E1	W2	N1	SE1	SW6
E5	W1	SW2	SE2	SE1	W3	N1	W6
SE3	SE4	NE1	NE3	W3	S2	S2	N3
S1	NW1	E2	SW1	N2	W3	W5	W1
SE1	✱	S1	NE3	W3	S1	SE1	W3
E4	W1	N3	SE1	E2	NW2	NW5	N3
E3	NE2	E5	N4	N4	W3	NW6	N2

PUZZLE 114

This diagram represents a treasure map. You are allowed to stop on each square only once (though you may cross a square as often as you like). When you stop on a square you must follow the instructions you find there. The letters stand for points of the compass (N = North, S = South, etc), the numbers for the amount of steps you have to take. The finishing point is the square with the asterisk.

Can you find the starting point? There is one complication. You will find that you never land on some of the squares at all. If you cross out those squares on which you have landed you will see that those on which you have not form a letter. Which one is it?

See answer 68

PUZZLE 115

Can you unravel the reasoning behind these diagrams and find the missing letter?

See answer 150

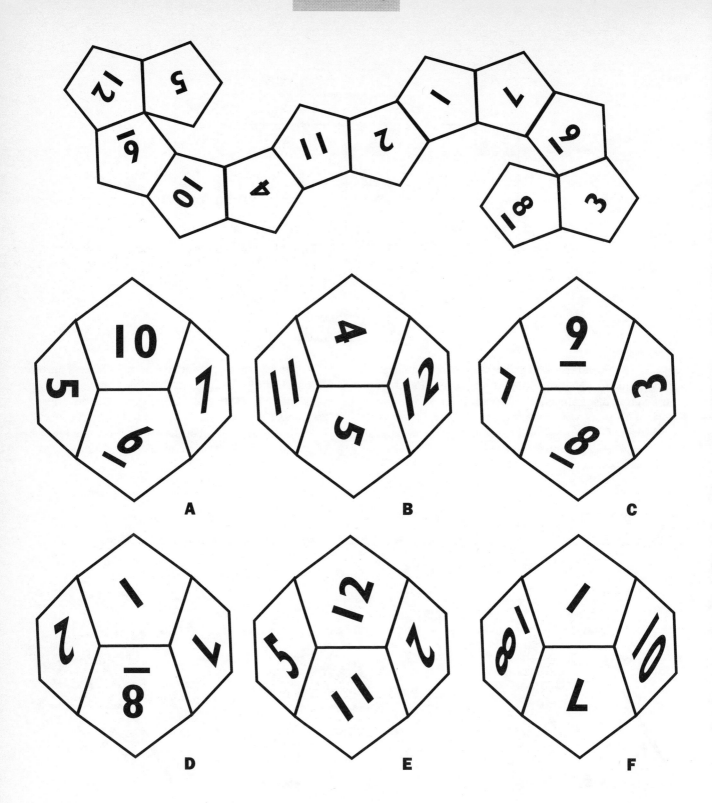

PUZZLE 116

Can you work out which two models cannot be made from
the above layout?

See answer 122

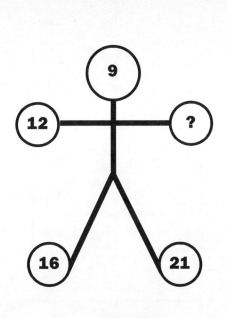

PUZZLE 117

Can you work out which number should replace the
question mark?

See answer 146

PUZZLE 118

Can you find the missing letter?

See answer 151

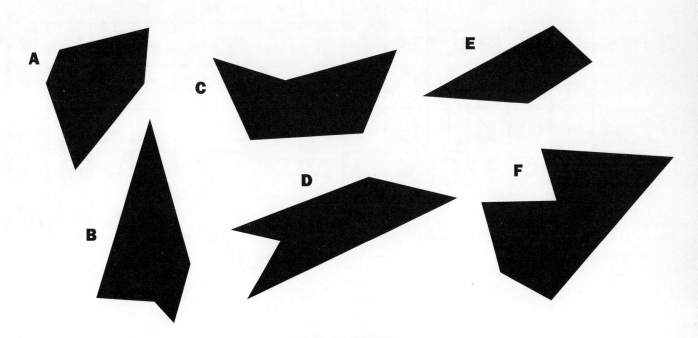

PUZZLE 119

The pieces, when fitted together correctly, make up a right-
angled triangle. However, one of them is not needed. Can
you work out which one it is?

See answer 58

```
O R O O E R A M I O R I G A A G
R E M R G O O R I G A M O R G A
I G A E G A O O O A M R I I O M
G A G G O O R M R G I O G G O I
A M E R R R I I A E O M A A A O
M O R A G I G G G R R A M R G R
O R I M A G A A I G I G O O I I
M A G I M A O R M O G I R I R G
O R I G I O R O O A A R G A O A
O G A M G R A O I I M O I M M M
O R I G A M O M O M O M A O A O
O I M A G E R I R M A A M R G R
O R E G A N O G I G A G I G I I
G A R O M I G O G O G G I A R G
I O R A I G A R A R I I O R O A
M O R I G A M O M O O R G R O M
```

PUZZLE 120

In this grid the word Origami, written in a straight line, appears only once in its entirety. Can you spot it? It can be written in a horizontal, vertical or diagonal direction. As an addition, there is also hidden a similar looking word that adds a little seasoning to the puzzle. It is, again, written in a straight line. Can you find it?

See answer 65

19

91

11

17

23   53

41

3	3	9	3
5	8	2	1
4	3	8	1
8	2	1	?

PUZZLE 121

Can you find the odd number out?

See answer 128

PUZZLE 122

This square follows a pattern. Can you unravel it and replace the question mark with a number?

See answer 19

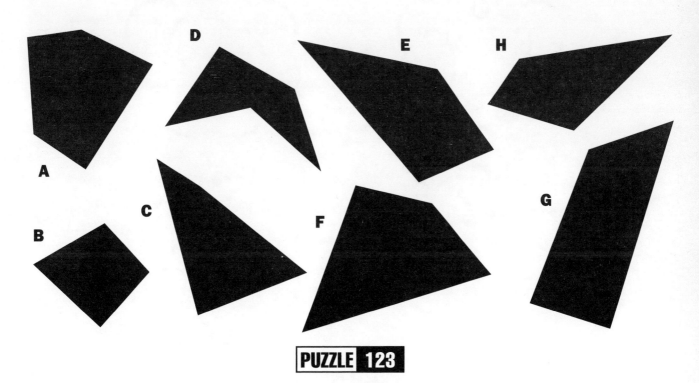

PUZZLE 123

The above pieces, when fitted together correctly, form a square. However, one wrong piece is among them. Can you work out which one it is?

See answer 73

PUZZLE 124

Take a letter from each flower in the order shown. You will get the surnames of five composers. Who are they?

See answer 118

N4	NW6	W9	W6	E3	NE5	N1	NE3	E1	E4	N4	E3
N6	W8	SW1	W5	NW4	E4	NW4	NE4	NW1	N2	E10	N5
W4	N3	NW2	N1	SW2	NE2	E6	N1	W2	N3	W1	NE5
NW3	SW2	S2	E2	N4	N2	W4	E2	E2	NE2	N4	E3
S1	S2	S1	S2	NE2	S2	*	E6	N3	SE2	N2	E5
W11	SW4	S3	W1	S4	S1	SW4	S4	SE1	S1	E8	N2
W5	NW1	S2	W3	E4	SW1	S4	N1	S2	E5	E2	S2
S7	S1	S7	SW7	E1	SW6	W3	SW4	SW1	E8	E5	SE7

PUZZLE 125

This diagram represents a treasure map. You are allowed to stop on each square only once (though you may cross a square as often as you like). When you stop on a square you must follow the instructions you find there. The letters stand for the directions on a compass. However, there is a complication which is for you to find out. The numbers indicate the number of squares you have to move.

The finishing point is the square with the asterisk. Can you find the starting point? You will also find there are some squares that you don't land on at all. If you cross out those squares on which you land you will see that those on which you do not form a number. Which one is it?

See answer 145

PUZZLE 126

23	6		8	17
?				5
7				3
7	4		9	34

PUZZLE 127

A [1]   B [3]   C [2]   D [1]

Can you work out what the missing number is?

See answer 45

Can you spot the odd diagram out?

See answer 152

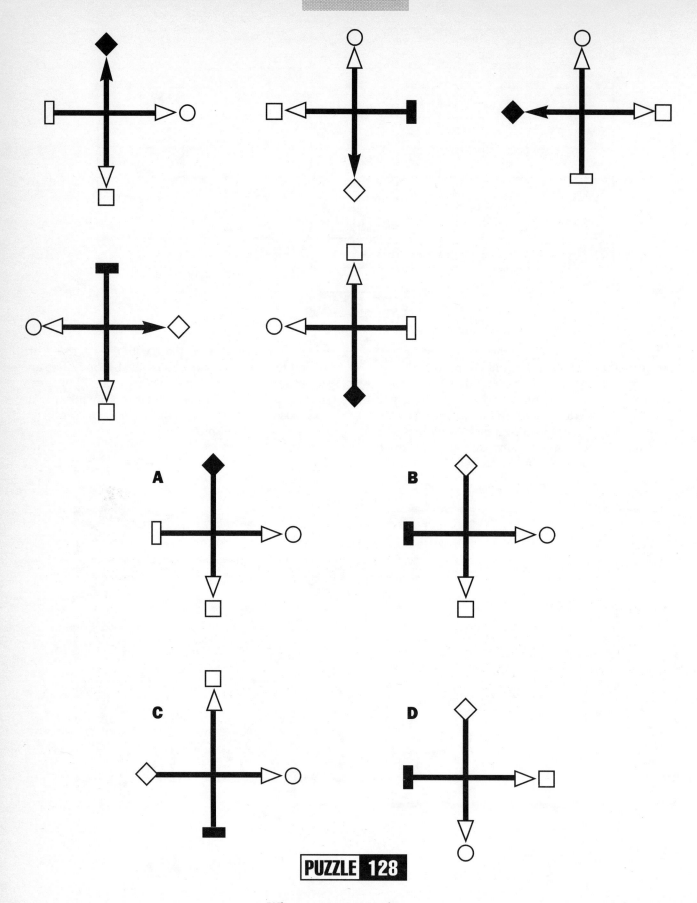

PUZZLE 128

What comes next in this series?

See answer 79

4	3	2	?
3	7	1	2
8	2	8	2
1	2	5	4

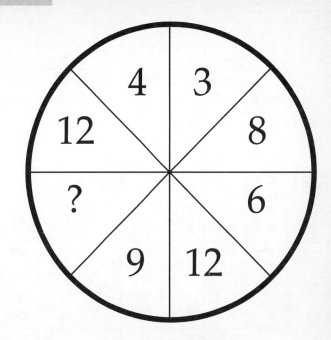

PUZZLE 129

This square is made up according to a pattern. Can you work it out and fill in the missing number (1 – 9)?

See answer 26

PUZZLE 130

Can you unravel the reasoning behind this wheel and find the missing number?

See answer 112

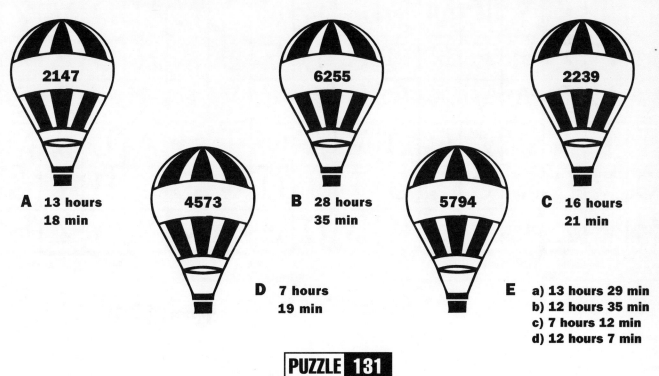

A 13 hours 18 min

B 28 hours 35 min

C 16 hours 21 min

D 7 hours 19 min

E a) 13 hours 29 min
   b) 12 hours 35 min
   c) 7 hours 12 min
   d) 12 hours 7 min

PUZZLE 131

Each of these balloons was taken for a flight, which lasted a different length of time. Can you work out how long the flight of balloon No. 5794 lasted?

See answer 29

N	O	Q	R	D	F	G	S	J	T	U	V	K	G	L	T
V	A	W	U	D	X	Q	R	Z	D	F	M	P	H	J	R
S	E	B	C	M	O	T	A	V	N	W	K	Y	I	A	K
M	B	G	O	Z	V	J	Y	M	D	L	T	L	Q	C	E
O	G	L	B	R	I	N	K	L	V	Q	J	H	L	G	N
B	P	D	F	K	P	S	C	A	C	T	M	D	Q	M	K
Q	S	U	W	A	C	L	A	K	S	W	U	X	Z	B	F
H	L	B	R	Q	J	M	H	R	G	E	R	V	W	S	D
R	S	O	K	P	C	N	D	T	Y	R	P	G	O	U	X
D	V	K	M	R	T	F	A	F	O	U	E	F	X	T	C
L	T	X	Y	K	M	D	H	B	C	I	N	U	O	V	Z
B	G	Z	H	E	R	O	Q	L	E	D	A	R	Q	P	A
G	U	D	A	V	K	S	U	F	V	Y	F	J	T	A	E
T	L	N	W	X	O	Q	V	A	M	T	S	A	L	J	M
O	R	B	Y	C	F	S	T	J	Q	U	P	D	H	I	G
H	K	Z	L	O	Q	K	B	D	G	X	V	Y	A	Z	B

PUZZLE 132

In this grid there are hidden pairs of letters, adjacent to each other in the alphabet. They can be written in a horizontal, vertical or diagonal direction. How many can you spot?

See answer 67

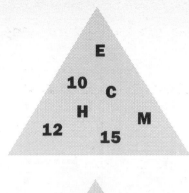

PUZZLE 133

Can you spot the odd one out in the bottom triangle?

See answer 31

PUZZLE 134

Can you find the missing letter in this square?

See answer 43

PUZZLE 135

Can you replace the question mark with a letter?

See answer 154

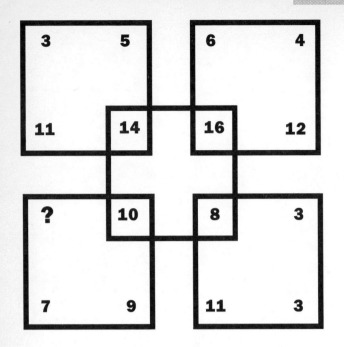

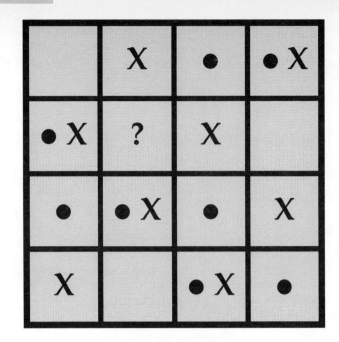

PUZZLE 137

PUZZLE 136

Can you find the missing number?

See answer 149

Can you unravel the logic behind this diagram and work out what the square with the question mark should look like?

See answer 34

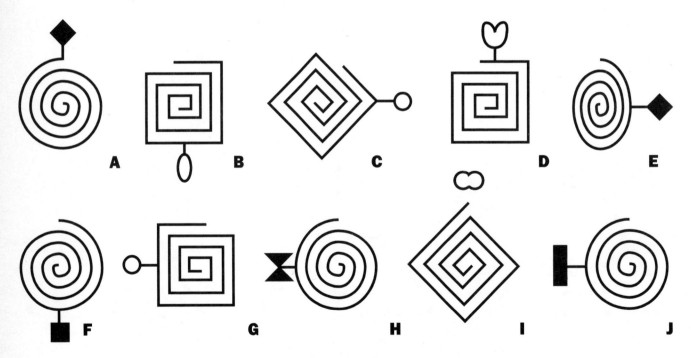

PUZZLE 138

Can you find the odd one out?

See answer 123

**It is said
that Lucretia Borgia
could split an apple**
in such a way that, when she
shared it with someone else,
the subject of her generosity
would be dead within
hours.

How did she do it?

See answer 42

PUZZLE 140

Pick one letter from each of the flowers in the order shown.
You will get the names of five American cities. Which ones
are they?

See answer 131

SEW	SP	ET	SER	ET	SWY	WX	SEW	SS	SQ	SS	WX
EY	SP	NEY	SES	SWX	WW	SWW	SEW	WY	SP	SP	SU
SX	SEU	SU	EU	SY	EX	WU	WW	SWX	NEX	WP	SQ
EQ	SY	EW	NX	WW	SWY	SW	SWU	WY	NX	SWW	NY
SY	EY	ES	NEV	SV	SW	SS	SEY	NEW	WY	SU	ST
EO	NU	SY	SWX	NEY	SWX	WU	EX	SY	NW	NW	WQ
NET	SX	NV	EX	NY	NV	EV	SV	NEW	WU	WP	NWT
NV	SEX	WX	EV	SWV	NWX	NT	SWX	SWY	SWV	WY	NW
EU	SEX	NR	NES	SEX	NWY	WT	SWY	NWW	NWT	NEY	SY
NET	SEY	NET	WW	SY	WY	NS	NU	NWR	NW	WX	∗
NEY	NV	ER	EX	WV	NQ	SEY	NU	NQ	WY	NU	WX
NET	EX	NX	NW	WX	NEW	NW	NX	NWU	NW	WX	WS

PUZZLE 141

This diagram represents a treasure map. You are allowed to stop on each square only once (though you may cross a square as often as you like). When you stop on a square you must follow the instructions you find there. The first one or two letters stand for points of the compass (N = North, S = South, etc). What the last letter stands for is for you to find out. The finishing point is the square with the asterisk. Can you work out where the starting point is?

See answer 57

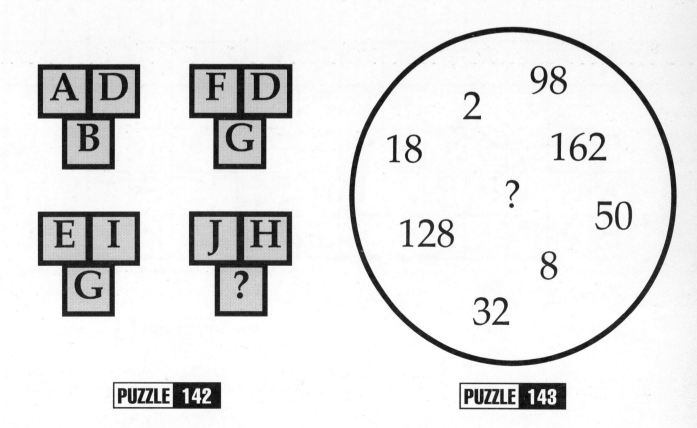

PUZZLE 142

Can you complete the last diagram?

See answer 157

PUZZLE 143

Can you find what number is missing from this circle?

See answer 142

P	A	R	S	I	S	P	A	R	S	P	A	R	P	I	S
S	A	P	R	S	P	I	S	P	A	R	S	P	A	R	S
R	A	P	S	A	R	P	I	S	P	R	A	S	P	S	I
I	S	P	A	R	I	P	S	A	R	I	S	P	S	P	A
A	S	P	A	R	S	P	A	R	S	I	P	A	R	S	I
P	A	R	S	I	S	P	A	R	S	P	A	S	I	S	R
P	R	A	S	I	P	A	S	R	P	R	A	S	R	I	S
R	S	A	S	I	P	A	R	S	I	S	P	A	I	S	S
R	S	A	I	S	R	A	S	R	A	I	S	P	R	A	S
R	I	S	I	P	S	A	P	R	A	I	R	S	I	P	I
A	R	P	R	A	I	R	S	I	P	S	A	P	R	A	S
I	A	P	A	P	A	R	A	R	I	P	I	S	A	I	P
S	P	R	I	S	S	I	P	P	S	A	R	P	R	S	A
R	P	I	R	S	I	P	S	A	P	R	A	I	R	S	R
I	A	S	A	P	R	A	I	R	S	I	P	S	A	P	I
S	P	A	R	I	P	A	S	I	R	P	A	R	I	P	A

PUZZLE 144

In this grid the word Paris, written in a straight line, appears only once in its entirety. Can you spot it? It can be written forwards or backwards in a horizontal, vertical or diagonal direction.

See answer 71

PUZZLE 145

These shapes, when fitted together correctly, make up a
letter. Can you work out which one it is?

See answer 77

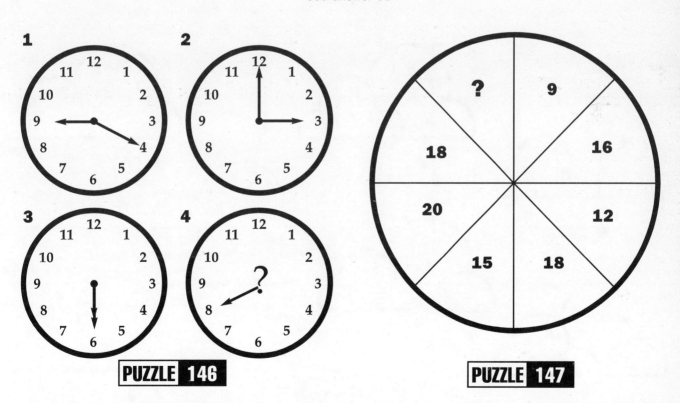

PUZZLE 146

PUZZLE 147

From the above clockfaces, can you work out what
number the minute hand on clock 4 should
be pointing at?

See answer 51

Can you unravel the reasoning behind this wheel and
find the missing number?

See answer 116

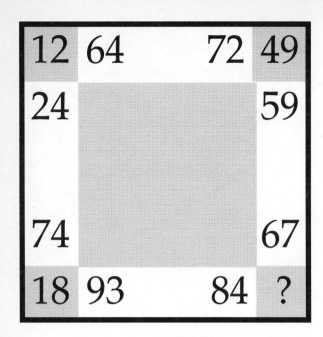

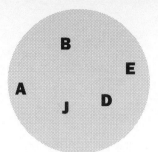

PUZZLE 148

Can you replace the question mark with a number?

See answer 53

PUZZLE 149

Can you work out which is the odd letter out in each circle?

See answer 121

PUZZLE 150

Pick one letter from each cloud in the order shown. You should find the names of five pop or rock artists and one extra name. Who is it?

See answer 62

LEVEL 3

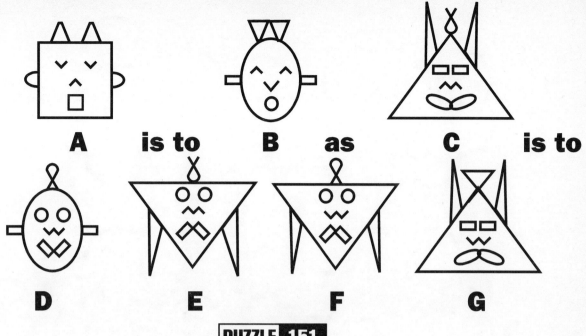

A is to **B** as **C** is to

D **E** **F** **G**

PUZZLE 151

See answer 140

1. A Y P O M R P
   E C T U Q V V

2. Q C W K M M L
   U M E O S Q R

3. A C D A G B J
   E M N E O H R

4. Z H Q Y S H R Q
   D J U G W J V U

5. Z K A   C H J A
   H S M   I V T G

6. A E J A H I Z R B   Z Y H C
   E K T E V O B V H   F C N G

7. K S N D P J H G M
   O W X L T T V S Y

8. L O Z L C A   F T D A B
   R U B P K I   N V N E H

9. S A C B P W Y H A   Q K R L
   Y I K H X E E P I   U S X T

10. R H Q P T C Q
    V J U V V G U

PUZZLE 152

Mrs Jones was about to go shopping when she stopped
for a chat with a neighbour. Her cheeky son stole her
shopping list and encoded it for a joke. When she arrived
at the supermarket the list above is what she found.
What was on her original list?

See answer 158

285

PUZZLE 153

Pick a letter from each flower in the order shown.
You will get the surnames of five pop and rock stars.
Who are they?

See answer 95

A. Mercedes 14.08

B. Rover 9.09

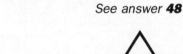

C. Renault 9.07   **D. Volvo 5.12**   **E. Citroen ?**

a) 3.09
b) 24.13
c) 24.14
d) 14.03

PUZZLE 154

Each car was filled with petrol at different times. Can you unravel the logic between the car and the time and work out when the Citroen was filled?

See answer 48

PUZZLE 155

Can you unravel the reasoning behind this wheel and fill in the missing matchstick man?

See answer 50

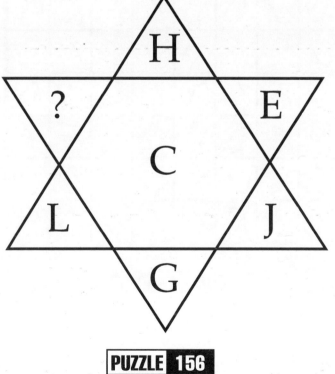

PUZZLE 156

Can you unravel the logic behind this star and find the missing letter?

See answer 119

21	18	22	27
23	?	24	33
20	29	28	30
26	31	35	32

PUZZLE 157

Can you find the missing number in this square?

See answer 89

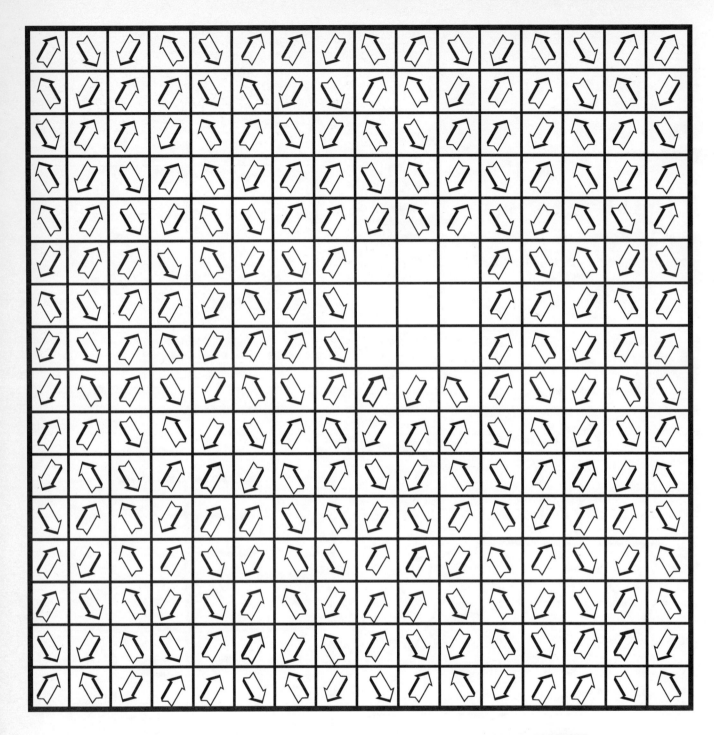

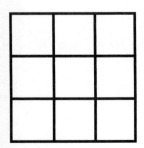

PUZZLE 158

Can you work out the pattern of this grid and fill in the missing section?

See answer **96**

Answer 1

38. Regard the alphabet as a circle. The number is double the number of spaces between the letters.

Answer 2

Start at the top right and move across the square in a horizontal boustrophedon. The pattern is: miss 1 square, turn by 180°, turn by 90° clockwise, miss 1, turn by 90° clockwise, turn by 180°.

Answer 3

A.

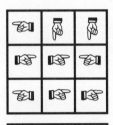

Answer 4

The pattern sequence is shown below. Starting at the bottom right, work in a diagonal boustrophedon (clockwise start).

Answer 5

The pattern is:

Start at the bottom right and work through the square in a vertical boustrophedon.

Answer 6

7. Regard the alphabet as a circle. The number is a third of the number of spaces between letters.

Answer 7

8. Starting at the top left corner add the first three numbers and place the sum on the inside of the second number. Moving around the square in a clockwise spiral, repeat with the next three numbers, etc.

Answer 8

Reading across segments 1 and 1a, 2 and 2a, etc. the dots move around the circle in a vertical boustrophedon.

Answer 9

He was a goldfish whose bowl got broken, with fatal results.

Answer 10

8. The two numbers added together give the number the minute hand points at on the next clock. The hour hand points at the number three spaces before.

Answer 11

10. Multiply the two numbers on the outside of each segment, divide the product by 1,2,3 …8 respectively and put the new number in the middle of the opposite segment.

Answer 12

Start at the top right and move in an anti-clockwise spiral. The dot moves around the square in a clockwise direction.

Answer 13

Row 1, Column 1. The letter is based on the alphabet backwards, however with Y = 1, X = 2, W = 3, A = 25, Z = 26. Its value represents the number of spaces you have to move.

Answer 14

The pattern sequence is shown below. It starts at the top right and works down in a diagonal boustrophedon (anti-clockwise start).

Answer 15

The shapes form a series in order of value:

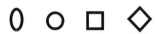

Of the two shapes at the edge of a segment, the one with the higher value moves into the middle. A vertical arrow is turned by 180°, a horizontal arrow is turned by 90° clockwise.

Answer 16

50. The letters represent alphanumeric values where the alphabet is numbered backwards (A = 26, Z = 1). Add all the outside numbers and swap the totals in horizontal pairs.

Answer 17

A chest of drawers.

Answer 18 – See Page 291

Answer 19

5. Three numbers in a horizontal line add up to the fourth number.

 Answer 20 The pattern sequence is:

Start at top left and follow the pattern in a clockwise spiral.

Answer 21

His wife and given birth prematurely. He made her breakfast and prepared a bottle for the baby.

Answer 22

B.

Answer 23

Costner, Cushing, Dunaway, Garland, Hepburn. The extra one is Domingo.

Answer 24 – See page 292

The extra word is Arrivederci.

Answer 25

5. Add both numbers in one segment, add the digits of that sum and place new number in the next segment going clockwise.

Answer 26

8. Three numbers in a vertical line are added together to make up the forth number.

Answer 27

Both hands should be pointing at the 10. It is based on the 24 hour clock. The two hands on the first clock multiplied result in a product of 36. 12 + 24 (the equivalent of 12 on the 24 hour clock) equals 36. The same is repeated with clocks 3 and 4. (4 x 8 = 10 + 22).

Answer 28

Hockney, Matisse, Gauguin, Hogarth, Vermeer. The extra one is Erasmus.

Answer 29

A. Multiply the first and last digit, subtract the second digit for hours, add the third digit for minutes.

Answer 30

		2
9		7
4	8	3

Answer 31

3. Each letter has a partner in the other triangle, which is its value in the alphabet backwards (A = 26, Z = 1). The number equivalent for C should be 24 (the letter for 3 is X).

Answer 32

The two vases were the only surviving example of work by a famous potter. The man already owned one and by smashing the other he ensured his vase would be unique.

Answer 33

The starting point is at Row 1, Col 1. The number is 31. Start at the finishing point and work back.

Answer 34

It should be blank. Start at the bottom right and go round the square in an anti-clockwise spiral. The pattern is: ● **X** blank ● **X** ●

Answer 35

D	3
F	7

The pattern starts at the top right and goes in diagonal stripes from left to right.

Answer 18

I	D	I	A	I	D	D	A	I	A	I	I	D	A	I	D
D	I	A	I	A	D	A	A	D	A	I	I	A	D	A	I
A	A	D	I	I	A	D	D	A	D	D	A	I	D	I	A
I	A	A	I	D	I	D	D	D	I	A	D	A	A	D	A
D	A	D	A	I	D	I	A	D	D	A	D	D	A	I	D
I	A	A	D	A	D	A	I	A	D	D	A	D	I	D	A
A	D	I	A	I	I	D	D	A	I	I	A	D	A	I	D
D	A	I	D	D	A	D	D	D	A	I	D	I	D	I	D
D	A	D	A	D	D	A	D	D	A	A	D	A	A	D	I
I	A	D	D	A	I	A	D	D	A	A	D	D	A	D	I
D	A	A	D	A	D	A	D	D	D	D	I	A	I	D	I
A	D	A	A	D	A	D	A	D	A	D	A	D	A	D	A
I	A	A	D	A	A	I	A	I	D	A	A	D	D	A	D
D	I	D	A	D	D	D	I	D	A	A	D	I	D	D	A
I	D	A	D	D	D	A	A	I	D	I	D	A	A	I	A
A	I	A	D	A	A	D	I	D	A	D	I	I	D	I	D

Answer 36

7. Multiply the two numbers on the outside of each segment, divide their product by 2 and place the new number two segments ahead in the middle.

Answer 37

83. Add the values of the letters in each box, based on the alphabet backwards (i.e. Z = 1, a = 26) and place the sum, with the digits reversed two squares ahead.

Answer 38

C and **F**.

Answer 39

D. The rest of the letters make the word APOLOGETIC.

Answer 40

C. Add together the values of the letters (Z = 1, A = 26) and subtract the individual digits from the sum.

Answer 41

Anouilh, Moliere, Ionesco, Osborne, Marlowe. The extra name is Connery.

Answer 42

She rubbed poison on one side of the knife blade.

Answer 43

K. Add the values (based on the alphabet forward) of the letters, convert their value into a new letter (based on the alphabet backward) and put it two squares ahead.

Answer 24

```
D R I V E R I D V E R D D R I V
R D R I V E R D R I V E R V E R
I V E R D V E R D D R I V E R V
V D R I V E R D E R C D E V V E
E D R I V E E D E R C I E V V E
D R I V E V R V D E R I V E R D
V D E R I D I V E R D R I V E R
D R I R V E R D R I D R D V D E
D R R V D R E V E R D R I V E
D A D R I V E D R I V D R I V E
I R D R E V I R D R E V I R D R
V E R D D R I V E R D R I V E D
V I V I V E V R D E V D E V I R
E R E R E D E D R R I R V E R I
R D R D R R R R I D R I I R D V
I I D I D I D E V I D V R D R E
```

Answer 44

9. Multiply the two outer numbers in each segment, and divide the product by 2 and 3 alternately. Place the new number in the middle of the opposite segment.

Answer 45

4. Multiply the two numbers in the bar, deduct the sum of the same numbers, and put result in the next square but one.

Answer 46

Celsius, Doppler, Faraday, Hawking, Pasteur.
The extra one is Kerouac.

Answer 47 – See opposite page

There are 44 pairs.

Answer 48

B. Based on the values of the letters in the alphabet (Z = 1, A = 26), take the first and last letter of the make of the car.

Answer 49

The starting point is Row 1, Col 1. The hidden letter is shaped like an L.

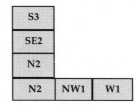

S3		
SE2		
N2		
N2	NW1	W1

5	3	6	4	4	3	5	7	5	7	9	2	2	5	8	3
9	8	9	6	1	5	8	6	6	8	3	7	6	7	4	4
2	1	5	7	8	3	1	3	5	1	6	6	8	9	8	6
7	6	2	9	1	1	8	3	1	5	1	7	5	3	4	1
8	5	6	6	2	4	4	8	3	8	4	7	1	6	1	8
7	6	2	2	5	2	3	7	4	5	8	5	7	6	3	1
7	9	3	1	8	4	5	4	7	7	9	4	8	5	6	3
3	6	8	8	2	9	8	8	2	5	7	2	1	8	3	5
5	6	9	6	5	3	4	7	4	7	4	2	6	6	5	5
1	6	3	2	3	4	5	8	1	1	2	4	9	3	2	7
5	8	9	7	1	8	3	6	9	3	6	3	5	4	9	4
8	4	5	6	7	1	5	1	8	5	8	3	1	2	5	7
7	2	2	9	2	2	4	7	4	9	4	1	8	6	7	8
2	4	3	9	5	6	7	8	5	8	3	2	7	5	6	1
5	9	4	3	4	2	6	1	7	3	4	9	2	6	9	1
3	2	5	8	1	3	2	5	3	8	3	5	3	1	2	7

Answer 47
44 pairs

Answer 50
Add the limbs of the figures on the outside of each segment and put the new figure, minus one limb into the middle two segments before.

Answer 51
Between the 4 and 5. The two numbers the two hands point to on each of the clocks multiplied has a product of 36. 4½ x 8 = 36.

Answer 52
The hidden letter is X, and the pattern is a vertical boustrophedon starting from the bottom left.

Answer 53
72. Add the two numbers in each bar, multiply the digits of that sum and put the product three squares ahead.

Answer 54 – See page 294
There are 55 pairs.

Answer 55
D. Take the values of the first two letters of each starting town, the first based on the alphabet forward (A = 1, Z = 26) and the second on the alphabet backward (A = 26, Z = 1). Add the values together. The new letter of that value will be the first letter of the new town.

Answer 56
Their mother had produced triplets. However, being poor she had been unable to bring them all up and had given one up for adoption. Nevertheless, the family resemblance was so strong that the men recognized their long lost brother.

Answer 54 55.

```
A G K A V E D C B V D N P R U V
W C Q D H K F L G M R S A B Q Y
Z K E X A L H O I A B G B Q C R
V R A W T B I T K N K A O B G U
B C D G X A E Y M Z B M B F M N
D O Z F A J R J K L T W A W X Y
F A E O H R S A O G A C F G T A
H K L A X Y Z B R F J F O P Q R
J S T U A B C O V D Q X S T U V
L M N G F J D U Z A V L M N T O
P Q R M O Q A T V Y D E F R G H
I J N X Y Z B V C D E F A B C D
S K O A B C F X G H X Z K L M N
O U P R Y W S T U K L A B C A B
P A W F G H I N A E X D P V X E
Q B E Y A C K Q D F Z L M A R C
```

Answer 57
Row 1, Col 1. The last letter represents the number of steps you have to go, based on the alphabet backward, however with Y = 1, X = 2, W = 3, A = 25, Z = 26. Start at the finishing point and work back.

Answer 58
C.

Answer 59 – See opposite page

Answer 60
The hidden letter is F. The pattern is diagonal stripes starting from the top right and going up from right to left.

Answer 61
B. In the first name, each consonant is worth 1, and each vowel 2; in the second name, consonant = 3, vowel = 4.

Answer 62
Hendrix, Houston, Madonna, Manilow, Presley. The extra one is Tolkein.

Answer 63 – See Page 296
There are 51 pairs.

Answer 64
B and **E**.

Answer 59

G	A	R	A	R	D	D	E	P	G	A	R	D	I	E	U
E	G	E	R	A	D	G	R	A	E	P	E	G	D	I	G
R	D	A	D	R	D	E	D	R	R	A	D	E	R	E	E
A	E	R	A	G	E	R	I	D	G	E	R	R	A	U	R
R	P	R	D	E	P	P	E	G	E	R	A	A	P	D	A
D	E	E	D	R	A	A	U	A	R	D	U	R	E	E	R
G	U	I	R	A	R	D	I	E	U	I	E	D	E	E	D
G	E	R	A	R	D	E	G	E	P	A	R	D	P	E	R
D	R	A	R	E	G	P	G	E	R	A	R	I	I	E	U
D	D	D	P	G	I	A	D	D	E	P	A	E	A	I	D
E	R	E	E	E	D	R	R	D	I	E	U	U	R	G	A
P	A	P	D	R	R	D	G	E	R	A	R	D	G	D	E
A	R	A	D	A	A	I	G	E	R	A	R	D	D	E	P
R	E	R	R	R	P	E	G	D	U	A	E	I	D	R	A
D	G	G	A	D	E	G	E	R	A	R	D	D	E	P	A
I	E	E	R	D	D	D	R	A	R	E	G	E	I	D	R

Answer 65 – See Page 297

The extra word is Oregano.

Answer 66

He was captain of a river boat ferry. The globe he went round was a decorative one he had in his cabin.

Answer 67 – See Page 298

There are 60 pairs.

Answer 68

Row 1, Col 1. The hidden character is A. Start at the finishing point and work backwards.

Answer 69

G.

Answer 70

D. The striped section moves clockwise by 1, 2, 3 and 4 sections (repeat). Each time it moves by 2 and 4 sections the pattern is reflected. The dot moves 2 sections clockwise and 1 section anti-clockwise alternately.

Answer 71 – See page 299

Answer 72

Rossini, Puccini, Debussy, Berlioz, Corelli. The extra one is Cezanne.

LEVEL 3 — ANSWERS

The grid is a large number search puzzle (answer to Answer 63).

18	3	16	7	10	3	14	15	2	13	7	6	12	19	2	8
16	5	12	10	14	7	9	19	12	6	13	3	8	7	7	6
16	18	3	16	12	14	7	4	13	12	15	9	14	5	13	4
12	8	8	3	7	11	6	8	5	11	9	13	11	7	6	12
15	8	11	19	10	10	7	14	4	12	5	7	16	13	9	15
13	14	11	4	3	10	17	9	18	7	3	6	12	5	14	19
11	4	9	11	18	4	18	12	9	12	14	15	14	17	2	6
17	5	4	18	3	17	6	8	19	17	4	15	8	11	12	15
4	6	8	19	15	11	19	12	12	13	11	8	4	3	14	3
13	5	1	19	6	8	15	2	17	13	7	15	11	14	17	12
9	1	2	13	4	6	5	8	19	12	9	8	17	7	15	4
5	12	2	18	11	8	15	6	3	4	2	1	4	6	16	12
17	18	9	12	5	13	2	8	6	16	10	14	3	4	12	11
8	6	13	16	5	11	12	8	9	14	7	3	8	9	13	6
5	6	19	1	7	8	15	4	5	15	3	6	15	8	8	11
9	18	2	4	3	1	19	8	13	16	12	18	14	19	2	12

Answer 63
51.

Answer 73
D.

Answer 74
20. Take two numbers in adjacent circles. If both are odd, add them. If both are even, multiply them. If one number is odd and one is even take the difference. Put the new number in the overlapping section.

Answer 75
C. All the others, when reflected on a vertical line, have an identical partner.

Answer 76
Belmondo, Pfeiffer, Rampling, Redgrave, Travolta.

Answer 77

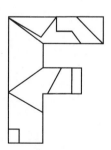

Answer 78
D and **E**.

Answer 79
E. The symbols turn by 180° and 90° alternately. The circle and square swap places, the diamond and rectangle swap shading.

Answer 65
Oregano

O	R	O	O	E	R	A	M	I	O	R	I	G	A	A	G
R	E	M	R	G	O	O	O	R	I	G	A	M	O	R	G	A
I	G	A	E	G	A	O	O	O	A	M	R	I	I	O	M
G	A	G	G	O	O	R	M	R	G	I	O	G	G	O	I
A	M	E	R	R	R	I	I	A	E	O	M	A	A	A	O
M	O	R	A	G	I	G	G	G	R	R	A	M	R	G	R
O	R	I	M	A	G	A	A	I	G	I	G	O	O	I	I
M	A	G	I	M	A	O	R	M	O	G	I	R	I	R	G
O	R	I	G	I	O	R	O	O	A	A	R	G	A	O	A
O	G	A	M	G	R	A	O	I	I	M	O	I	M	M	M
O	R	I	G	A	M	O	M	O	M	O	M	A	O	A	O
O	I	M	A	G	E	R	I	R	M	A	A	M	R	G	R
O	R	E	G	A	N	O	G	I	G	A	G	I	G	I	I
G	A	R	O	M	I	G	O	G	O	G	G	I	A	R	G
I	O	R	A	I	G	A	R	A	R	I	I	O	R	O	A
M	O	R	I	G	A	M	O	M	O	O	R	G	R	O	M

Answer 80

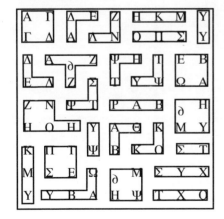

Answer 81
19. Write the alphabet in a circle. The numbers represent values of letters based on the alphabet backwards (A = 26, Z = 1). Start at A, miss 2, D (=23), miss 2, G, etc.

Answer 82
C. A and D, and B and E are pairs. When reflected against a vertical line and turned, they are identical.

Answer 83
D. These are the first letters of Do, Re, Mi, Fa, So, La, Tee, etc.

Answer 84
72. Halve the number on the top left, multiply the number on the top right by 3. Multiply the two resulting numbers with each other, and put the product in the bottom square.

Answer 85
A la Recherche du Temps Perdu by Marcel Proust.

Answer 67
60.

Answer 86

K. K is the same number of spaces in the alphabet from H and N, O and G, and E and Q.

Answer 87

I. These are the second letters of the numbers one to five.

Answer 88

B. Each column contains faces with 4 different types of hair, pairs of ears, eyes, mouths and face shapes.

Answer 89

25. Starting at the top left hand corner, work through the square in a diagonal boustrophedon pattern (clockwise first), subtracting 3 and adding 5 alternately.

Answer 90

11. Multiply the number of sides of each number by 3, and then subtract the number printed.

Answer 91

W. Starting from P go back 3 spaces in alphabet (M), forward 3 (S), back 5 (K), forward 5 (U), back 7 (I), forward 7.

Answer 92

The colours of the rainbow alternate with random colours. However, yellow and green have been transposed.

Answer 93

S. D is the 4th letter from the start of the alphabet, W is the 4th from the end. F is the 6th from the start, U the 6th from the end, etc.

LEVEL 3 — ANSWERS

Answer 71

P	A	R	S	I	S	P	A	R	S	P	A	R	P	I	S
S	A	P	R	S	P	I	S	P	A	R	S	P	A	R	S
R	A	P	S	A	R	P	I	S	P	R	A	S	P	S	I
I	S	P	A	R	I	P	S	A	R	I	S	P	S	P	A
A	S	P	A	R	S	P	A	R	S	I	P	A	R	S	I
P	A	R	S	I	S	P	A	R	S	P	A	S	I	S	R
P	R	A	S	I	P	A	S	R	P	R	A	S	R	I	S
R	S	A	S	I	P	A	R	S	I	S	P	A	I	S	S
R	S	A	I	S	R	A	S	R	A	I	S	P	R	A	S
R	I	S	I	P	S	A	P	R	A	I	R	S	I	P	I
A	R	P	R	A	I	R	S	I	P	S	A	P	R	A	S
I	A	P	A	P	A	R	A	R	I	P	I	S	A	I	P
S	P	R	I	S	S	I	P	P	S	A	R	P	R	S	A
R	P	I	R	S	I	P	S	A	P	R	A	I	R	S	R
I	A	S	A	P	R	A	I	R	S	I	P	S	A	P	I
S	P	A	R	I	P	A	S	I	R	P	A	R	I	P	A

Answer 94

N. The letters spell Wittgenstein.

Answer 95

Carlisle, Costello, Harrison, Knopfler, Morrison.

Answer 96

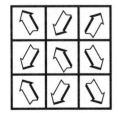

The pattern sequence is as below. It starts at the bottom right and works up in a horizontal boustrophedon.

Answer 97

M. The value of the letter on the bottom left, based on its alphabetical position, minus the value of the letter on the bottom right, results in the letter in the middle. Incidentally the outer letters spell Mark Twain backwards but this is of no significance.

Answer 98

F. Each shape changes into a shape with two extra sides. The order of the shapes is reversed.

Answer 99

20. Left hand x right hand ÷ waist = head. Left foot x right foot ÷ waist = head.

Answer 100

PUTTEN. The initials can be rearranged to form Paris.

Answer 101

P. Write the alphabet in a circle. NOP are the letters diametrically opposite ABC.

Answer 102

C. The letters spell Henry Mancini backwards.

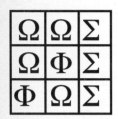

Answer 103

The pattern sequence is:

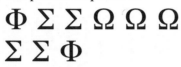

It starts at the bottom right and works up in a diagonal boustrophedon.

Answer 104

11. Divide the number of sides of the letter by 2 and add the value of the letter, based on its position in the alphabet.

Answer 105

Brezhnev, Disraeli, Thatcher, Adenauer, Pompidou.

Answer 106

U. The letters spell Art Garfunkel.

Answer 107

R. These are the second letters of the days of the week.

Answer 108

56. Take ⅔ of the number in the top left square and multiply it by twice the number in the top right square. Put the new number in the bottom square.

Answer 109

M. Starting with the middle triangle and letter A move round the diagram in a clockwise direction. Move then on to the diagram on the right and last to the diagram on the left. Miss three letters with each move.

Answer 110

C. It is the only circle with an asymmetrical shape.

Answer 111

A. The edges of all the symbols in one square added together, increase by 2 with each square (i.e. 12, 14, 16, 18, 20)

Answer 112

16. The numbers form two series: 3, 6, 9, 12 and 4, 8, 12, 16.

Answer 113

9. The alphabet equivalents make up the name Nagasaki.

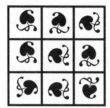

Answer 114

The pattern sequence is shown below. It starts at the top left and works downwards in a vertical boustrophedon.

Answer 115

32. All the others have a partner, with the digits being reversed.

Answer 116

14. Alternate numbers form two series: 9, 12, 15 and 18, and 14, 16, 18 and 20.

Answer 117

A Midsummer Night's Dream by William Shakespeare.

Answer 118

Bruckner, Gershwin, Schubert, Schumann, Sibelius.

Answer 119

I. Start at C and move forward by 5 letters and backward by 3 letters alternately in a clockwise direction.

Answer 120

T. E is the 5th letter from the start of the alphabet, V is the 5th from the end. D is the 4th from the beginning, W is the 4th from the end, etc.

Answer 121

J and **Z**. The values of the letters in the bottom circle are squares of the values of the letters in the top circle. J squared is 100.

Answer 122

B and **F**.

Answer 123

D. An anti-clockwise spiral points up or left, a clockwise spiral down or right. A round shape has a small shape with straight lines attached, a straight-sided shape has a small shape with round lines attached to it.

Answer 124

410. In all the others the first two digits added result in the third digit.

Answer 125

359. Reading left to right and bottom to top, subtract 17 each time.

Answer 126

729. The numbers 5, 6, 7, 8 and 9 are cubed.

Answer 127

A and **N**. The series is B, D, F, H, J (2, 4, 6, 8, 10). Add 1, 2, 3, 4, 5 respectively to the values to get the letters in the second triangle.

Answer 128

91. All the others are prime numbers.

Answer 129

56. (Head x left foot) ÷ waist = right hand; (head x right foot) ÷ waist = left hand). (14 x 15) ÷ 5 = 42; (14 x 20) ÷ 5 (56).

Answer 130

D. The whole figure is reflected on a horizontal line. Any shape with straight lines is then rotated by 90° clockwise and a dot in a round shape disappears.

Answer 131

Columbus, Honolulu, Portland, San Diego, Syracuse.

Answer 132

5 and **625**. The cubes of 7, 9 and 13 go into the bottom circle, the squares of 18, 26 and 54 go into the top circle.

Answer 133

11. It is a series of prime numbers.

Answer 134

S. Add the values of the letters on the top and right, and the values of the letters on the left and bottom. Subtract the second sum from the first, and put either the new number or alternately the letter based on the value of that number into the middle.

Answer 135

O and **V**. The others spell Charlie Chaplin.

Answer 136

E. The squares with lines from the bottom left to the top right have arrows pointing up or right. Squares with lines from the bottom right to the top left have arrows pointing down or left.

Answer 137

Z. In alternate shapes go: top, left, middle, right, bottom, and left, top, middle, bottom, right. In both cases miss out one letter.

Answer 138

M. Add 9 to the value of each letter in the first circle. C + 9 = L.

Answer 139

D. The formula is: left + (middle x right) = top + (middle x bottom), but in D, the answers are 26 and 25 respectively.

Answer 140

F. A round shape turns into a shape with straight sides and vice versa. Anything pointing down changes to pointing up and vice versa.

Answer 141
The formula is (right x left – top) x black fraction of circle = bottom.

Answer 142
72. These are twice the squares of numbers 1 to 9.

Answer 143
K. Starting with the middle square and moving in a clockwise direction, miss 2 letters in the first diagram, miss 3 in the second one, etc.

Answer 144
N. in the lower triangle. The others spell George Orwell.

Answer 145
The starting point is at row 3 Col 9.
The hidden number is 100.

W8									
N3									
SW2									
S2									
SW4									

W5	NW4	E4
N1		NE2
E2		N2
S2		S2
W1	S4	S1

NE4	NW1	N2
N1		N3
E2		NE2
E6		SE2
S4	SE1	S1

Answer 146
27. The numbers increase by 3, 4, 5, 6 in an anti-clockwise direction.

Answer 147
24 and **Q**. Take the value of the letters in the top triangle, based on the reversed alphabet (Z = 1, A = 26) and take 5 away. Put the new numbers in the bottom triangle. Take the value of the letters in the bottom triangle, based on the alphabet forwards (A = 1, Z = 26), and add 3. Put the new numbers in the top triangle. For Q to fit these criteria, the number 20 would need to be in the upper triangle, and for 24 to fit, the letter would need to be U.

Answer 148
D. The formula is: (right x shaded fraction of left) – (top x shaded fraction of bottom) = middle shape's number of sides. Therefore, in example D: (18 x 2/3 [12]) – (12 x 3/4) [9] = 3. The answer shape should be 3-sided, so it is the odd one out.

Answer 149
4. Add the two top outer numbers from the upper boxes and the two bottom numbers from the lower boxes and put the sum in the inner box diagonally opposite. The third outer number is obtained by subtracting 3, 4, 5, and 6 from the adjoining answer, starting from the top left and reading clockwise. The answer is obtained as follows: 6 + 4 (top right's two outer top numbers) = 10 (bottom left's inner numbers) – 6 = 4.

Answer 150
T. It spells Marcel Proust.

Answer 151
C. It spells Henri Toulouse-Lautrec.

Answer 152
A. Multiply each shaded fraction with the shaded fraction opposite. The number in the middle is the ratio of the two resulting fractions. A is the odd one out because ⅔ x ½ = ⅓; ½ x ¾ = ⅜, and the ratio is not 1.

Answer 153
Z. Add the values of the three outside numbers, based on their position in the alphabet, and place their sum in the inner box opposite.

Answer 154
Y. It spells Aldous Huxley.

Answer 155
7. Add the three numbers on the outside of each square (A). Add the digits of the sum (B). Divide A by B and place in the small square.

Answer 156
V. It spells Anton Chekhov.

Answer 157
L. Start at the top left of each diagram, move to the top right, bottom and on to the new diagram. Move forward by 3 letters, back by 2, forward by 4, back by 2.